History of

BRITISH
ATHLETICS

Also by Melvyn Watman

The Encyclopaedia of Athletics

MELVYN WATMAN

History of
BRITISH
ATHLETICS

Illustrated

ROBERT HALE · LONDON

SBN 7091 0255 0

Robert Hale Limited
63 Old Brompton Road
London S.W.7

PRINTED IN GREAT BRITAIN BY
CLARKE, DOBLE AND BRENDON LTD.,
CATTEDOWN, PLYMOUTH

CONTENTS

CONTENTS

ILLUSTRATIONS

8 ILLUSTRATIONS

ACKNOWLEDGEMENTS

The above photographs were supplied by Alfieri Picture Service (facing page 48 *bottom*), Adolphe Abrahams (49 *top*), H. W. Neale (49 *bottom*, 96, 97 *top*, 113 *left*, 177), Sport and General (64 *left* and *right*, 97 *bottom*, 112 *top*, 192 *top*), Keystone (112 *bottom*), Central Press (113 *right*), Peter Tempest (192 *bottom left*), Ed Lacey (176, 192 *bottom right*), Fionnbar Callanan (193).

On the jacket: Sydney Wooderson (Central Press) and Lynn Davies (R. V. Good).

FOREWORD

A s well as being a very good friend, Melvyn Watman is to me one of the most knowledgeable, sincere and thorough authorities in athletics today. It therefore gives me great pleasure to be associated with this unique history of British athletics.

Mel has done a colossal amount of research, more perhaps than even this book can indicate. The result is a detailed history of the sport in this country. It is something which not only fulfils a long felt need among active athletes who enjoy reading about their predecessors, but by everyone connected with the great sport of track and field athletics.

Whilst agreeing with what Mel says in his introduction that 'there is a risk of each new generation scorning the times and distances of the old champions' you cannot argue with watches and tapes. These are the black and white figures making track and field the most uncompromising of all sports. Perhaps the only fair comparisons are those taken amongst one's contemporaries.

The author pays tribute to all the great British athletes of yesteryear; and you will, I am sure, wish me to thank Melvyn Watman for a very informative and entertaining book.

LYNN DAVIES

PREFACE

IN this volume, the first to chronicle the history of British athletics since *Get To Your Marks!* by Ross and Norris McWhirter in 1951, I have concentrated on the evolution of performances and attempted to keep them in perspective *vis-à-vis* world standards of the day. Thus certain events claim far more space than others, and if more words have been written about the mile than on all eight field events combined this is merely a reflection of Britain's contribution to international athletics progress rather than any prejudice on my part.

Bearing in mind the enormous range of the subject, a book of this size runs the risk of superficiality but there is, I hope, justification for a concise history of this nature. Athletics is a sport which is dominated by statistics and there is a risk of each new generation scorning the times and distances of the old champions, who, in many cases, would be 'also-rans' if the stopwatch and tape measure were the only criteria. Perhaps the only reasonable method of comparing athletes of different eras is to assess their degree of superiority over contemporaries and measure the duration of their records; and this I have tried to do.

The question of what constitutes 'British' has posed problems in writing this book. Basically, I have included anybody of note who has been an integral part of the athletics scene in England, Scotland, Wales and Northern Ireland—plus, prior to the treaty of December 6th 1921, what is now the Republic of Ireland. Therefore prolonged 'visitors' like Jack Lovelock and McDonald Bailey are included, as are the early Irish stars, but Ron Delany for instance is not.

Another difficulty has been the subject of records. Only in the last few years have there been official United Kingdom records; previously there was a conglomeration of meaningless records such as British (National), open to anyone from the Empire and Commonwealth competing in this country, and English (Native). Per-

formances made abroad or at metric events were not considered!
Consequently often when I have referred to some mark as a UK,
British or national record the performance in question may never
have been officially ratified as such but has satisfied statisticians as
to its authenticity. Similarly, there were no official world records
prior to 1913 but, thanks to exhaustive research by Peter Lovesey
and Bob Sparks in particular, I have been able to label many an
earlier performance as a world record or best performance.

I have derived an immense amount of satisfaction during the two
years it has taken me to prepare and write this book and it is my
fervent hope that some of the pleasure and excitement I experienced
will be shared by readers.

MELVYN WATMAN

London,
October 1967

ACKNOWLEDGEMENTS

IN collecting material for this book I have drawn heavily on many sources but I am particularly indebted to Harold Abrahams, who made the whole of his massive collection of books, magazines, clippings and programmes available to me, and Peter Lovesey, who supplied much nineteenth-century data. I would also like to thank Ken Finding, of the *News of the World*, for arranging for me to sift through the late Joe Binks' collection of material; Les Higdon, of the Amateur Athletic Association; P. W. Green, managing editor of *Athletics Weekly*; and the National Union of Track Statisticians, a body of which I am proud to be a member.

I have made extensive use of the files of several specialist magazines and national newspapers as well as a number of books. The following publications were particularly valuable:

MAGAZINES
Athletics Arena, Athletics Weekly, Athletics World, World Athletics, World Sports.

BOOKS
Abrahams, H. M.—*The 'Western Mail' Empire Games Book* (*Western Mail & Echo*, 1958); *XVII Olympiad 1960* (Cassell, 1960).

Abrahams, H. M. and Bruce Kerr, J.—*AAA Championships 1880–1931* (AAA, 1932).

Amateur Athletic Association—Miscellaneous programmes and handbooks.

Association of Track and Field Statisticians—Miscellaneous handbooks.

Bannister, R. G.—*First Four Minutes* (Putnam, 1955).

British Olympic Association—Miscellaneous Olympic Reports.

Buchanan, I.—*An Encyclopaedia of British Athletics Records* (Stanley Paul, 1961).

Burke's Who's Who in Sport and Sporting Records (1922).

Butler, G. M.—*Sydney Wooderson and Some of his Great Rivals* (1946).

Croome, A. C. M. (ed.)—*Fifty Years of Sport at Oxford, Cambridge and the Great Public Schools* (Walter Southwood, 1913).

Downer, A.—*Running Recollections* (Gale & Polden, 1908).

Guiney, D.—*Ireland's Olympic Heroes* (Philip Roderick, 1965).

Harris, N.—*The Legend of Lovelock* (Nicholas Kaye, 1965).

Jamieson, D. A.—*Powderhall & Pedestrianism* (W. and A. K. Johnston, 1943).

London, J.—*The Way to Win on Track & Field* (D.P. Ltd., 1948).

McWhirter, N. D. and A. R.—*Get To Your Marks!* (Nicholas Kaye, 1951).

McWhirter, N. D. and A. R., & Buchanan, I.—*British Athletics Record Book* (McWhirter Twins, 1957 and 1958).

Meyer, H.A. (ed.)—*Athletics by the Achilles Club* (Dent, 1951); *Modern Athletics by the Achilles Club* (Oxford University Press, 1958).

National Union of Track Statisticians—Miscellaneous handbooks.

O'Donoghue, Tony—*Ireland: The Best Performers of All Time* (1962).

Pallett, G.—*Women's Athletics* (Normal Press, 1955).

Pash, H. F. (ed.)—*Jubilee Souvenir of AAA, 1880-1930.*

Pearson, G. F. D. (ed.)—*Athletics* (Nelson, 1963).

Peters, J. H. & Edmundson, J.—*In The Long Run* (Cassell, 1955).

Pirie, D. A. G.—*Running Wild* (W. H. Allen, 1961).

Pozzoli, P. R.—*British Women's Athletics* (Arena, 1965).

Quercetani, R. L.—*A World History of Track & Field Athletics* (Oxford University Press, 1964).

Race Walking Association—*The Sport of Race Walking* (1962).

Richardson, L. N.—*Jubilee History of the International Cross Country Union, 1903–53.*

Shearman, M.—*Athletics* (The Badminton Library, 1898 edition).

Shrubb, A.—*Running and Cross Country* (Health & Strength, 1908).

Smith, G.—*All Out for the Mile* (Forbes Robertson, 1955).

Tisdall, R. M. N. & Sherie, F.—*The Young Athlete* (Blackie, 1934).

Watman, M. F.—*The Ibbotson Story* (*Athletics Weekly*, 1958); *The Encyclopaedia of Athletics* (Robert Hale, 1964 and 1967).

Webster, F. A. M.—*Athletics of Today* (Warne, 1929); *Great Moments in Athletics* (*Country Life*, 1947); *Olympic Cavalcade* (Hutchinson, 1948).

Whitfield, C.—*Robert Dover and the Cotswold Games* (Sotheran, 1963).

M.W.

1

EARLY HISTORY

ALTHOUGH the sport of track and field athletics in a form recognisable to us today is barely one hundred years old, men have run, jumped and thrown implements in competition against one another for thousands of years. Possibly the most ancient of all sports festivals were the Tailteann Games, which are thought to have been established as long ago as 1829 BC. Staged in County Meath, Ireland, this annual thirty-day gathering included such events as foot racing and stone throwing and it survived in all its splendour until the Norman invasion in AD 1168.

The first Olympic Games of which there is documentary evidence took place in Greece in 776 BC, but some historians believe the four-yearly cycle began 600 years earlier. As the Greek civilisation declined so too did the Olympic Games and in AD 393 they were abolished altogether by decree of the Roman emperor Theodosius.

Little more is heard of athletics until the Middle Ages. Scottish Highland Games, which have maintained their appeal to the present day, date back to the fourteenth century or earlier; while some form of organised physical activity was known in twelfth-century England for during the reign of Henry II (1154–1189) open spaces near the City were provided so that Londoners could practise 'leaping, wrestling, casting of the stone, and playing with the ball'. It appears that 'casting of the stone'—the forerunner of shot-putting—developed into such a popular pastime that it endangered England's military might since in order to prevent archery practice from falling into disuse Edward III issued an edict in 1365 prohibiting weight-putting!

Henry V, who reigned from 1413 to 1422, proved a much more sports conscious monarch. According to a contemporary observer he 'was so swift a runner that he and two of his lords, without bow or other engine, would take a wild buck in a large park'. Prior to his marital problems the solidly built Henry VIII (reigned 1509–1547) appears to have been the decathlon champion of his day . . . he is described variously as an outstanding runner, jumper, weight putter and hammer thrower.

Benefiting from the sovereign's example, footracing became an important sport in the sixteenth century. There was, however, a cleavage of opinion among Establishment figures as to the precise social status of such an activity. On the one hand Sir Thomas Elyot wrote in his manual of education for gentlemen: 'Running is both a good exercise and a laudable solace [pastime]'; on the other, Roger Ascham expressed the opinion that 'running, leaping and quoiting be too vile for scholars.' The author of *Compleat Gentleman* (1622) referred to hammer throwing as 'not so well beseeming nobility but rather soldiers in a camp' but, in his eyes, running and jumping were 'commendable'.

The rural population of England was not concerned with such niceties and continued to enjoy the sporting activities that were a feature of fairs and religious festivals. Running, jumping and hammer throwing were popular pursuits, along with grinning contests, shin kicking, sack jumping, donkey racing and climbing the greasy pole.

In his book *Robert Dover and the Cotswold Games* Christopher Whitfield has traced the extraordinary story of such a rustic sports meeting. The Cotswold Games, believed to have been held in Gloucestershire since Saxon times, were much like any other up and down the country until transformed by a barrister named Robert Dover (1582–1652), a man who—anticipating Baron de Coubertin by nearly three centuries—was fired by the desire to revive the ancient Olympic ideal. So effectively did he succeed that one writer suggested the competitors 'imagined that they had stepped back into a classical past where they were the companions or equals of the mythical heroes of old'. Several poets rhapsodised over Robert Dover's 'Olympicke's'.

The Puritans tried to stamp out physical recreation but following the Restoration in 1660 sport rose to new heights of popularity. Footracing attracted a huge following, as borne out by Samuel Pepys who on July 30th 1663 wrote: 'The town talk this day is of nothing but the great footrace run this day on Banstead Downs between Lee, the Duke of Richmond's footman, and a tyler, a famous runner. And Lee hath beat him; though the King and Duke of York and all men almost, did bet three to four to one upon the tyler's head.'

Pedestrianism, as professional footracing came to be known, flourished throughout the eighteenth century. Mostly the contests were between footmen, who were employed by the wealthy to carry messages and make advance travel arrangements—for until the advent of improved roads at the end of the eighteenth century a good runner could make better time than a man on horseback. Vast sums were wagered on the outcome of these matches.

How good were the top runners in pre-Victorian times? Trustworthy information is hard to come by. For example, a contemporary chronicler informed his readers: 'A butcher of Croydon, on December 1st 1653, ran twenty miles from St Albans to London in less than an hour and a half, and the last four miles so gently that he seemed to meditate, and not to ensult on the conquest, but did make it rather a recreation than a race.' This is clearly nonsense when one considers that among the superbly trained athletes of to-day not one has yet come close to running ten miles in 45 minutes, let alone twenty miles in 90 minutes. Only a little more credible are such widely heralded exploits as a footman winning a four miles race at Woodstock Park in 1720 in 18 minutes, and an un-named runner covering a mile between Charterhouse Wall and Shoreditch Church gates in 1770 in four minutes.

Rather more likely is that one Mr Walpole, a butcher from Newgate Market, did win a mile race along the City Road in 1787 in 4 minutes 30 seconds; that Joseph Headley, a pedestrian (Professional runner), did record 9 minutes 45 seconds for two miles in Yorkshire in 1777; and that in the following year other 'peds' by the name of Wild and Evans did cover four miles in 21 minutes 15 seconds and ten miles in 55 minutes 18 seconds respectively.

It was during the second decade of the nineteenth century, round about the time of the Battle of Waterloo, that the seeds of modern amateur athletics were sown. From 1812 an annual sports day was held at the Royal Military College, Sandhurst, and in 1817 a Major Mason founded the world's first athletic club, the Necton Guild, in Norfolk. Athletics really began to blossom when the public schools, recognising the sport's value in bringing out some of the best qualities in a boy, added it to the curriculum. The Crick Run, a tough cross-country race, was inaugurated at Rugby in 1837; annual sprint, hurdle and steeplechase races were staged at Eton from 1845. The universities' interest originated in 1850 with a track

B

meeting at Exeter College, Oxford, and the same year Exeter College Athletic Club—the oldest in existence—was formed.

For a while, organised amateur athletics was confined to public schoolboys, undergraduates and officer cadets, but by the 1860s young men of all backgrounds were finding opportunities to indulge in the sport—though not without opposition from some quarters. The Amateur Athletic Club, which organised an annual national championship meeting until driven out of existence by the formation in 1880 of the Amateur Athletic Association, was founded in 1866 'to supply the want of an established ground (Lillie Bridge) upon which competitions in amateur athletic sports might take place, and to afford as completely as possible to all classes of gentlemen amateurs the means of practising and competing against one another, without being compelled to mix with professional runners'.

There were three categories of athlete in those times: the professional, the 'gentleman amateur' and the 'amateur'. To this day professionals and amateurs have been kept apart in competition but for several years the AAC and similar organisations also would have nothing to do with the 'amateur', who happened to work for his living. Gradually the age-old barriers of class and privilege were broken down. The turning point, perhaps, was when W. J. Morgan, a walking champion in the mid-1870s, had his entry accepted for a meeting organised by the influential London Athletic Club. Several of the club's senior and more reactionary members threatened to resign in protest against such heresy (Morgan was actually a wage earner!) but eventually they were persuaded to accept the situation. It was a victory for commonsense as well as democracy and from then on athletics in Britain never looked back.

We, though, shall be looking back . . . at the outstanding personalities and events of a century of exciting, fascinating and colourful athletic endeavour.

2

THE SPRINTS

OF all the various activities that go to make up the sport of athletics, sprinting is the most fundamental. Even the most refined training methods can do little to alter the speed of muscle contraction—the key to fast running—and as the famed American coach Dean Cromwell once wrote: 'The star sprinter is born and not made and no one without natural fleetness of foot can ever become a champion.' Not surprisingly, therefore, there has been relatively less progress made during the past century in the sprints than in those events where dedicated training and attention to technique can compensate for a lack of inherent natural ability.

One hundred years have elapsed since 'even time', i.e. 10 seconds for 100 yards, was first recorded under apparently authentic conditions by an amateur. Such a time is respectable even today, yet when the Cambridge cricket 'Blue' Charles Absalom achieved that 10 seconds on March 19th 1868 the crouch start, not to mention starting blocks, had yet to be thought of, tracks were inferior in quality to those of the modern era, and the runner was encumbered by 'shorts' flapping around his knees, elbow-length vest and weighty shoes.

Ten seconds was accomplished on several other occasions prior to the first such timing in the United States, in 1877. W. M. Tennent performed the deed in June 1868, J. G. Wilson in 1870, William Dawson in 1872, George Urmson in 1873, record breaking long jumper Jenner Davies in 1874 and Irishman B. R. Martin in 1876. William Phillips in 1878 and Scotsman James Cowie in 1884, both members of the world's oldest (1864) open club, London AC, also joined the ranks of even-timers before the Jamaican Arthur Wharton was credited with the first 10.0 marks under championship conditions. The occasion was the 1886 AAA Championships at Stamford Bridge and Wharton clocked 'evens' in both heat and final. He later became one of the earliest professional soccer players (he kept goal for Preston North End) and in 1889 covered 126 yards in 12.6 at the famous professional meeting at Powderhall, Edinburgh.

The most successful British 100 yards specialist of the nineteenth century was Charles Bradley, from Huddersfield; winner of the AAA title four years running between 1892 and 1895. His performance at the 1893 meeting at Northampton was particularly remarkable. Having been warned that the slightly downhill track and wind assistance would rule out any records Bradley persuaded the officials to reverse the direction of the race and, uphill and into the wind, he proceeded to win in a record-equalling 10.0. Bradley turned in another 10.0 at the 1895 Championships but better was to come at Stoke the following month when he dead-heated with the Jamaican-Scot Alf Downer in 9.8. This was acknowledged by the Americans as equalling the world's best first set by John Owen (USA) in 1890 (there were no official world records until the International Amateur Athletic Federation began listing them in 1913) but the AAA never ratified the performances . . . which were to remain unbettered by a Briton until Eric Liddell's controversial 9.7 in 1923. Bradley, incidentally, used a standing start; he preferred the old method to the crouch—or hand spring start as then known— which had been introduced into Britain in 1889 by Tom Nicholas, the AAA 440 yards champion of 1890.

Bradley, who had been a well known cricketer before taking up sprinting, was a strongly built man of medium height. He was a consistent performer and probably broke 10 seconds again when in September 1895 he finished a yard behind the sensational American schoolboy Bernie Wefers (9.8) in the memorable New Yorker AC v London AC match after leading at the halfway mark. He gained the satisfaction, though, of beating the other New Yorker, John Crum, who had himself clocked 9.8 earlier in the season. British sprinting suffered a grievous blow when both Bradley and Downer were permanently suspended by the AAA in 1896 for accepting appearance money.

Downer, described as 'a swarthy and sinewy stripling', became an outstandingly successful professional and at Powderhall in 1898 he recorded 12.4 for 128½ yards, 4½ yards inside 'evens'. Some years later Downer provided an interesting insight into professional athletics in his book, *Running Recollections*. Referring to Scottish meetings, he revealed: 'No one, who is "on the job", ever dreams of waiting for the report of the pistol, or whatever the signal may be, but is generally running some five yards (this is no exaggeration) when the signal is given.' Professional sprint times in the nineteenth century were notoriously suspect, in any case. For example, a widely hailed 9.25 100 yards by the American George Seward in London in 1844 was in fact run on a turnpike road from a ten-yard flying start. Nevertheless, one must mention the dazzling and apparently authentic times credited to Harry Hutchens of Putney. His collection included 12.4 for 131¼ yards in 1879, 14.5 for 150 yards in 1887, 21.8 for 220 yards in 1885 and 30.0 for 300 yards in 1884.

Back to the amateurs. Until the advent of the great Willie Apple-garth shortly before the First World War performances at the fur-long lagged behind those at the shorter sprint—mainly because the event was so rarely contested, omitted as it was from the Oxford v. Cambridge match and not accorded AAA Championship status until 1902. The first man to better 23 seconds was Edward Colbeck with 22.8 in 1867, a time matched by John Reay six years later. Fred Elborough ran 22.6 in 1876 and there the record stood until even-timer James Cowie, who was also twice AAA 440 yards cham-pion, hacked it down to 22.2 in 1885. William Phillips, who was to die of a heart disease only five years later, had registered 22.0 on a straight track (equivalent of about 22.4 around a turn) in 1878.

The next record holder was Charles Wood, three times a runner-up in the AAA 100 yards and the first British quarter-miler to break through the 50-seconds barrier. From an upright start, Wood bracketed his name with Cowie's as a 22.2 performer in 1886 and the following season, on the Stamford Bridge straightaway, he returned 21.6 from scratch in a handicap race. His most feared rival was Ernest Pelling, who set an English 200 yards record of 19.8 in a heat at Stamford Bridge in 1887. He clocked 19.6 in the final but despite protests from Pelling that the wind was blowing against the runners the time was disallowed as a record on grounds of wind assistance. The following year he covered the 250 yards straight in 24.8. Pelling was one of the first British sprinters to adopt a crouch start and won the AAA 100 yards in 1889 using this method. It is amusing to note that the *Sporting Life* reported that 'Pelling adopted the Nicholas style with his hands on the ground when the pistol cracked, but got away very smartly'.

Jack Morton was the first world class British sprinter of the present century. He achieved two notable feats in 1904: he beat America's legendary Arthur Duffey (the first man to run 100 yards in 9.6) at the AAA Championships in July and clocked a legitimate 9.8 in September. Regrettably, Britain did not send a team to that year's Olympic Games in St Louis where Morton would have stood a fine chance of a medal in the 100 metres which was won in 11.0 (equivalent of a 10.1 100 yards) against the wind by Archie Hahn (USA). Morton won Canadian titles at 100 (10.0) and 120 yards (12.0) in 1905 and retained his AAA crown for the next three years, defeating Olympic silver medallist Nathan Cartmell (USA) in 1907. His own Olympic opportunity came at London's White City in 1908 but at 29 he was past his best and was eliminated in the semi-finals. The winner of the 200 metres at these Games, Robert Kerr of Canada, was actually born at Enniskillen, Co. Fermanagh. He was only four when his family emigrated but in 1909 he returned to represent Ireland against Scotland and England.

Curiously, the next two Britons to clock 9.8 for 100 yards per-formed the trick in Vienna: Vic d'Arcy in 1911 and Scotsman Harold Macintosh in 1913. But the man who dominated British sprinting immediately before the outbreak of war was d'Arcy's fellow Polytechnic Harrier, Willie Applegarth. A diminutive man who ran with machine-like precision, Applegarth had been a cham-pion all-rounder at school and in 1910, at the age of twenty, he made a promising debut in the AAA Championships by filling third place in the 100 yards behind F. L. Ramsdell (USA) and South Africa's Olympic 100 metres champion, Reggie Walker.

Applegarth was less successful the following year, placing only fifth in the 100, but in 1912 he established himself as the nation's premier sprinter. At the AAA Championships he was second in the 100, won in 9.8 by South African George Patching who 15 days later was to finish fourth in the Olympic 100 metres, and in the 220 he took the title in 22.0 with Patching third. Applegarth was elimin-ated in the Olympic 100 metres semi-finals at Stockholm (he was second to the USA's Donald Lippincott with only the winner qualifying) but made amends by gaining a bronze medal—Britain's first in an individual sprint—in the 200 metres. Drawn in the inside lane, Applegarth ran in storming fashion around the turn and entered the straight slightly ahead but he could not sustain the effort and two Americans (Ralph Craig, the newly crowned 100 metres champion, and Lippincott) surged past. The British runner, in fact, had his work cut out to hold third place from Germany's Richard Rau, unofficial holder of the world's 100 metres best with 10.5. Craig won in 21.7, with Lippincott showing 21.8 and Applegarth, in his eighth race in five days, a valiant 22.0 (worth 22.1 for 220 yards).

In between the two individual sprints, Applegarth became the proud possessor of a gold medal in company with David Jacobs, Macintosh and d'Arcy. With Applegarth on the anchor leg, the British quartet won the inaugural Olympic 4 × 100 metres relay final by two yards from Sweden in 42.4. The clear-cut favourites, the USA, had been disqualified in the semi-finals.

Applegarth struck his best form of the 1912 season in September when on successive weekends he set English records at 200 yards (19.4) and 220 yards around a turn (21.8). The latter mark equalled John Crum's 17-year-old world's best in spite of a strong head wind in the straight and the fact that Applegarth split a shoe during the race. Next year he became the first home athlete to score an AAA sprint double, his times being 10.0 and 21.6—the furlong time being a new world's best. Later in the season he added his name to the English 100-yards record list with a couple of 9.8s.

He enjoyed an even finer double at the 1914 Championships: the 100 in 10.0 and the 220 in 21.2. The furlong mark, around the Stamford Bridge bends, proved to be the greatest achievement of a distinguished career. It stood as the world record for the curved event until 1932 and as the United Kingdom best until as recently as 1958! The official watches registered 21.2, 21.2 and 21.4; second, 4½ yards behind, was Olympic relay colleague d'Arcy. That final pre-war campaign of Applegarth's was notable also for a 10.6 100 metres (equivalent of 9.7/9.8 for 100 yards) in Copenhagen, only a tenth of a second outside Rau's best on record. Twenty-one years were to elapse before any Briton ran the distance faster. At the height of his fame Applegarth turned professional and in no time established himself as 'world champion'. In November 1914 he chalked up a 100 yards victory over the seemingly unbeatable 'Blue Streak' from Australia, Jack Donaldson (credited with a shade inside 9.4 in 1910) in fractionally under 10.0 and five months later downed Donaldson in a 22.25 furlong. Applegarth settled in the United States after World War I and died there in 1958 . . . still holder of the AAA Championships 220 yards record.

No sooner was post-war athletics into its stride than a glittering new star emerged in the person of Harry Edward, a tall and stylish sprinter from British Guiana who carried Polytechnic's colours. As a 19-year-old, Edward had beaten Rau in a 21.7 200 metres in Berlin in 1914 but, despite internment in Germany during the war, he came back better than ever. An AAA double of Applegarthian proportions (10.0 and 21.6) in 1920 indicated that he would give a good account of himself at the Antwerp Olympics, and so he did. Notwithstanding an atrocious start he placed third in the 100 metres behind the American cracks, Charles Paddock (winner in 10.8) and Morris Kirksey; while in the 200 metres he collected another bronze medal in spite of his thigh being strapped up due to hamstring trouble. The USA filled first two places in this race also: Allen Woodring (22.0) won from Paddock.

Edward retained both his national titles the following year and at the 1922 Championships he thrilled the spectators with a unique triple. He succeeded in the 100 (10.0), 220 (22.0) and 440 (defeating 1920 Olympic silver medallist Guy Butler in 50.4) . . . all within the space of one hour on a heavy track! Yet such was the richness of British sprinting in the twenties, undoubtedly the golden era as far as these events are concerned, that just as Edward departed from the scene on marched two of the most glorious names in all British athletics history: Eric Liddell and Harold Abrahams.

The story of Liddell's remarkable career is given in some detail in the next chapter; suffice here to mention that at the 1923 AAA Championships the Edinburgh University divinity student scored a brilliant double. He won the 100 in the new British record time of 9.7, just a tenth shy of the world record and unsurpassed by a UK sprinter until 1958, and the furlong in 21.6. The 100 yards timing was received in some quarters with scepticism, mainly because two Englishmen who were considered even-timers at best finished within a yard of the Scot, but everything was according to the rules and the time was officially ratified. Liddell, of course, concentrated on the quarter in 1924 but his bronze medal in the Olympic 200 metres behind the Americans Jackson Scholz (21.6) and Paddock two days before his 400 metres triumph must not be overlooked.

Sixth and last in that 200 metres final, running—in his own words —'like a selling plater', was the man who 48 hours earlier had become the first and only Briton to capture an Olympic sprint title. Harold Abrahams, born in Bedford on December 15th 1899, had been an athlete of unusual ability from an early age. Encouraged by his elder brothers, Adolphe and Sidney (the AAA long jump champion in 1913), young Harold was only ten when he made a successful racing debut at what was then the mecca of British athletics, Stamford Bridge. It was there four years later, in 1914, that he watched his first AAA Championships. 'I well remember the thrill', he recalled many years afterwards, 'of seeing Willie Apple-garth in the inside string [lane] tearing round the bend in the 220-yards race with his strides following one another with incredible rapidity.' Little did he guess then that one day he would supplant his idol as the foremost speedster in British track history.

By 1918 Abrahams was beginning to make himself known to the public; that year he won both the 100 yards and long jump at the Public Schools Championships. During a short spell in the Army the 19-year-old Lt. Abrahams had the opportunity of meeting his boyhood hero, the 29-year-old CSM Applegarth, in an exhibition 100 yards race in 1919. The younger man, given a start of two yards, won by six in 10.0. Two months later he went up to study law at Cambridge and in December 1919 he beat AAA champion William Hill over 100 yards. He recorded 'evens' in the 1920 inter-varsity clash and later in the season, at the Antwerp Olympics, he succeeded in winning his 100 metres heat in 11.0 but was eliminated in the next round.

The highlight of Abrahams' 1921 season was equalling the world's best time of 7.4 for the rarely contested 75-yards event (the course at Stamford Bridge was, however, found to be eight inches short) but on the same track the following weekend he had no answer to Harry Edward, who beat him in both AAA sprints. Abrahams achieved little of consequence in 1922 but enjoyed a successful pre-Olympic campaign. His final appearance in the 'Battle of the Blues' was a memorable one. He took the 100 in 10.0, 440 in a career best of 50.8 (ahead of the 1921 American champion, Bill Stevenson) and long jump with an English record of 23 feet $7\frac{1}{4}$ inches to bring his aggregate of victories in the series to an unprecedented eight. His clash with Eric Liddell in the AAA 100 yards was awaited with eager anticipation but, by a stroke of misfortune, it never took place. Abrahams, victim of a septic throat, failed to reach the final which Liddell proceeded to win in a sensational 9.7. Two weeks after the championships, Abrahams ran the fastest furlong of his life: 21.6 along the Wembley straightaway.

Under the direction of the celebrated Polytechnic Harriers coach, Sam Mussabini—the man who had previously guided Applegarth and Edward towards their sprinting triumphs—Abrahams trained diligently during the winter of 1923-4 with the Olympics in mind.

He recalls: 'I used to train two or three times a week. Sam was "dead nuts"—that was the expression we used—on the arm action

with the arms kept low, bent at the elbows (we used running corks
for a good grip), and maintained, which I believe to be absolutely
sound, that the action of the arms very largely controls the poise of
the body and action of the legs. My training sessions consisted
largely of perfecting the start and practising arm action over and
over again. No starting blocks in those days, and we took meticulous
care with the placing and digging of starting holes and the accurate
control of the first few strides. I always carried a piece of string the
length of first stride and marked the spot on the track, at which
I gazed intently on the word "set". Our partnership was ideal,
because Sam was not an autocrat. We discussed theory for many
hours and argued and argued until I knew that his theories were
sound—not because of his experience and knowledge, but because
my mind was satisfied with his reasons. We paid infinite attention
to my length of stride. Speed, of course, is a combination of length
of stride multiplied by the rapidity with which a stride is taken. I
used to put down pieces of paper on the track at measured distances
and endeavour to pick them up with my spikes as I ran. I shall
always believe that the vital factor in my running in Paris was that
by conscientious training I had managed to shorten my stride an
inch or two and get an extra stride into my 100 metres. Then Sam
encouraged me to work on a "drop" finish.'

Such assiduity (it was almost unheard of in those days for a
sprinter to train three times a week) was to pay off handsomely and
an early indication of his dramatic improvement was provided at
an inter-club match at Woolwich on June 7th 1924 when he raised
his English long jump record to 24 feet 2½ inches and clocked a
wind-assisted 9.6 100 yards. The time was equal to the world record
but it was never taken too seriously by the man concerned, who
knew better than most the fickleness of sprint times. Two weeks
later he became the only man to score a double in the AAA 100
yards (9.9) and long jump (22 feet 8½ inches) championships.

To his dismay, Abrahams was selected to compete in the 100
metres, 200 metres, long jump and relay in Paris. 'A Famous International Athlete' (Abrahams himself, actually!) sounded off in the
Daily Express: 'H. M. Abrahams is chosen for four events, which
is unfortunate. From the point of view of the Olympic Games this
athlete should leave the long jump severely alone. The authorities
surely do not imagine that he can perform at long jumping at two
o'clock and running 200 metres at 2.30 on the same afternoon. Let

us hope that Abrahams has been told by the authorities to concentrate his efforts on the 100 metres.' The authorities did, in fact, excuse Abrahams from long jumping.

And so to Stade Colombes. 'Truthfully', Abrahams has written, 'I did not think I had any chance of a gold medal, nor did anyone else. I never really gave it a thought, though my trainer Sam Mussabini sent me a note just before the Games opened saying he thought I would win. But I had no anxieties, which was a godsend.' He was not being unduly pessimistic, merely realistic. Quite apart from the cream of the rest of the world's sprinters the American opposition was truly formidable. There was the immortal Charles Paddock, the reigning Olympic 100 metres champion and then the greatest speed merchant the world had known; Jackson Scholz, fourth in the 1920 final and a 10.6 100 metres performer; Loren Murchison, a finalist in both the 1920 sprints and double American champion in 1923; and promising Chester Bowman, who in later years was to blossom out as a 9.6 100-yarder. All Abrahams could point to was a genuine 9.9 100 yards (equivalent of 10.7/10.8 for 100 metres, whereas Paddock had once been credited with 10.2 for the slightly longer 110 yards) and an irregular 9.6.

There was a huge entry for the 100 metres of seventy-five (cf. seventy-three at Tokyo in 1964). The first round posed no difficulty and Abrahams cruised to victory in a sedate 11.0. Any resemblance to the Abrahams of 1920 ended there and then, for in the second round he won through to the semi-finals with a totally unexpected 10.6 . . . equalling the Olympic record set in a heat at the 1912 Games by Donald Lippincott (USA). Obviously he had timed his peak to perfection.

Next day, July 7th, at 3.15 p.m. he settled in his holes (remember, starting blocks were not patented until 1927) and rose to the set position. Here . . . 'I did a very stupid thing which nearly lost me the race. I saw a runner on my right move slightly. The pistol went (I thought there might be a recall), I took my mind right off the work in hand, and started badly as the result.' Left an estimated yard and a half down in a field that included such luminaries as Paddock, Bowman and Australia's 'Slip' Carr, a lesser man might have panicked. Instead, Abrahams revealed the physical and mental qualities of a world champion in the making by smoothly making up the lost ground and not merely qualifying in second or third place but winning in 10.6! Now, for the first time, he realised he

was capable of winning the final and consequently for the next
3¾ hours he 'felt like a condemned man feels just before going to
the scaffold'.

The draw for the final, at 7.05 p.m., was Paddock, Scholz, Murchison, Abrahams, Bowman and Arthur Porritt, a Rhodes Scholar
from New Zealand. Abrahams went to his mark with Sam Mussabini's parting words installed in his subconscious: 'Only think of
two things—the report of the pistol and the tape. When you hear
the one, just run like hell till you break the other.'

Britain's Dr E. Moir, the starter, got the field away to a perfect
start at the first time of asking. By the halfway mark Abrahams
was showing fractionally ahead of Scholz and Bowman and—
'scudding like some vast bird with outstretched wings, a spectacle
positively appalling in its grandeur'—the 24-year-old London Athletic Club and Achilles star soared through the tape in that by now
famous drop-finish of his two feet clear of Scholz. The time once
again was 10.6, or 10.52 to be exact. Porritt finished well to take the
bronze medal ahead of Bowman, with Paddock fifth and Murchison
last.

The first European ever to win the blue riband event of sprinting has always acknowledged the debt he owed Mussabini. 'Under
his guidance I managed to improve that decisive one per cent, which
made all the difference between supreme success and obscurity.'
Understandably there had to be a reaction following Abrahams'
rags-to-riches transformation as a 100 metres runner and in the
200 metres, though he did well even to reach the final (he clocked
a personal best of 22.0 in a heat), he was never in the hunt and
trailed home a weary last. Scholz was the winner in 21.6, followed
by Paddock and Liddell. An eventful week in Paris was completed
for Abrahams by a silver medal in the 4 × 100 metres relay along
with Walter Rangeley, Lancelot Royle and W. P. Nichol.

Such landmarks as a 9.6 100 yards and 25-feet long jump might
have fallen to Abrahams the following season but in May 1925 he
seriously damaged his leg while jumping and never competed again.
'I wonder if, in a sense, that was not another piece of good bad-
luck', he once wrote. 'How many people find it almost impossible
to retire at the right time. Would I have gone downhill, and tried
to go on? That was the decision I never had to make; it was made
for me. Rather painfully, but it was made.' He took over as an
administrator where he left off as a competitor and has remained

in the forefront of British athletics for over forty years. He has served on the AAA's General Committee since 1926 and as honorary treasurer of the British Amateur Athletic Board since 1948.

Happily, it was not too long after Abrahams' departure from competition before British sprinting threw up new candidates for international honours in Jack London and Walter Rangeley. Both won silver medals at the 1928 Olympics in Amsterdam.

London, who like Harry Edward hailed from British Guiana (he was brought to England at the age of three months) and was a member of Poly Harriers, finished two feet behind Canada's Percy Williams (10.8) in the 100 metres, after having tied the Olympic record of 10.6 in winning his semi-final. A strapping fellow, 6 feet 2 inches tall, London was truly a natural athlete; back in 1925 he had run the 100 in 'evens' at his first serious attempt and in 1927, without any special training, he had topped the British high jump rankings with a leap of 6 feet 2 inches. His vanquished rivals in the Olympic final included such stars as Georg Lammers (Germany), whose fastest time was 10.4; Frank Wykoff (USA), who was destined to win a gold medal in three consecutive Olympic sprint relays; and Wilfred Legg (South Africa), the AAA 100 yards champion. London, who placed only fourth at the AAA Championships, had a previous best 100 metres time of 10.7.

London, the first Briton to use starting blocks, admitted in his book *(The Way to Win on Track and Field)* that he broke all the rules of good sprinting technique. Even Mussabini failed to cure him of his bad starting, over-striding and too upright carriage. One day after Sam had died, London relates, he was practising starts when Albert Hill, the great middle distance runner turned coach, came over and made a few comments. He suggested the front foot be brought back eight inches and the hands kept down. 'Believe it or not,' wrote London, 'in that one lesson he gained me three-quarters of a yard on my start alone!' Hill became his coach and London attributed all his chief successes to Hill's guidance. London bowed out as an international in 1931 and later made a name for himself in show business circles.

Walter Rangeley proved far more durable; indeed his longevity as a top-flight sprinter was quite astonishing. In 1921 he placed third in the 100 and 220 at a 'national junior championships' organised by Manchester AC; in 1924 he gained a silver medal in the Olympic 4×100 metres relay; in 1928 he exceeded all expectations by taking second place in the Amsterdam 200 metres . . . and yet it was not until 1935 that he registered his fastest 100 metres time, a UK record of 10.5! His best furlong mark was 21.4 in 1934. Rangeley, a polished mover who rounded off his career at the age of 34 with fourth place in the AAA 220 final, encountered extremely tough opposition in that Olympic final of eleven years previously—not that Olympic medals have ever been won 'cheaply', not at least since 1908. He entered the straight in fourth position but a prodigious finishing burst carried him past defending champion Scholz and Germany's great Helmut Kornig to within only two feet of Percy Williams, the winner in 21.8.

Although not of the stature of their contemporaries London and Rangeley, Ernest Page and Stanley Englehart achieved a measure of success. The finest hour for both men came during the inaugural British Empire Games at Hamilton, Ontario, in 1930. In the absence of Williams, Englehart won the 220 in 21.8 from Olympic finalist John Fitzpatrick (Canada); while 20-year-old Page filled second place behind Williams (9.9) in the 100 yards, ahead of Fitzpatrick and Wilfred Legg. From the stopwatch point of view, Englehart's worthiest accomplishment was a 21.4 furlong in 1934, inches ahead of Rangeley; Page's a 10.6 100 metres in Paris in 1938.

The two outstanding dashmen of the thirties, though, were that closely matched pair, Cyril Holmes and Arthur Sweeney. Their numerous clashes were a constant source of excitement to spectators at the major pre-war meetings. They tangled on sixteen occasions between 1936 and 1939, the score being 7-4 for Holmes at 100 yards/metres and 3-2 for Sweeney in the longer sprints.

Sweeney, six years the elder, was born in Dublin but lived practically all his tragically short life in England (he was killed in a flying accident in 1941). He burst into the top rank of British sprinters in 1934 when, after winning the RAF titles in 10.1 and 22.1, he split two of Europe's leading men in the AAA 100. Jozsef Sir (Hungary) won in 9.9, mere inches in front of Sweeney, who in turn finished a foot ahead of Holland's Chris Berger, destined to win the first European 100 metres championship less than two months later. Regrettably, Britain was not represented at that historic meeting in Turin. The smoothly striding Sweeney made a brilliant international debut against France, taking both sprints—the 200 metres in a speedy 21.4. A few days later, at London's White City, he scored a triple victory at the Empire Games: the 100 in

10.0, the 220 in 21.9 (with Rangeley third) and the anchor leg for England's winning 4 × 110 yards relay team.

At the following season's AAA Championships Sweeney got the better of the ungainly Dutchman Martinus Osendarp, one of the most successful European sprinters of all time, in the 100 yards but was decisively beaten in the 220. Two months later, though, he tied Applegarth's hallowed figures of 21.2 (which still existed as the European record) a yard behind Martinus Theunissen (South Africa) in Johannesburg. Holmes also ran a 21.2 furlong in 1935, but on a straight track—which saves about 0.4 seconds *vis-à-vis* the curved event.

Their first AAA duel occurred in 1936. Sweeney, one of the best starters in the business, showed ahead in the early stages of the 100 final but Osendarp overhauled him to win by a whisker in 9.8. Place times were not taken but Sweeney almost certainly must have duplicated the 9.8 he clocked in a semi-final. Holmes, a newcomer to this class of competition, finished a highly creditable third, half a yard down. Britain's leading sprinter at the Berlin Olympics, however, was neither Sweeney (who returned 10.6 and reached the 100 metres semi-finals) nor Holmes (who pulled up lame in a heat) but a 20-year-old Oxford freshman, Alan Pennington. He was timed at 10.6 in his second round heat and was only narrowly eliminated in the semi-finals by Jesse Owens (USA), Frank Wykoff (USA) and Lennart Strandberg (Sweden). Surprisingly, Britain's speediest 100-yarder in 1936 was Godfrey Brown, of quarter-miling fame, credited with 9.7 on the slightly down-sloping Fenner's track at Cambridge.

The 1937 season was a good one for British sprinting, with Holmes and Sweeney scoring maximum points in all their international match races. The exploit of the year was Sweeney's victory over Germany's redoubtable Erich Borchmeyer, co-holder of the European 100 metres record of 10.3, in a time of 10.4 at Wuppertal. This, the equivalent of 9.5 or 9.6 for 100 yards, stood as a UK best for nineteen years. Holmes and Pennington each recorded a wind-assisted 10.4: Holmes in losing by inches to the American champion Perrin Walker in Stockholm and Pennington in finishing behind Ben Johnson (USA) in Paris.

Holmes, who had been convinced of the importance of relaxation after watching Jesse Owens in Berlin, came into his own during the last two pre-war seasons. At the Empire Games in Sydney in February 1938 he succeeded the absent Sweeney in both events, his times of 9.7 and 21.2 equalling the British records; while in Zurich just three weeks before the start of the holocaust he dead-heated with the American star Clyde Jeffrey in a personal best 100 metres time of 10.5. Jeffrey, destined to equal the 100 yards world record of 9.4 the following year, later stated that a photo of the finish showed Holmes to be a clear winner. Holmes did not compete at the 1938 European Championships where Sweeney placed fifth in the 100 metres and Pennington third in the 200 metres. Both races were won by Osendarp, in 10.5 and 21.2.

Holmes managed to keep in good shape during the war and in August 1945 he scored a double (9.9 and 22.2) in the RAF v. Army v. AAA v. US Armed Forces match, a meeting that drew no less than 54,000 sport-starved enthusiasts to the White City. Holmes went on to become an English rugby international and his mantle settled on the shoulders of the man who followed him home in both races at that first post-war White City fixture . . . Emmanuel McDonald Bailey. As an 18-year-old, Bailey had made his AAA Championships debut in 1939. He progressed no further than the semi-finals of the 220 on that occasion, a state of affairs he was to rectify in no uncertain manner in later years.

Bailey, who recorded 9.8 and 21.2 in his native Trinidad during the war years, established himself as one of the greatest crowd pleasers in British athletics history. Between 1946 and 1953 no important meeting was complete without the sight of this tall, slim Polytechnic Harrier in full flight. If any sprinter personified 'poetry in motion' it was McDonald Bailey. His high-level consistency over a long period was astonishing; more often than not running against mediocre opposition on sluggish tracks and in unfavourable weather conditions he turned in dozens of clockings in the range of 9.6–9.8 for 100 yards and 21.1–21.5 for 220. In 'Mac' Bailey Britain had the good fortune to possess one of the world's most distinguished sprinters of that era and one wonders what he might have achieved had he been resident in the United States, with the good tracks, weather and competition he would have encountered there. As it was, he almost invariably recorded his greatest times abroad, notably his world record equalling 10.2 for 100 metres in Belgrade in 1951.

Bailey made an indelible impression on the 1946 AAA Championships, the first for seven years, by notching the first sprint double since 1932. He made an outstanding debut for Great Britain by taking the 100 yards against France in 9.7, a good three yards ahead

of Jack Archer, whom he had beaten easily also in the Championships. These convincing victories indicated his standing in Europe,
for less than three weeks after the French match Archer captured
the European 100 metres crown in Oslo in 10.6. Bailey, who was
ineligible for these Championships, clocked a breathtaking 10.3 in
Sweden a few days later—a tenth of a second outside the official
world record shared by Americans Jesse Owens and Hal Davis—
in defeating Archer by fully four yards.

Although Archer clearly was not in the same class as Bailey (who,
apart from the top Americans, was?) his success against the cream
of Europe's sprint talent was a splendid and unexpected achievement. Archer, who had been an even-timer in 1939 when only 17,
went to Oslo with a best 100 yards time of only 9.9 but, following
in the glorious tradition of Harold Abrahams and Jack London, the
big occasion inspired him to such a degree that he reeled off 100
metres times of 10.6 in heat, semi-final and final. He won with a
metre to spare.

Bailey enjoyed another devastating season in 1947 and posted
marks of the calibre of 9.6 (and a wind-assisted 9.4) for 100 yards,
10.3 for 100 metres and 21.2 for 200 metres. Unfortunately while
heading for a sensational 100 yards time—certainly a 9.5, perhaps
even a world record tying 9.4—at the White City in the inter-county
final he pulled a thigh muscle 20 yards from the tape while travelling
at about 25 m.p.h. Clasping his leg, he hopped the remainder of
the distance in agony and anguish . . . and still managed to hold
on to win by a yard from 18-year-old John Wilkinson in 10.0!
Wilkinson displayed tremendous promise at the end of the season:
on the lightning fast 500 metres track in Cologne he clocked 21.3
for 200 metres (the fastest by a European that year); at the World
University Games in Paris he won both the 100 (10.5) and 200
metres (22.2 into the wind); and on the same track in the match
against France he took the 200 metres in 21.3. Unhappily, Wilkinson
proved to be injury prone and he never fulfilled his immense
promise.

It was during 1947 that a 21-year-old Coldstream Guard, Lt.
Alistair McCorquodale, embarked upon his brief and brilliant
career. He won the Army 100 yards title in 9.9 and placed fifth in
the AAA final, sound but modest achievements that were no indication of what was to follow in 1948. With his considerable raw power
properly harnessed, thanks to coaching by former Olympic hero Guy

C

Butler, McCorquodale was the revelation of the year of the Wembley Olympic Games. He emerged from the shadows when at the Southern Championships he placed second to the famous Welsh rugby star Ken Jones and ahead of an injury-plagued Bailey. The following week, in spite of a poor start, he headed Bailey again in 9.9 and at the AAA Championships he finished second to Australia's John Treloar in the 100 and won the 220 yards.

That the burly Scot had timed his peak to perfection became evident in the first heat of the Olympic 100 metres; he ran the great American star Barny Ewell (co-holder of the world record of 10.2) to inches as both were timed in 10.5. He clocked another 10.5 in the second round and both he and Bailey fought their way into the final. McCorquodale then proceeded to thrill the huge crowd by the way he dared to match strides with his famed transatlantic rivals, men who could have given him a five-yard start only a few months earlier. He did not win a medal . . . but how close he came. Harrison Dillard (USA) won in 10.3 from Ewell and Lloyd La Beach (Panama), with the inspired Briton in fourth place just eleven-hundredths of a second (about four feet) behind the winner. One position behind him was the favourite, Mel Patton (USA), the first man to run 100 yards in 9.3. McCorquodale was not officially hand-timed but the electrical apparatus indicated 10.4, equal to Sweeney's UK record. Later in the Games he, together with Archer, Jones and Jack Gregory, gained a silver medal in the relay—and that, more or less, was the end of his track career. He preferred cricket. 'Had he carried on with his athletics career he would have been a force to reckon with anywhere in the world,' said McDonald Bailey. The Trinidadian, meanwhile, had finished sixth and last at Wembley, yet when asked in 1950 to single out his most pleasing performance he chose that. 'Why? Because I had to battle not only against the opposition but against nature, and to reach the final was a just reward. To do this when I was supposedly "finished" and against mental strain, worry, tension and illness, leaves me extremely gratified.'

The 1949 season marked a return to normality, i.e. Bailey 'streets' ahead of all domestic rivals. While in Iceland he recorded spectacular times of 9.5 for 100 yards and 10.2 for 100 metres. The latter, equal to the world record, was adjudged to be wind-assisted but there was no wind gauge in operation and Bailey always thought it to be a genuine performance. Bailey matched his best acceptable

100 metres time of 10.3 in 1950 as well as breaking through in the longer sprint with two 200 metres clockings of 20.9. On top of that, he made history by gaining his fourth AAA double (and was destined to defend both titles successfully for another three years!). Home grown talent seemed to be at a low ebb but, as in 1946, the challenge of the European Championships brought out the best in one sprinter at least. He was Brian Shenton, who had taken up sprinting in 1941, 'retired' the following year in the belief that he was too small to get anywhere, and reappeared in 1946. He competed without much distinction in the 1950 Empire Games and was picked for Brussels only at the last moment to replace the injured Wilkinson in the 200 metres. Running yards faster than ever before, Shenton reeled off 21.5 in heat, semi-final and final, leading all the way from the outside lane in the latter to win by three yards. Shortly afterwards, Shenton produced yet another 21.5 in the match against France but, keeping things in perspective, he found himself six yards behind Bailey's 20.9. Shenton went from strength to strength following his unanticipated triumph and was a mainstay of the British team for many seasons. His best times came late in his career: 9.7 for 100 yards (equalling the UK best) in 1957 and 21.2 for 200 metres in 1956.

Shenton's fastest 100 metres was a creditable 10.6 in Belgrade in 1951—but it probably did not feel that fast for he found himself further behind Bailey than usual. But Bailey was enjoying his day of days: 'carried by the electrifying urge of the 40,000 crowd' he took full advantage of the perfect conditions to tie the world record of 10.2, owned among others by his boyhood hero, Jesse Owens.

Carrying his age lightly, 31-year-old Bailey, whose gazelle like speed and grace had made him a household name and second only to the lure of a four-minute mile as a box-office attraction, shaped up as a potential winner of the 1952 Olympic 100 metres; perhaps also of the 200 metres for there were few to equal him as a curve runner whereas his starting prowess was relatively ordinary. Largely self-coached (he learnt much from Holmes in 1945) and one of the first British sprinters to make use of weight training, Bailey was a stylist of the classic school but it was just his textbook carriage that may have cost him the Olympic 100 metres crown in Helsinki. Although drawn in one of the worst two lanes, which had been saturated by rainwater dripping from the overlapping grandstand roof, Bailey was on terms with Lindy Remigino (USA) and Herb

McKenley (Jamaica) ten yards from the finish. But whereas his two rivals lunged for the tape Bailey maintained his upright form, ran through the tape as coaches insist, and lost the race. 'It was one of those times,' commented Bailey ruefully, 'when if I'd stuck out my chest I might have won.' As it was, the little known Remigino snatched the verdict by one inch from McKenley, with Bailey another nine inches behind. All three were credited with 10.4. Bailey resolved to win the 200 metres or bust; in fact he tied up in the straight to finish fourth behind the American trio in 21.0. Nobody questioned the ability of Bailey to have become an Olympic champion; it was his lack of high pressure competition that cost him so dearly.

Bailey wound up his long career in 1953, shortly after gaining his seventh AAA sprint double (a record that might well last for eternity), in order to turn professional rugby footballer. His departure left a void in British sprinting that was not to be filled satisfactorily for five years. During the interim the most notable performers were Brian Shenton, silver medallist in the 1954 Commonwealth 220; George Ellis, third in both sprints in the European Championships a few weeks later (Ellis, who in 1951 had become the first British junior to break 'evens' officially, ran a 1:53.2 half-mile in 1962!); and Roy Sandstrom, who recorded a genuine 10.3 100 metres in Budapest in 1956 but never again bettered 10.5, or 9.7 for 100 yards.

A wonderful new sprint talent emerged in 1958, Peter Radford by name. A serious kidney disease contracted when he was five confined him to a wheelchair for two years but, like so many other eventual world beaters, this bitter childhood experience equipped him with the grim determination and perseverance that are among the qualities so necessary to excel in sport. By the age of 14 he was already returning such times as 10.4 for the 100 and 24.0 for 220. The following season (1955) he followed up third place in the Midland youths 440 yards championship (54.4) with victory in the English Schools intermediate 100 yards. In 1956, still only 16, he returned 'evens' and in 1957, by now under the influence of AAA National Coach Bill Marlow, he was down to 9.9 and 21.8

Radford opened his momentous 1958 campaign with a wind-assisted 9.7 at Easter on his home track at Aldersley, Wolverhampton. Sceptics, understandably wary of unsubstantiated schoolboy times, were completely won over when he appeared at the important

London Athletic Club schools meeting later in the month. The surprise of seeing a bearded schoolboy paled in comparison to the sensation he created with his spectacular knee lift as he flashed to victory in 10.0. Obviously this frail looking (5 feet 10 inches tall, weighing 141 pounds) teenager had an exciting future in store but few were prepared for his rate of progress. At Aldersley in June he became the first Briton to run 100 yards in an authentic 9.6 and less than an hour later, against the wind, he clocked 21.4 a yard behind the country's premier furlong specialist, Dave Segal.

Representing one's country at such a young age can be a severe ordeal but Radford came through with flying colours. He performed splendidly at the Commonwealth Games in Cardiff, placing fourth in the 100 yards (missing the bronze medal by one-hundredth of a second) and assisting England to victory in the relay. A few days later, at the White City, he recovered brilliantly from a poor start to defeat all three Commonwealth medallists in 9.8. Yet better still was to come. He snatched third place in the European 100 metres final in Stockholm in 10.4, scored the greatest sprint double in British athletics history with UK metric record times of 10.3 and 20.8 against France (both were world junior 'records'), and ended in October with a British 220 yards record of 21.0 plus a wind-aided 9.4 century! As a postscript he was credited with a phenomenal 5.5 for 50 metres, an indoor world's best, in Germany.

Radford consolidated his position in 1959. He turned down numerous tempting scholarship offers from American universities but did travel to the United States for his first major competition of the season. Pitted against the co-world record holder (at 9.3), Dave Sime, he flashed into a yard lead at the halfway mark only to lose in a photo finish as both men were timed in a wind-assisted 9.5. Later his knees 'gave way', as he described it, in his first straight 220 race and he faded to third in 21.1. The following month he posted two national records in a week: 10.3 for 100 metres in Paris inches behind dead-heating Jocelyn Delecour (France) and Armin Hary (West Germany), and 9.4 for 100 yards on his favourite track, Aldersley. The 9.4 also constituted a European record but the European Commission of the IAAF refused to ratify the mark since the course was found to be three-quarters of an inch short! Later he collected his first AAA 100 yards title (curiously, the 220 always eluded him).

It was in the furlong, though, that Radford achieved his greatest

performance in 1960. The occasion was the Staffordshire Championships at Aldersley, attended by a mere 200 spectators. That Radford
was in tremendous form was obvious; he had opened his season
with a 10.5/21.0 metric double and in succeeding weeks had registered 9.6 for 100 yards, 10.4 for 100 metres, 21.0 for 220 yards
twice (equalling the UK record) and 30.0 for 300 yards. Conditions
at Aldersley on May 28th were just perfect and, in the absence of
any pressure, Radford was ideally relaxed—which is half the battle
for a sprinter seeking fast times.

This was the sequence of events on that memorable afternoon:
2.30—100 yards heat in 9.4, equalling the UK and European records
and only a tenth outside the world standard; 3.30—100 yards final
in 9.3, the wind blowing at 2.37 metres per second as against the
maximum allowed for records of two metres; 4.30—220 yards heat
in 23.2; 5.00—220 yards final in world record (for around a turn)
of 20.5. The 20.5 timing also constituted a world record for the
fractionally shorter 200 metres distance. Thus Radford, at the age
of 20, became the first British-born sprinter to set a world record
since Willie Applegarth's exploit in 1914. 'The start was perfect,'
recalled Radford, 'and I picked up speed round the sharp bend.
Normally I fade a little going into the straight but this time I felt
a new surge of energy and kicked right through to the tape.'

Radford, who thought he could improve his time by another fifth
of a second, never again encountered such a favourable combination
of circumstances and subsequently failed to better 20.9 for 200
metres, but over 100 metres he came almost as close to winning the
Olympic gold medal in Rome as had Bailey eight years earlier in
Helsinki. Radford's frequently mediocre starting ability let him
down when he could least afford it but an incredible burst over the
final 30 or 40 yards carried him into third place behind Hary
(10.2) and Sime (10.2) in a UK record equalling 10.3. If only he had
got away to a decent start . . . but athletics history is littered with
tantalising hypotheses. As world record holder, Radford appeared
to stand a great chance of winning the 200 metres but the combination of being slightly jaded after his 100 metres experience and
rather perverse seeding resulted in his being eliminated in the semi-
finals. Later in the Games, Radford joined forces with Dave Jones,
Dave Segal (the 1958 European 200 metres silver medallist) and
Nick Whitehead for bronze medals all round in the relay.

Although Radford produced the occasional good mark in later

seasons he never managed to recapture his very best form, nor has any other British sprinter attained such heights. Nonetheless, there have been a number of dashmen of good European class, including no fewer than three Jones's. Dave Jones twice tied the UK 100 metres record of 10.3 (1961 and 1963), set an unofficial world's best of 13.9 for 150 yards (1961), clocked 20.9 for 200 metres (1961 and 1963) and a windy 20.8 for 220 yards (1961), won four AAA furlong titles and placed second in the 1962 Commonwealth 220 yards. Welshman Berwyn Jones clocked 10.3 for 100 metres in 1963 prior to embarking on a successful Rugby League career and was rated the world's number four by the American magazine *Track and Field News*. Another Welshman, Ron Jones, recorded 9.5 in 1963 and 1965, enjoyed the rare distinction of running the world's fastest human, Bob Hayes, to a yard in the 1963 Britain v. U.S.A. match, and in his 34th year was still one of Britain's foremost sprinters in 1967. Other noteworthy speedsters of the sixties include Dave Segal, who while at college in the USA ran 9.5 (1960) and 20.6 for the straight 220 (1961 and 1962); Alf Meakin, a 9.5 performer in 1961; Lynn Davies, Wales' Olympic long jump champion, who returned 9.5 in 1964; Barrie Kelly, winner of the 60 metres at the inaugural European Indoor Games in 1966; and Menzies Campbell, of Scotland, who set a UK 100 metres record of 10.2 in 1967 and clocked 20.7 for 200 metres.

3

THE QUARTER-MILE

THE honour of winning the first two English quarter-mile championships, in 1866 and 1867, befell an Eton schoolboy by the name of J. H. Ridley but the real trail blazers of the period were Charles Guy-Pym, who was timed at 50.5 in 1865, and Edward Colbeck, who was unlucky not to go down in history as the first man to break 50 seconds for the distance.

Colbeck's best time of 50.4, at the 1868 English Championships, was made under extraordinary circumstances. Halfway through the race he collided with a sheep which had wandered on to the Beaufort House track in West London, a reporter of the day noting that the unfortunate animal stood motionless in Colbeck's path . . . 'being presumably amazed at the remarkable performance which the runner was accomplishing'. The sheep came off the worse in this chance encounter for its leg was broken while Colbeck, despite losing an estimated eight yards (about one second in time), went on to set a record that withstood all assaults for eleven years. Clearly of robust constitution, the tall long-striding Colbeck won the 880 yards in 2:02.0 and finished second in the 100 yards the same day. The following year Colbeck retained his title in an ambling 53.6, six-tenths of a second slower than a time posted earlier in the season by W. G. Grace of cricketing fame.

Jack Shearman equalled Colbeck's record in 1877 but it was not until 1886 that a British runner officially ducked under the 50-second barrier. The pioneer was Charles Wood, the noted sprinter, who recorded 49.8 in winning the AAA title but even that was small beer beside the achievement of the American 'Lon' Myers, an emaciated and disproportionately long-legged man who was the outstanding short distance runner of the nineteenth century. Myers, weighing a mere 110 pounds for a height of 5 feet 8 inches, had clocked 48.8 in October, 1881, three months after taking the AAA crown in 48.6—a time that was disallowed as a record due to a drop of over six feet between the start and finish of the race. Second in the championship race at Birmingham was the ill-fated William Phillips (49.2), who succeeded in matching strides with the master for 350 yards.

More remarkable still, apparently, was the Irishman Tom Malone. Following a modestly successful amateur career—he ran 120 yards in 12.0 in 1879 and won the AAA long jump in 1882—he emigrated at the age of 25 to Australia in 1882. Out there he enjoyed a great professional career during which he was credited with 47.6 for 440 yards (a time no amateur beat until 1916), 9.6 for 100, 21.5 for 220, 1:53.5 for 880, and such field event marks as a 6 feet 0½ inch high jump, 23 feet 4½ inches long jump, 48 feet 6 inches triple jump and 42 feet 1 inch shot-put!

The example of Myers, the first to treat the quarter as a prolonged sprint rather than a middle-distance race, rubbed off on the Rev. Henry Charles Lenox Tindall, a Kent county cricketer and former Cambridge 'Blue'. At the age of 26 he came up with a very special performance in the successful defence of his AAA title in 1889 . . . 48.5. Admittedly the shape of the Stamford Bridge track as it was then was advantageous—only one bend following a straight of 280 yards—but there can be no belittling Tindall's achievement. The mark stood as a world's best for eleven years and as an AAA Championship record until 1937! Off to a slow start, Tindall did not bother to take the lead until after 100 yards but then, to quote *The Sporting Life*, he 'turned on the steam in earnest' to win by seven yards from Ernest Pelling. What's more, Tindall returned to take the 880 the same afternoon in 1:56.4, excellent time for the era. 'Come, tell us where to find Tindall's fellow beyond the white cliffs of "perfide Albion",' enthused *The Sporting Life*.

Tindall's record was equalled by Edgar Bredin in 1895 at Stamford Bridge, which had three years earlier been converted into a standard two-turn 440 yards track. Bredin was a fine competitor, winner of three AAA titles in the half and two in the quarter, but he sustained a major defeat in the historic New York AC v. London AC match at Manhattan Field in September 1895. The winner in 49.0 was the home team's Thomas Burke, the man who was to win the inaugural Olympic 400 metres in Athens the following year, while the runner-up was Bredin's second string Gilbert Jordan. Although he had never previously bettered 50 seconds, Jordan ran the race of his life to lose only by inches. It was in 1896 that the

29-year-old Bredin—quoting Montague Shearman, the 1880 AAA 440 champion—'voluntarily joined the professional ranks, a step which was received with great surprise, as he was a gentleman by birth and education'. But then Bredin was no conventional figure; during his time he was a tea planter in Ceylon and a 'Mountie' in Canada. As a professional, Bredin's finest successes came in 1897 when he beat the American Charles Kilpatrick (holder of the world's amateur 880 record of 1:53.4) over 600 yards in 1:13.0 and 880 in 1:55.75.

With the loss of Bredin, British quarter-miling fell into the doldrums for a number of years and it was not until 1906 that 49 seconds was beaten again. It is worth recording, however, that R. W. Wadsley (the AAA 100 yards champion in 1899) inflicted a rare defeat on the celebrated American Maxie Long in the 1901 Championships . . . time 49.8. Long was the reigning Olympic champion and had in 1900 smashed the world's best shared by Tindall and Bredin with a sensational 47.8. Wadsley never really consolidated this performance although in 1902 he achieved the distinction of winning the first ever AAA furlong title.

The world of athletics first began to take notice of a London-born Scot by the name of Wyndham Halswelle in 1905. This dashing young lieutenant in the Highland Light Infantry, a veteran of the Boer War, succeeded in winning the AAA title in a modest 50.8. Next year, fresh from setting a Scottish 440 record of 49.6 *en route* to a 1:11.8 600 yards, he achieved the extraordinary feat of capturing four Scottish championships in one afternoon: the 100 in 10.4, 220 in 23.2, 440 in 51.4 and 880 in 2:00.4. Two weeks later, in London, he improved to 48.8 in retaining his AAA laurels. Halswelle confined himself to the short sprints in 1907, wisely sharpening up his speed in preparation for the 1908 Olympic 400 metres. His form as the Games neared was brilliant. In the space of a fortnight he recorded a world's best 300 yards time of 31.2, set a British 440 record of 48.4 that was to survive for twenty-six long years (it should be noted that 'The Sheffield Blade' Dick Buttery was credited with a professional record of 48.25 way back in 1873, not to mention Tom Malone), and romped away with the AAA title in 49.4 at the newly opened White City. It was to this venue, then known as the Great Olympic Stadium and claimed to be 'the largest, most costly and best appointed the world has yet known', that Halswelle returned later in July for the fourth of the modern Olympic celebrations.

Halswelle, the favourite, began well by winning his heat in 49.4 and fared even better in the semi-finals with victory in the Olympic record time of 48.4. The next fastest qualifier, at 49.0, was W. C. Robbins, one of three Americans to join Halswelle in the four-man final the following day on the three-laps-to-the-mile track. The draw resulted in J. C. Carpenter taking the inside position, then Halswelle, Robbins and J. B. Taylor. The race was not run in lanes (or 'strings' as known in those days) and consequently something of a free-for-all developed. Halswelle was baulked by Robbins within the first 50 yards but that was nothing compared to what was to happen later.

Here, in Halswelle's own words, is what occurred. 'I did not attempt to pass the Americans until the last corner, reserving my efforts for the finishing straight. Here I attempted to pass Carpenter on the outside, since he was not far enough from the kerb to do so on the inside, and I was too close up to have crossed behind him. Carpenter's elbow undoubtedly touched my chest, for as I moved outwards to pass him he did likewise, keeping his right arm in front of me. In this manner he bored me across quite two-thirds of the track, and entirely stopped my running. As I was well up to his shoulder and endeavouring to pass him, it is absurd to say I could have come up on the inside. I was too close after half-way round the bend to have done this; indeed to have done so would have necessitated chopping my stride, and thereby losing anything from two to four yards. When about 30 or 40 yards from the tape I saw the officials holding up their hands, so I slowed up, not attempting to finish all out.'

The judges declared 'no race' and an official inquiry into the alleged obstruction was held that evening. Dr A. R. Badger, a vice-president of the AAA stationed as an umpire on the bend just before the beginning of the finishing straight, said in evidence: 'The position of Robbins at that point was that he was leading and about a yard in front of Carpenter. Robbins and Carpenter were in such a position as to compel Halswelle to run very wide all round the bend, and as they swung into the straight Halswelle made a big effort and was gaining hard; but running up the straight the further they went the wider Carpenter went out from the verge, keeping his right shoulder sufficiently in front of Halswelle to prevent his passing. When they had run 30 yards up the straight Carpenter was about 18 inches off the outside of the track. I at once ran up the track, waving my hands to the judges to break the worsted.'

As referee, Mr D. Scott Duncan, a member of the British Olympic Council and secretary of the Scottish AAA, was positioned on the cycle track immediately opposite the winning post. He told the inquiry: 'Swinging into the straight Halswelle commenced to gain on the two men in front, whereupon Carpenter made straight for the outside edge of the track, while Robbins nipped through on the inside. The boring by Carpenter continued, and the umpires held up their hands and signalled a foul. The worsted was broken, but I do not know by whom. Three of the judges, Messrs Parry, Penny-cook and Fisher, consulted with me, and on the evidence of the umpires the race was declared void, and the words "no race" were signalled on the telegraph board and announced by mega-phone.'

The outcome was that Carpenter, whose 'winning' time has been quoted as anything from 47.8 to 48.6, was disqualified and a re-run ('in strings') ordered for two days later. Regrettably, Halswelle was the only taker, for Taylor and Robbins—in a gesture of sympathy for Carpenter—boycotted the re-run. Thus the spectators were offered the bizarre spectacle of their man running the distance solo in 50 seconds dead for his gold medal.

Halswelle did not race again after that season (he was to be killed in action in 1915) and apart from a 1:11.0 600 yards, equalling the world's best, by Edwin Montague in 1908 a complete decade was to flit by before another British quarter-miler reached world class. Ireland could point to Beauchamp Day, who twice clocked 47.8 in Australia in 1907, but he was a professional.

The second decade of this century may have been a dead period but the 1920s and 1930s were palmy days indeed. One outstanding quarter-miler followed another . . . Guy Butler, Eric Liddell, God-frey Rampling, Godfrey Brown, Bill Roberts. This golden era began in the Olympic year of 1920. Early in the season Devonshire-born Bevil Rudd, a chain smoking South African Rhodes Scholar at Oxford, and Guy Butler, Cambridge's 1919 AAA champion, dead-heated at the annual varsity clash in 49.6. This pair locked horns on two even more important occasions that year, with Rudd emerging the victor at the AAA Championships and the Olympics them-selves. Both these tall, powerfully built men came from sports-loving families: Rudd's grandfather won the Harrow School mile in 1862,

Butler's father was a Cambridge cricket 'Blue' and English rackets champion in 1889.

The rain-sodden track at Antwerp held Rudd's winning 400 metres time down to a mediocre 49.6 (he had returned 48.6 for 440 yards earlier in the year), with Butler closing fast at the end to gain the first of his four Olympic medals—the most ever obtained by a British athlete. There was certainly nothing hollow about the placings, for the cream of the world's quarter-miling talent was present. Frank Shea (USA), a sub-48 seconds 400 metres performer, placed fourth while 440 yards world record holder (at 47.4) Ted Meredith, another American, did not even make the final. Butler and John Ainsworth-Davis, a surprising fifth, together with Cecil Griffiths and R. A. Lindsay later collected a set of gold medals for winning the 4 × 400 metres relay. Rudd represented South Africa although he had previously run for England in a match against Scotland and Ireland.

Rudd retired in 1921 but Butler was still one of the world's best when the next Olympics came around in 1924. Unfortunately a 'game' leg which held him back for much of his distinguished career put paid to his chances of going one better than in Antwerp. Obliged to use an upright start with his thigh encased in a bandage, Butler did extraordinarily well to reach the 400 metres final in Paris at all. Yet such were his fighting qualities that he returned an estimated 48.0 (a European and UK best) in his semi-final and went on to finish third in the final in 48.6. He was lying second until overtaken in the last few strides by Horatio Fitch (USA). Under any other circumstances such a magnificent and plucky feat would have received the attention and acclaim it merited but on this occasion it tended to be overlooked in the excitement surrounding the winner of the race . . . Eric Liddell.

More than forty years after the event Liddell's success still reads like a fairy story. If ever a man was inspired by the supreme test of Olympic competition, that man was Eric Liddell. The son of a Scottish missionary, Liddell was born at Tientsin, China, on January 16th 1902. At the age of five he was brought to Britain and in 1920 he enrolled as a divinity student at Edinburgh University. The following year, aged 19, he landed his first Scottish sprint titles and won the 100 yards in the then annual triangular international match between England, Scotland and Ireland. He made little progress as a runner in 1922, in which year he gained the first of his 'caps' as a rugby three-quarter, but the next season he established himself as one of the fleetest sprinters in British history by capturing the AAA double in 9.7 and 21.6. In view of the 100 yards time being only one tenth of a second slower than the world record, Liddell was immediately hailed as Britain's white hope for the 1924 Olympic 100 metres crown and it came as a blow, therefore, when Liddell announced that he would not contest that event in Paris as the heats were to be run on a Sunday. He decided instead to aim for the 200 and 400 metres.

The quarter-mile is one of the most demanding events in the athletics schedule. Adrian Metcalfe, as eloquent a writer as he is gifted an athlete, has described the 440 in these terms: 'It is a sprint which also possesses those features one admires most in middle-distance events: stamina, the need to fight till the tape, the virtual masochism of pleasure through prolonged pain—a race in which one's body reaches to one's internal conflict. Physically the race is simple. But to make oneself do it . . . that is the challenge which, if overcome, yields the tremendous satisfaction.'

Liddell accepted the challenge. His first truly international class quarter-mile race was the AAA championship on June 21st 1924, which he proceeded to win in the personal best but frankly commonplace time of 49.6 from two good Oxford University opponents in D. M. Johnson of Canada and Bill Stevenson, the 1921 USA champion. 'People may shout their heads off about his appalling style', wrote Harold Abrahams of Liddell the quarter-miler. 'Well, let them. He gets there.' Be that as it may, his chances of winning through against the cluster of Olympic entrants credited with times in the 48-seconds region seemed fairly remote—even allowing for the 'guts' he had shown in the previous year's triangular international when, knocked over soon after the start, he picked himself up, hared off in pursuit, won the race in 51.2 . . . and promptly blacked out.

That Liddell was in the form of his life was made evident when on July 9th he gained the bronze medal in the Olympic 200 metres behind the USA's Jackson Scholz and Charles Paddock; but still the world remained unsuspecting. On July 10th Liddell cruised through his first round 400 metres heat in 50.2 far behind Holland's Adrian Paulen (subsequently to become one of Europe's most prominent athletics administrators); and later in the day won his quarter-final in a personal best of 49.0. Next day he caused a minor stir by taking the second semi-final in 48.2, only four-tenths of a second slower than Fitch's Olympic record in the first semi. Six men lined up for the final a few hours afterwards: two Americans (Fitch and Coard Taylor), two Britons (Liddell and Butler), a Swiss (Joseph Imbach) and a Canadian (Johnson). Liddell was drawn in the dreaded outside lane—a particular disadvantage for a relative novice at the event—but made light of this handicap as he sportingly shook hands with his rivals prior to the start.

At the crack of the pistol Liddell sprinted away like a man possessed; moving at a pace altogether unprecedented for a 400 metres race he flashed past the halfway mark in an unheard of 22.2, a good four yards clear of Butler, his nearest opponent. Liddell's head was thrown back, his arms all over the place, his knee drive exaggerated . . . the experts shook their heads knowingly; they were watching a classic example of a sprinter misjudging his effort. It was inevitable that he would 'blow up' in the finishing straight if not earlier. Any other man would have done so but the inspired 22-year-old Scot was in the process of making history. Somehow he summoned up hidden reserves of stamina and, incredibly, even managed to increase his lead in the final stages. At the tape he had no less than eight-tenths of a second to spare over Fitch, with the gallant Butler a close third.

The time was almost as sensational as the manner of his victory . . . 47.6 or only a fifth outside the best time on record. In fact Liddell's time, absurdly, was officially ratified as a world record because, reasoned the IAAF, Ted Meredith's 47.4 was made over 440 yards ($2\frac{1}{2}$ yards further) and not 400 metres! As a European and UK best, Liddell's mark stood for a dozen years and it represented a gain of some 1.7 seconds over Liddell's pre-Olympic fastest. To be scrupulously fair, it must be pointed out that the Stade Colombes track at the time of the Games measured 500 metres round, an advantage of perhaps a fifth of a second compared to a two-turn 400 metres circuit.

A few days later Liddell bowed out from the international scene with another glorious run, returning under 48 seconds for his 440 yards leg in the British Empire v. USA match in London. He took over for the final stage of the mile relay five or six yards down on Fitch, and won by a stride. Next season was his last, for after gaining a splendid treble at the 1925 Scottish Championships (10.0, 22.2, 49.2) he joined his father as a missionary in China. There he is reputed to have run 400 metres in 49.0 in 1929 and it was there, the land of his birth, that the Rev. Eric Liddell met his death on February 21st 1945 in a Japanese prison camp.

Guy Butler, who in Liddell's absence anchored Britain into third place in the Paris 4 × 400 metres and thus earned his fourth Olympic medal, continued his career to such good effect that at Stamford Bridge in 1926 he equalled the world 300 yards record of 30.6. On the same track the following weekend he took the AAA furlong in his best time of 21.9. As Butler contested only the 200 metres at the 1928 Olympics Britain's 400 metres hopes at Amsterdam rested on John Rinkel, whose fastest was only 49.4. Rinkel, a 21.6 220 performer, added his name to the pleasingly large number of British athletes who have soared to unforeseen heights in the cauldron of Olympic competition by snatching fourth place in the final in 48.3, barely three yards in arrears of the winner. Shortly afterwards, in the traditional British Empire v. USA match, Rinkel ran close to 47 seconds for his 440 yards relay leg. It is mere conjecture but had he gone for the 400 metres it seems likely that Douglas Lowe could have earned a medal (the bronze went at 48.2), for the great half-miler almost invariably beat Rinkel and in the Amsterdam 4 × 400 metres relay he turned in the fastest stage of the race: 47.6. His best official 440 time was 48.8. The other prominent Briton of the late twenties was Roger Leigh-Wood, who recorded a 48.5 quarter in South Africa in 1929.

On to the stage now stepped that lion-hearted competitor, God-frey Rampling. Coached in his early days by the legendary Walter George, Rampling first attracted attention in May 1928 when he won the 880 yards in 2:02.2 at a service cadets meeting. The time, even for a 19-year-old, was nothing special; the manner of his running was. The ubiquitous Harold Abrahams happened to be on hand and here is how he described the race for the *Sunday Times*: 'The judgment displayed by the winner, G. L. Rampling, was certainly somewhat primitive. He led at the end of the first quarter in 55.8 (not much slower than Dr Peltzer's first lap in his memorable half-mile record) and then proceeded to get slower and slower, just reaching the tape five or six yards ahead of C. M. Threlfall, who must have been 25 yards behind 220 yards from home.'

As Second Lieutenant Rampling, of the Royal Artillery, he gained a 440 (50.0) and 880 (1:57.8) double at the 1930 Army Championships but it was in 1931 that he really began to make his mark

Harold Abrahams wins the 1924 Olympic 100-metres title in 10.6 sec.

Versatile Godfrey Brown (left), best known as a quarter-miler, defeats
Arthur Sweeney in the 1936 Kinnaird Trophy 100 yards in 9.9 sec.

Arnold Strode-Jackson came through with a late burst to win the 1912
Olympic 1,500-metres crown in 3 min. 56.8 sec.

Derek Johnson defeats Brian Hewson in the half-mile at the Britain v.
West Germany match in 1955

on the nation's athletics. During a brilliantly successful season he won the AAA quarter in 48.6, the Army furlong title in a career best of 22.0 and his first two international races—against France (48.0 400 metres) and Italy (48.8 440 yards). He saved his best running, though, for the fixture against Germany in Cologne. This was a relays match and Rampling seized the opportunity to create a world-wide reputation in this form of competition. In both his races, the 4 × 400 metres and 1600 metres medley, contested within an hour, he came from behind to defeat the redoubtable Adolf Metzner—his 'legs' being timed at 47.0 and 46.6 respectively. The world record at the time stood at 47.0 by 'Bud' Spencer (USA), which shows just how good Rampling's performances were.

Just as he was shaping up as a potential Olympic medallist Rampling had the misfortune to contract a blood disease which was to ruin his chances in Los Angeles and hold back his progress until 1934. He managed to make the 1932 Olympic team but, painfully short of top-class competition, he was unable to do himself justice. All the same, he failed only by inches to qualify for the final which was won in the world record time of 46.2 by Bill Carr (USA). Typically, Rampling refused to be over-awed by the phenomenal American when they clashed on the final leg of the relay. Despite taking the baton ten yards down on Carr, he made a race of it and cut the lead by half as a result of a furious first furlong. However, as in that cadets half-mile four years earlier, Rampling over-reached himself in his enthusiasm and paid the penalty by 'dying' in the closing stages. Carr drew effortlessly away to win by some 25 yards, his stint occupying 46.2. Rampling, who held on grimly for second, was clocked in 48.1, compared to 47.6 by 800 metres champion Tom Hampson on the second stage and 46.7 on the third by the 1928 400 metres hurdles gold medallist Lord Burghley—neither of whom ever beat 49 seconds in level competition!

Rampling carried all before him on his return to the 'big time' in 1934, the most notable achievement being his victory in the Empire Games quarter at the White City in the British record time of 48.0. Unfortunately Britain was not represented at the first European Championships that summer, which was particularly frustrating for Rampling as the 400 metres title went to his old rival Metzner in 47.9.

Little was seen of Rampling in 1935 and the ascendancy was gained by Bill Roberts, who had finished second in the previous

D

year's Empire Games. Roberts won all three of his international match races: against Finland (48.8 for 440 yards notwithstanding a pause at the 220 mark when a fly flew up his nose!), France (48.5 for 440) and Germany (47.7 for 400 metres). Runner-up (48.4) in the last mentioned race was a 20-year-old Cambridge undergraduate making his international debut . . . Godfrey Brown. The younger brother of Ralph Brown, the AAA 440 yards hurdles champion in 1934, he was no stranger to athletic success. Between 1932 and 1934 he had won the Public Schools 880 yards title three years running (winning the long jump also in 1933 with a leap of 20 feet 11¼ inches) and early in the 1935 season he had won the quarter for his university against the AAA in 48.1. Prospects for the Berlin Olympics of 1936 were looking distinctly promising what with the experience of Rampling, the established ability of Roberts and the youthful promise of Brown.

It was Brown who set the pace during the opening phase of the all-important season. He met with success at all distances from 100 yards (he clocked 9.7 on the slightly downhill Fenners track and defeated no less a person than Arthur Sweeney at the Kinnaird Trophy in 9.9) to the 880, in which he was Midland champion. Indeed, at the AAA v. Cambridge match, he followed up his 9.7 '100' with other victories in the 440 (49.1) and 880 (1:56.0); while at the Kinnaird, the unofficial English inter-club championship, he also took on Rampling at the quarter for the first time and beat him by inches in 48.3.

The 'big three' clashed for the first and only time at the AAA Championships before a White City crowd of 40,000. It was a fine race, although the driving rain ruined the times. Roberts went out fast, too fast, for he cracked in the final straight and both Brown and Rampling sailed past. Brown won by about four yards from Rampling in 48.6 with Roberts inches behind in third place. The trio reached the 400 metres semi-final stage in Berlin intact. Roberts won his second round heat in 47.7 while Brown and Rampling finished second in theirs in 48.3 and 48.0 respectively. The first semi saw Roberts safely through as he placed second to Archie Williams (USA) in a relatively sedate 48.0. Brown and Rampling had a tougher task in the other race, for it needed 47.4 to make the final. Brown succeeded with second in 47.3 (clipping 0.3 from Liddell's UK record) but Rampling was edged out of third place in spite of returning 47.5, the fastest time of his career.

The draw for the final, staged in practically perfect conditions the same day, was—reading from the inside—John Loaring (Canada), Bill Fritz (Canada), Jimmy LuValle (USA), Roberts, Williams and Brown. The British champion got away very smartly and held the lead at the first bend but, endeavouring to relax, he eased off a shade too much along the back straight. The outcome was that with 150 yards left to run Williams held a lead of two or three yards. Brown strove valiantly to overcome the deficit and all along the finishing stretch he was edging closer to the American . . . but his mighty efforts resulted in glorious failure. At the tape Williams was still ahead: by seven inches to be precise! The photo finish timing apparatus credited Williams with 46.66 and Brown with 46.68, which makes nonsense of the differential in the official stopwatch times (46.5 for Williams, 46.7 for Brown). As a European record, Brown's time lasted until 1939; as a British best it survived until the European final in 1958! An equally tense Anglo-American struggle ensued for the bronze medal, with Roberts failing by less than a foot to catch LuValle. Both men were given 46.8 (46.84 to 46.87 electrically).

Two days after this epic race Brown and Roberts won themselves a gold medal apiece in the 4 × 400 metres relay, along with Freddie Wolff and Rampling. Back at the White City the following week Roberts defeated Williams on the first leg of the British Empire v. USA 4 × 440 yards relay and Brown, on the anchor, was timed in an astonishing 45.9. More about these stirring events in the chapter on relays.

With Rampling retired from major athletics, Brown and Roberts continued to dominate British and European quarter miling in 1937. Brown's successes included an exceptional clocking of 19.2 for 200 yards amid the slush and snow of Fenners in February, a barn-storming American tour which yielded personal bests at 440 (47.7) and 880 (1:52.2), a 47.2 400 metres in Stockholm, and victory at the World University Games. As for Roberts, he won against France (47.5 400 metres) and Germany (48.2 440 yards) and deposed Lenox Tindall as AAA Championship record holder with a time of 48.2, three-tenths inside the 48-year-old figures.

Roberts struck the first blow in 1938 when, in Brown's absence, he won (or did he?) the Empire Games 440 title at the second attempt. In a desperately close race in Sydney he was awarded the verdict over fellow Olympic finalist Fritz in a personal best of 47.9

but it is reported that a judge admitted later that he had erred and in fact Fritz ought to have been placed first. During the summer, though, Roberts was no match for Brown who went through the whole season undefeated. The climax was his runaway victory (in 47.4) in the European 400 metres championship in Paris. His winning margin over runner-up Karl Baumgarten (Netherlands) was a good half-dozen yards. The one man who could have tested him was Germany's Rudolf Harbig, who clocked 46.8 that year, but he went for and won the 800 metres. It may be significant that the week after the Championships Brown beat the American 46.6 quarter-miler Ray Malott in 47.1 for 400 metres, and Malott had earlier defeated Harbig. Four days later, having travelled from Milan to Oslo, Brown returned the second fastest 400 metres time of his career (46.9) in spite of encountering hamstring trouble at the 300 metres mark. There is little doubt that Brown was the world's number one that year for at the White City he defeated both Fritz and Jim Herbert, Malott's runner-up in the American championship, in a 47.6 quarter. This was a British record but not officially an English one, since Brown was born in India.

As Roberts did not compete and Brown had not trained too seriously, the title of Britain's leading quarter-miler was transferred to Alan Pennington, the 10.6 100 metres performer, in 1939. He set a somewhat meaningless English native record of 48.0, a foot or two ahead of Brown, but Britain's supremacy in Europe was terminated for the race was won by Italy's Mario Lanzi in 47.6. The point was hammered home in Cologne when, despite a sparkling 47.3 for 400 metres in the Germany v. Britain match, Pennington was thrashed by the now great Harbig, who had the previous week established a world record of 46.0. Brown trailed in last in 48.7, the only time he was ever beaten by the opposition in an international match.

Brown, Pennington and Roberts all resumed their track careers after the war. The first two did not progress very far along the comeback trail but Roberts produced some remarkable performances for a man of his age. He placed fifth in the 1946 European Championships and bowed out in 1948, aged 36, with the captaincy of the Olympic team and a 48.5 clocking for 400 metres, the twelfth best in Europe that year.

The great figure in British quarter-miling circles in those days was Jamaican Arthur Wint. Although he ran for his native island at the Olympics he was a mainstay of the British international team for several seasons and, with clubmate McDonald Bailey, was the greatest crowdpuller in domestic athletics. He was an awe-inspiring sight when in full flight, his towering height (6 feet 4½ inches) and prodigious stride perpetually drawing gasps of wonder and admiration from spectators.

Wint was only 18 when, in 1938, he achieved his first international success by winning the 800 metres at the Central American Games in 1:56.3 and placing third in the 400 metres hurdles. Liberally endowed with natural talent, Wint could point to such marks as 9.9 for 100 yards, 21.2 for 220, 48.3 for 440, 1:56 for 880, 55.4 for 400 metres hurdles, a 6 feet 2 inch high jump and 24 feet 0 inch long jump when he came to England in 1944 as an officer in the RAF. He began to impress his personality on the British athletics scene as soon as the war was over and in 1946, besides AAA titles at 440 and 880, he won both the 400 and 800 metres at the Central American Games and clocked 47.0 in Sweden.

That time of 47.0 remained Wint's fastest prior to the Wembley Olympics of 1948 and, although recognised as a strong contender for a medal, he was given little chance of beating his compatriot and former schoolmate Herb McKenley, a man who had set world record figures of 46.0 for 440 yards two months earlier. Whatever hopes Wint might have entertained seemed to be dashed when he streaked to a brilliant but extravagant clocking of 46.3 in his semi-final—with the final to follow only 1¾ hours later. But McKenley, who cruised through his race in 47.3, was aware that his friend was in the greatest form of his life (three days earlier Wint had finished second in the 800 metres in his best time of 1:49.5), attempted to run the legs off him . . . and committed a fatal error of pace judgment. At the 200 metres mark he was eight yards up in 21.4, only three-tenths slower than the winning 200 metres time, but he began to tie up when the finishing straight was reached and the 28-year-old London medical student threshed his way past twenty yards from the tape to win in 46.2. Wint never ran quite that fast again but at the 1952 Olympics he won himself another two medals: a silver again in the 800 metres and a gold in the 4 × 400 metres relay. Such was the affection and esteem in which he was held by the British public that at the White City in September 1952 he was prevailed upon to run a lap of honour to mark his retirement from international competition.

Britain possessed a number of quarter-milers of good European calibre during the Wint era, the most successful being Derek Pugh. Quite unexpectedly he took the bronze medal at the 1946 European Championships in 48.9 for only three months earlier his best 440 yards time stood at a mediocre 50.6. He was an altogether more formidable proposition by the time of the next European Championships in 1950 and on that occasion he produced a storming finish to triumph in a personal best of 47.3, the fastest since the heyday of Brown and Roberts. In fact, prior to his victory, Pugh was ranked second in the country to Les Lewis who had placed a very close second in the Empire Games 440 yards in 48.0 and who had defeated Pugh in the AAA Championships, but Lewis finished only fifth in Brussels.

Brown's British 440 record of 47.6 came under severe fire in 1955 when Peter Fryer and Mick Wheeler practically dead-heated in 47.7 at the AAA Championships and it finally succumbed the following season when Peter Higgins—whose advisers had included Brown and Guy Butler—returned 47.5. The record would probably have been carried under 47 seconds in due course by Wheeler had he not decided to retire following the Melbourne Olympics at the ripe old age of 21. Who knows what he might have achieved in his best years, the mid-twenties; suffice to record that after an absence of eight seasons he made a remarkable comeback in 1965 to clock 47.8 for the quarter!

British quarter-miling enjoyed its finest moments since pre-war days when, at the 1958 European Championships in Stockholm, John Wrighton and John Salisbury filled first two places in 46.3 and 46.5 respectively—both of them inside Brown's hallowed UK record. As in 1950 the 'wrong man' succeeded. Salisbury appeared to possess the better qualifications in view of his AAA title in 47.2 and his fourth place (47.1), one ahead of Wrighton, in the Commonwealth Games, but on the day Wrighton proved the stronger and, after taking the lead at the halfway mark, held off his team-mate all the way along the finishing straight.

Wrighton, 6 feet 3 inches tall and with a pronounced forward lean when running, was just a moderate sprinter when Arthur Wint spotted him and recommended him to move up to the one-lap event. It was good advice and he improved steadily each season, ducking under 48 seconds for 400 metres for the first time in 1956. His pace judgment, however, tended to be erratic and he was known on occasion to cover the first furlong in under 22 seconds, which was perilously close to his fastest for that distance. He admits that it was not until 1958 that he learnt how to distribute his effort properly.

Neither Wrighton nor Salisbury, nor their two colleagues in the victorious European 4 × 400 metres relay team, Ted Sampson (who, 'out of the blue', had posted a British 440 record of 46.8 in a Commonwealth Games heat) and Scotsman John MacIsaac (who clocked 47.3 at these Cardiff Games), ever improved upon their 1958 performances. By 1960 a fresh crop of youngsters had thrust their way to the top. They were headed by Robbie Brightwell, who as a junior had placed fifth in the 1958 European 200 metres final.

Conscious that a best 100 yards time of 9.7 was not fast enough to enable him to reach the heights as a furlong runner, Brightwell was persuaded to move up a distance in preparation for the 1960 Olympics. 'There are', he remarked, 'no attractions for quarter-miling as far as I am concerned—just force of circumstances. If I was good enough in the sprints I would sit tight and count my blessings.' Reluctant or not, Brightwell lost little time in establishing himself as Britain's fastest ever quarter-miler. In the very first individual 440 yards race of his life, in June 1960, he won in 47.6, although in spite of such a formidable debut he felt that 47 seconds represented his limit for the season. He under-rated himself. He finished second (47.0) in the AAA 440 behind India's Commonwealth champion Milkha Singh and in the match against France he recorded 46.5 for 400 metres. He rose magnificently to the occasion at the Rome Olympics, reducing the UK record to 46.2 in his quarter-final and 46.1 in his semi-final, failing by inches only to win through to the final. Quite a performance by a 20-year-old in his first season at the event!

Even allowing for the promise of still younger runners like Malcolm Yardley, with 46.6 for 400 metres at the age of 19, and Barry Jackson, with 47.0 for 400 metres while still 18, there seemed no reason to doubt that Brightwell was at the start of a long period of British quarter-miling leadership. Sure enough he commenced his 1961 campaign in storming fashion. Running in Moscow on July 1st he demolished Olympic finalists Manfred Kinder (West Germany) and Milkha Singh by five yards in 46.2 and four days later, in Helsinki, he beat the two leading Americans, Ulis Williams and Adolph Plummer, in 46.6. He was on top of the world . . . for

forty-eight hours. On July 7th came stunning news from Oslo:
Brightwell's UK 400 metres record had been lowered to 45.8 by 19-
year-old Adrian Metcalfe, whose previous best was 47.3 for 440
yards! Metcalfe's time was received at first with a certain amount
of scepticism—after all, he had only taken up quarter-miling
seriously the previous October and it was only on June 13th that
he broke 48 seconds for the first time. But any doubts as to the
authenticity of the mark were swept away when it was made known
that second in that race was Milkha Singh. One had to be great to
beat him.

The first one-lap clash between these two strapping young men
was eagerly awaited but at the AAA Championships Brightwell
opted for the 220 and Metcalfe won the quarter on a flooded track
in 47.6. One week later they did meet at 440 but their personal rivalry
was submerged in the excitement of the first ever match between
Britain and the United States. It was a memorable race if hardly
pleasing to Brightwell who found his time of 46.8 sufficed only for
last place! Williams won in 46.3, narrowly ahead of Metcalfe whose
46.4 broke the UK and European records. Plummer, destined two
years later to hack the world record down to an amazing 44.9, was
third in 46.8. Next day Metcalfe became virtually a national hero
with a superb 440 yards relay anchor in 45.3.

This exciting pair tangled on six further occasions in 1961, Metcalfe winning four. The fastest race was in Dortmund where
Metcalfe, in the outside lane, reduced the national 400 metres record
to 45.7, the fastest in the world that season and the best on record
by a 19-year-old. Characteristically, he entered the home straight
two or three yards down but overhauled the opposition with a
vigorous finishing drive. Brightwell just edged Kinder for second
place in a personal best of 45.9.

Metcalfe, described by the American coach 'Jumbo' Elliott as
possessing 'the greatest potential I've ever seen in an athlete of his
age', had the world at his feet. Anything and everything was possible for the long striding (up to 9 feet 6 inches when suitably
relaxed) Yorkshireman. Asked what his target was for 1962 he had
replied: 'To run the legs off anyone I run against and if this means
doing under 45 seconds then I shall have to do it.' One believed
him. But, being human and therefore the 'slave of circumstance',
Metcalfe was destined to fail in his ambitious but perfectly feasible
plans to conquer the world. Injury and illness conspired to plague

him in subsequent seasons and never again was he to run faster than 46.2 for 400 metres—no mean performance, admittedly. His only notable placing in a major international championship was fourth in the 1962 European 400 metres but, as will be related in a later chapter, he scaled the heights once again as a relay runner on just the right day.

With Metcalfe displaying top class form only intermittently it was left to Brightwell to maintain Britain's considerable prestige in this event. And a good job he made of it. Faster than ever he was in his days as a sprint specialist (he cut his 200 metres time to 20.9) Brightwell enjoyed a magnificent season in 1962. He won the AAA title almost casually in 45.9 ('I thought it was about 47 seconds', he commented incredulously when informed of his time) —a European 440 record and only a fifth of a second outside the world record. He duplicated that time, but over 400 metres, in capturing the European title. Actually Brightwell misjudged his race on that occasion, for he ran the first 100 metres much too fast and was a sitting target in the final stages. Sheer guts enabled him to hold off Kinder. As mentioned earlier, Metcalfe was fourth (in 46.4) and Barry Jackson excelled himself in taking fifth place in 46.6. An attack of dysentery on the eve of the 440 yards final weakened Brightwell at the Commonwealth Games in Perth and he was beaten, though only just, by Jamaica's George Kerr.

A foot injury sustained while making a rare indoor appearance caused Brightwell to miss most of the 1963 season but in October he proved himself none the worse for his enforced lay-off by registering 46.2 for 400 metres. He made it known that 1964 would be his final season and that nothing short of the Olympic 400 metres title would satisfy him. To that end he trained as perhaps no other quarter-miler has ever trained, often running himself to a state of sickness or even collapse. He believed that the Tokyo victor would be the strongest and not necessarily the fastest man in the field; thus he concentrated on improving his stamina. That he succeeded in this aim was made crystal clear when, early in the season, he defeated Britain's leading half-miler John Boulter in the exceptional time of 1:48.1. After clocking a 46.5 quarter on a practically flooded track at Loughborough his target of 44.5 for 400 metres (0.4 inside the world record) began to look a more realistic proposition but the hyper-fast times being recorded by his American rivals (Mike Larrabee 44.9, Ulis Williams 45.0, Ollan Cassell 45.6) continued to elude him. His best for 400 metres was 'only' 46.0, achieved both in the American championships (where he was narrowly beaten by Larrabee) and in Warsaw, where he turned the tables on Larrabee but lost the race to Poland's Andrzej Badenski (45.7). He was, however, turning in some tremendous relay performances, most notably a 44.7 400 metres stint (from a flying start, of course).

Hopes of success were raised again when Brightwell won his Olympic semi-final on a soggy track in a UK record equalling 45.7. Larrabee took the other race in 46.0. But when it came to the final the inspiration had drained away; Olympic nerves had claimed another victim. Not that he ran badly; indeed he clocked 45.7 again but this time it was mechanical, devoid of passion, and by the time he entered the finishing straight he knew he had lost and there was no fight left. Larrabee won in 45.1; Brightwell was fourth, a failure in his own eyes. That was his last individual race but, happily, he redeemed himself with a truly heroic anchor leg in the relay.

Brightwell may have fallen short of his expectations in the Tokyo 400 metres although running as fast as he had ever done, but who would have predicted that Tim Graham—curiously, like Brown and Brightwell, born in India—would finish only a couple of yards behind his team captain? For that matter who would have predicted he would reach the final at all? Graham, who did not break 48 seconds for the quarter until 1963 and whose pre-Olympic 400 metres best was 46.7, created one of the minor sensations of the Games by filling sixth place in the eight-man final in 46 seconds flat. After all the excitement of the Metcalfe-Brightwell era, British quarter-miling since 1964 has proved relatively flat, the best time being Graham's 46.6 440 yards in 1967.

4

THE HALF-MILE

THE half-mile is an in-between event, not exactly a sprint yet not really middle distance either. The effective half-miler requires an ample measure of speed coupled with the endurance and nimble tactical skill of the miler—a combination of talents that, judging by the numerous successes chronicled in this chapter, has been bestowed upon many a British runner.

The current world record for 880 yards may be inside 1¾ minutes but for the pioneers two minutes was the magic figure. The first to hit the target was the Hon. Arthur Pelham, a 6 feet 4 inches tall Cambridge undergraduate possessed of an enormously long stride, who recorded 1:59.8 in 1873. Six years earlier his brother, the Hon. Francis Pelham (later the Earl of Chichester), had clocked 2:02.5 for what is considered the inaugural world 'record'. Walter Slade, better known as a miler, reduced the mark in 1876 to 1:58.2 but before the year was out Fred Elborough had returned 1:57.5. In this, the greatest 880 race contested up to that time, Arthur Pelham held a lead of several yards at the half distance but was overtaken 250 yards from home by Slade, who in turn was passed by H. W. Hill. Finally, 100 yards from the finish Elborough ploughed past everybody to win by three or four yards. Hill (1:58.0) was also inside Slade's previous figures, while Slade himself was timed in 1:58.8 and Pelham in 1:59.8.

Walter George, of whom much will be heard in succeeding chapters, made his contribution to British half-miling progress by returning 1:57.0 in 1880 and winning the AAA titles of 1882 and 1884, on the latter occasion taking the mile and four miles the same day! The giant of the nineteenth century in this event, though, was Frank Cross, who created a sensation in 1888 when on the then three laps to the mile track at Iffley Road, Oxford, he clipped a full second from the world record held by the almost legendary American star Lon Myers. His time, a revolutionary 1:54.4, remained unbeaten by a British runner until 1925!

The performance was all the more remarkable in view of the track's six-foot rise and fall and the fact that Cross, in the words of eye witness Arthur Croome (the noted hurdler), 'cantered home, past home in fact, for he went on from the finish to the top of the back stretch before pulling up'. Cross, a sturdily built man weighing upward of 170 pounds, was a sub-50-seconds quarter-miler, a 4:23 miler (AAA champion in 1887) and a casual 21-foot long jumper. He specialised in running hard from the gun, in contrast to the usual delaying tactics of that era.

Those two great quarter-milers, Lenox Tindall and Edgar Bredin, produced the finest 'halves' of the next few years. Tindall won the 1889 AAA title by a dozen yards in 1:56.4 and Bredin the 1893 race with over 20 yards to spare in 1:55.25. Alfred Tysoe, whose first AAA success curiously was won at 10 miles in 1897, was the first English half-miler to achieve significant international victories. He triumphed at the 1900 Championships over a former American titlist John Cregan in 1:57.8 and nine days later in Paris he defeated Cregan again to become Olympic 800 metres champion in 2:01.2, after covering the final 400 metres in a spectacular 56.2. Tysoe picked up another gold medal in the 5,000 metres team race, in which individually he finished seventh.

The Rev. H. W. Workman kept up the good work the following season, winning a race in Montreal in 1:54.8, the closest approach yet to Cross's British best and only 1.4 seconds outside the world record set by Charles Kilpatrick (USA) in the New York AC v. London AC match of 1895. Workman became AAA champion in 1904, the year in which Kinahan Cornwallis of the reputed ten-foot stride clocked 1:54.8, but neither man was able to challenge for the Olympic title since Britain did not send a team to the Games in St Louis. James Lightbody (USA) won the 800 metres there in 1:56.0, equal to 1:56.7 for 880 yards.

The next decade yielded slim pickings. On home ground at the 1908 Olympics the highest British placing in the 800 metres final was fifth by Theodore Just (American Mel Sheppard won in a world record 1:52.8) and four years later in Stockholm not one Briton even reached the final. The rot was stopped by Albert Hill, who like Tysoe first made a name for himself as a cross-country and long distance track runner. He was the first link in a chain of brilliant half-milers that graced British athletics between the two world wars. He won the North London cross-country championship in 1907

and the AAA 4 miles (20:00.6) in 1910 wearing the colours of
Gainsford AC and it was not until 1914, then a member of Polytechnic Harriers, that he emerged as a half-miler of some standing. In that year's AAA Championships he bettered 1:55 in
running American champion Homer Baker to less than three
yards.

The war deprived Hill of what should have been the best athletic
years of his life (he served for three years in France) but in 1919,
at the age of 30, he took up the threads of his track career. At the
AAA Championships that season he became the first man since
Frank Cross thirty-two years earlier to win the 880-mile double.
He won each race by a margin of fifteen yards, his times being
1:55.2 and 4:21.2. In preparation for the 1920 Olympics he skipped
his usual cross-country season and concentrated instead on improving his speed. Due to a severe strain of the shin muscles of his left
leg he was below form at the AAA Championships, in which he
was soundly beaten by Bevil Rudd (1:55.8 to 1:56.6), but the Games
themselves six weeks later found the 5 feet 10 inches, 160 pounds
protégé of Sam Mussabini in irresistible form.

In a race which he considered to be the tactical success of his
career Hill outsprinted the American champion Earl Eby by a yard
to win the 800 metres in the British record time of 1:53.4, with Rudd
—destined to win the 400 metres for South Africa three days later—
third and 19-year-old Edgar Mountain a fine fourth. Two days after
this final Hill returned to take the 1,500 metres in 4:01.8 to complete a double that was unrepeated in the Olympics until Peter
Snell's achievement in 1964. Moreover, Hill also gained a silver
medal as a member of the British squad in the 3,000 metres team
race, his individual placing being seventh. Hill bowed out in 1921
with British records of 3:05.8 for ¾ mile and 4:13.8 for the mile.
He turned professional and later won further fame as a coach, his
star pupils being Jack London and Sydney Wooderson.

Mountain, a long striding 'greyhound' type of runner, succeeded
Rudd as AAA champion in 1921 but although he posted a world's
best of 65.6 for 500 metres in Stockholm that summer he never
fully realised his immense potential. Cecil Griffiths took over as
top man in 1923 but was not eligible to compete in the Paris
Olympics because many years earlier he had raced for a money prize
and although reinstated by the AAA he was debarred by an IAAF
ruling of July 1923 from international competition. Griffiths, an

extraordinarily consistent performer, reached the AAA final every year from 1919 to 1928.

The direct heir to Hill's throne was Douglas Lowe. At the time Hill was making Olympic history Lowe was just 18 (he was born in Manchester on August 7th 1902) and was reigning Public Schools half-mile champion in 2:06.8. He went up to Cambridge in October 1921 and in no time was making his mark in university sport. Not only was he awarded his athletics 'Blue' as a freshman but he played outside right in the soccer team that beat Oxford two-nil. He made his AAA Championships debut in 1922, going unplaced in the final won in 1:55.6 by Mountain. Nevertheless, nine days before his twentieth birthday, he was picked to run for his country in the first full-scale international match ever held in London. The opponents were France and Lowe assisted in England's 57-42 victory by filling third place in the 800 metres behind colleagues Mountain (whose winning time was 2:01.6!) and Griffiths.

Lowe made considerable progress in 1923—he won against Harvard and Yale in 1:56.6—but there was as yet no indication of the extent to which he would improve the following year. Indeed, his results early in the Olympic season of 1924 were nothing special, and he met with two defeats in June. At the Kinnaird Trophy he lost to Griffiths, who turned in a 54.8-second lap following a funereal first quarter of 67.6; and at the AAA Championships he finished two feet behind Hyla (Henry) Stallard, who took the lead after a furlong, passed the quarter in 56.8 and held off Lowe in a near record 1:54.6.

Lowe travelled to Paris as second string to Stallard, well aware that his best chance for success rested on a fast pace throughout as his own sprint finish had twice been found wanting in recent weeks. He won both his 800 metres heat (1:58.0) and semi-final (1:56.8) in leisurely times, while Stallard took his semi in a brisk 1:54.2. H. Houghton also made the nine-man final, the other starters being the American quartet of Schuyler Enck, William Richardson, Ray Dodge and J. N. Watters, Switzerland's Paul Martin and Norway's Charles Hoff, better known as holder of the world pole vault record!

Right from the start Stallard set a swift pace. This suited Lowe perfectly, but as Stallard was quick to point out after the race his intention was to win and not simply draw out his second string. The position at 400 metres was Stallard, Martin, Enck, Dodge,

Richardson and Lowe. Two hundred metres to go and Stallard was still ahead with Lowe and Martin closing; one hundred metres left and the hare was caught. This left Lowe and Martin to fight for the gold medal and it was the 21-year-old Englishman, yet to win even his own national title, who proved the stronger and thus reaped the highest honour in athletics. His time of 1:52.4 took a second off Hill's British record, which also had been registered in an Olympic final.

The gallant Stallard also gave his all and was deprived of the bronze medal only in the final stride by Enck, both men returning 1:53.0. Little wonder that Stallard collapsed after crossing the line; in spite of everything he had just run the fastest race of his life. Happily, he gained a bronze medal in the 1,500 metres two days later, one place ahead of Lowe whose position and time (3:57.0) were remarkable for a novice at that distance.

The 1925 season had to be an anti-climax after such heady stuff, as borne out by the result of the AAA final: Griffiths first in a mundane 1:57.2. Stallard went for the quarter, which he won in 50.0 to become the only man to this day ever to win AAA titles at the 440, 880 and mile. As for Lowe, he was away in the USA where he took both the 880 in 1:53.4, thus breaking Cross's ancient British best, and the mile in 4.21.0 against Harvard and Yale.

Lowe scaled new heights in 1926 . . . but met his match in the person of Dr Otto Peltzer of Germany. Excitement ran high for the clash between these two superb athletes at the AAA Championships. Peltzer had covered 800 metres in 1:52.8, the world's fastest time in 1925, while Lowe had added to his list of honours by tuning up for the Stamford Bridge clash with a world record 600 yards of 1:10.4 (passing 440 yards in a personal best of 49.1) seven days earlier. The event attracted 27,000 spectators and none could have been disappointed, unless on chauvinistic grounds, for both men beat Ted Meredith's world record of 1:52.2. Wilfred Tatham, the 1924 440 yards hurdles champion, acted as pace-setter but before the first lap was completed Lowe was ahead, his halfway time a sizzling 54.6. He repelled Peltzer's persistent challenges along the back straight but found himself unable to counter the German's final sprint for home. Peltzer stormed in three yards ahead in 1:51.6, with Lowe's time untaken but estimated at 1:52.0. The ever present Griffiths was hardly noticed at all in the excitement, yet his calculated time of 1:53.5 in third place was the fastest of his long career.

Lowe's third great run in a month came in the France v. England match in Paris; unpressed he won the 800 metres in 1:52.6.

Somewhat belatedly, Lowe captured his first AAA title in 1927. Or rather titles, for 2¾ hours after disposing of Griffiths in a 1:54.6 half he came back to win the quarter in a personal best of 48.8. Another outstanding performance that season was his 1:53.8 880 in his native Manchester, thus officially breaking Cross's English record.

Lowe's chances of another Olympic success were improved still more at the 1928 AAA Championships, where he produced a throbbing second lap of 55.4 to defeat Hermann Engelhardt, Dr Peltzer's successor as Germany's top two-lapper, in 1:56.6. As in Paris four years earlier, Lowe ran no faster than necessary in the Olympic preliminaries at Amsterdam and it was to his advantage that whereas he was able to stroll through his semi-final in a relaxed 1:56.0 (eliminating Peltzer among others) three of his most dangerous rivals—Lloyd Hahn (USA), Phil Edwards (Canada) and Sera Martin (France)—were caught up in a hectic battle which necessitated their running 1:53 or faster.

Drawn in the inside position for the final, Lowe got away to a splendid start and was ideally placed all the way. Hahn, who had set a world record of 1:51.4 earlier in the year, led at 400 metres in 55.2 with Lowe beautifully positioned in second place (55.6) and Edwards just behind. The situation remained unchanged until the final bend, at which point Lowe accelerated clean away from his rivals to win by a full second in the Olympic and British record time of 1:51.8. Erik Byhlen (Sweden) was second in 1:52.8, Engelhardt third in 1:53.2, Edwards fourth, Hahn fifth and Martin (world record holder at 1:50.6) sixth. Rarely has a runner dominated his rivals so absolutely in an Olympic final; and, make no mistake, they were the world's cream.

As the official British Olympic Report put it—'To describe Lowe's victory as a wonderful effort is to employ mere words in an attempt to do justice to a performance which, from whatever angle one looks upon it, is unparalleled in the history of Olympic middle-distance running.' That was not all. Later in the Games, Lowe afforded the world a glimpse of his 400 metres ability with a 47.6 relay leg, a time faster than Ray Barbuti's winning time in the individual race although it must be conceded that Lowe had the benefit of a flying start.

(left) The first man to win the Olympic 800-metres title on two occasions (1924 and 1928), Douglas Lowe. (right) Tom Hampson (right), Lowe's successor in 1932, edges Luigi Beccali (who was to win the Olympic 1,500 metres) in the 880 yards at the 1931 England v. Italy match

Sydney Wooderson completing his fastest ever mile (4 min. 04.2 sec.)
behind Sweden's Arne Andersson in 1945

Lowe's last two races were among his greatest and proved a fitting finale to a glittering career. In the British Empire v. USA relays match he took over four yards down on 1,500 metres finalist Ray Conger and left him well behind with an 880 stage run in approximately 1:51 and, in conclusion, he defeated Peltzer in the British record time of 1:51.2 for 800 metres in Berlin in August 1928. He never raced again but continued to make a valuable contribution to athletics as an administrator, serving as honorary secretary of the AAA from 1931 to 1938.

Three Olympic 800 metres titles on the trot for Britain. By the law of averages it ought to have been years before the likes of Hill and Lowe would be seen again in British colours . . . but no, along came another supreme champion in the tall, bespectacled person of Tom Hampson. Born at Clapham (South London) on October 28th 1907, the son of a middle distance runner with Herne Hill Harriers, Hampson took to athletics with enthusiasm but apart from gaining a standard medal for bettering 2:10 at the 1926 Public Schools Championships he achieved little of distinction until the summer of 1929. While at Oxford he did not even earn a full 'Blue' and in his final year as an undergraduate, 1929, he was a poor last in the inter-varsity match with a time of outside two minutes. Luckily he was selected for the Oxford and Cambridge tour of the USA and Canada that summer for during the trip be blossomed forth with victories against Harvard and Yale in 1:57.6 and against Princeton and Cornell in 1:56.0. He never looked back after that.

His new found authority was evident in 1930 and he made his AAA Championships debut a resoundingly successful one by defeating the redoubtable Sera Martin by seven yards in the English native record time of 1:53.2, although this was still well outside Lowe's unofficial figures behind Peltzer. Third was the defending champion Cyril Ellis, who in the previous season had posted a world record of 2:11.2 for 1,000 yards after passing the half-mile *en route* in 1:54.0. Three days after slamming Martin again in the Britain v. France match Hampson sailed for Canada: destination Hamilton and the first British Empire Games. A series of delays stretched the travelling time to ten days, which was hardly an ideal preparation, but the evening of the 880 yards final found Hampson in his best form to date. A prodigious finishing sprint carried him to the tape no less than 20 yards clear of the next man, team-mate Reggie Thomas, with Canada's Alex Wilson third and the favoured

E

Phil Edwards (British Guiana) only fifth. Hampson's time of 1:52.4 was the fastest in the entire world that year.

Hampson retained his AAA crown by a wide margin in 1931 and won his races against France and Italy in slow time; otherwise the season was noteworthy only for a personal best mile time of 4:17.0. He knew what he was about, though, for like Lowe he was a master at timing his peak to coincide with the really important tests—and nothing short of an Olympic title would satisfy him. Accordingly, he planned his training in 1932 with the object of being fit enough to win the AAA title early in July but reserving his very best form for the supreme test in Los Angeles a month later.

A feature of Hampson's racing strategy in 1932 was his remarkable pace judgment. 'I was convinced,' he once wrote, 'having studied some of Professor Hill's researches and knowing the working of the "oxygen-debt" theory, that the Finnish runners were correct when they maintained that the most economical method of running was to keep as near as possible to an even pace throughout . . . I appeared early in the year running largely in miles and I remember the howls of "Nurmi" when I ran in a club match at Battersea Park with a watch in my hand.'

Even without a stopwatch Hampson's ability to run at a predetermined speed was uncanny. Hampson recalled: 'I found that only very rarely did my lap times show a discrepancy of more than two-fifths of a second, which showed that I had mastered the difficult subject of pace which had been my bane two years earlier. The only outstanding exception was the occasion of the match between the AAA and Cambridge at Fenner's. Here, purely for the purpose of seeing how I should get on, I ran my first quarter in 55 seconds. Unfortunately I dropped the others after that stage, so the fact that my second was a full minute, without any opposition but a nasty head wind in the straight, was hardly a fair test. But in the Surrey, Southern and AAA Championships and at the Oxford v. AAA match and the British Games the plan worked well. Another useful discovery was that I could run a pretty fair 440 on this method.'

Hampson's 880 times included 1:55.0 against Cambridge, 1:54.4 against Oxford, 1:55.4 in the Southern and 1:56.4 in the AAA Championships, in which he also finished second in the quarter.

Taking up the story again, Hampson wrote in the July 1935 issue of *Amateur Sport and Athletics* : 'The intervening period between the middle of July and the beginning of August was of course occupied by the journey to Los Angeles. For a person who had not reached a fairly advanced stage of racing fitness this would have meant a setback of a fortnight. As it was, I was able to regard it as a kind of holiday, and by taking a little exercise of some sort—skipping, trotting or walking on deck, a little P.T. in the gym, interspersed with visits to the ship's pool which did not altogether please the "old-timers"—I kept my fitness.

'Three days' break in Toronto enabled us all to regain our land legs, but the worst part of the journey was to come—the five days' train trip across America in the cramped confines of a tourist coach. Even here, however, we were able to stretch our legs with an occasional trot on the station platforms, and five days clear after our arrival in Los Angeles was sufficient to put on the finishing touches.

'With the actual racing there I cannot now deal. Suffice it to say that only the perfect atmospheric conditions in California could have produced the astounding performances and the numbers of records made. I do, however, derive a certain amount of satisfaction from knowing that I kept to a level pace by holding myself back while others were running much too fast in the first lap (imagine 24.4 for the first furlong of a half mile!); that except for the last two or three yards my style did not go to pieces; that the general plan of my training must have been roughly correct; and that 1:50 certainly could be beaten for 800 metres.'

In retrospect, it can be seen that Hampson ran a perfectly planned and executed race in Los Angeles—a classic example of the merits of even pace—but on the day his supporters must have been swallowing hard at seeing their man fully twenty yards behind the leader, Canada's Phil Edwards, at the half distance. British Guiana born Edwards, an old rival of Hampson's, cut out a sizzling pace to pass the 400 metres mark in 52.3. Hampson was having none of this and occupied fifth position in the field of nine in 54.8, dead on schedule for the 1:50 timing that he estimated would be sufficient for victory.

Shortly after the start of the second lap the bespectacled 6 feet 0½ inch, 150 pounds English schoolmaster began to pick off the men ahead and soon only Edwards was in front. Hampson passed the flagging leader along the back straight but the real race was only just beginning, for another Canadian, Alex Wilson (whom Hampson had outclassed two years earlier at the Empire Games), had been running at his heels all this time and went ahead as the pair reached the final bend. The men were locked in mortal combat all the way to the tape, first one and then the other edging in front, but it was Hampson who prevailed. By a margin of a foot or two he presented Britain with her fourth consecutive Olympic gold medal in this event and, in the process, became the first man to better the elusive 1:50. The time was a magnificent 1:49.7, almost a second inside Sera Martin's world record and fully two seconds faster than Hampson had ever run before. His lap times: 54.8 and 54.9. From the onlooking American Ben Eastman, who was to clock 1:49.8 for 880 yards two years later, came this tribute: 'He is the greatest middle distance man the world has ever seen.' Wilson, too, won his place in athletics history with a 1:49.9 timing in second place. Third, a dozen yards behind, came Edwards; with Britain's second string John Powell filling seventh place ahead of two former world record holders in Martin and Peltzer.

Hampson ran two relay legs at the Olympics before retiring, and proved himself to be a first-rate quarter-miler. Running the second stage in the 4 × 400 metres final he was timed in 47.6 for his stint and held his distance against the American, Ed Ablowich. A silver medal was his reward. Hampson maintained his keen interest in athletics for the rest of his life (he died in 1965). He was among the first ten senior honorary AAA coaches to be appointed and was an official at the Wembley Olympics of 1948.

Britain's great Olympic 800 metres tradition foundered at Berlin in 1936 and little comfort could be derived from the results of the Empire Games of 1934 and 1938 or the European Championships in the latter year, but in his one serious season's competition in the event Sydney Wooderson emerged as the world's fastest half-miler.

Wooderson, whose early career is dealt with in the next chapter, had never bettered 1:54 prior to 1938—the year in which he decided to set about breaking the world 880 yards record of 1:49.6 set by Elroy Robinson (USA) in 1937. His first major race at the distance was at the traditional Bank Holiday international meeting at the White City on August 1st, a race in which he defeated the Italian ace, Mario Lanzi, by a yard and a half in the British record time of 1:50.9. Fresh from a personal best quarter of 49.3 on a poor grass track 12 days earlier, Wooderson took little heed of Lanzi's impetuous start. The Italian covered the first furlong in an extravagant 25.0, with Wooderson nearly ten yards back in 26.2, but at the bell the diminutive Blackheath Harrier was neatly poised a stride or two behind: 53.1 to 53.5. With half a lap to go Wooderson moved up to Lanzi's shoulder and took his man in the final 100 yards. Following a UK 1,500 metres record of 3:49.0 in Glasgow on August 6th Wooderson returned to the White City on the 14th for a slow (1:55.8) but convincing 880 victory against France.

Six days later all was ready for a planned assault on Robinson's record. The scene was the University of London track at Motspur Park, the cinder path on which Wooderson had registered a world mile record of 4:06.4 almost exactly a year earlier. Everything was in his favour: the track was in first class condition, there was little wind about and the race was a specially framed handicap designed to draw Wooderson out to the maximum. This was in the days before the governing bodies banned paced record attempts. His six helpers were given starts ranging from 8 to 85 yards. Nothing was left to chance: the record challenger even started ten inches behind the line in case the track was found to be short.

The pace was hot from the outset—25.8 at 220 yards, 52.6 at 440. The watches showed 1:20.3 at 660 and he had 29.2 seconds left to cover the remaining half lap. The excited crowd of 5.000 dearly wanted to witness a record by Britain's favourite athlete and Wooderson did not let them, or himself, down. Sustaining his form brilliantly he consumed the final furlong in 28.9 for an overall time of 1:49.2. Fifty years after Frank Cross's 1:54.4 at Oxford a British runner was in possession of the world record again. There was a bonus, too, for at 800 metres he was timed in 1:48.4—another world record. Incidentally, he did not quite manage to win the race, for younger brother Stanley (off 85 yards) broke the tape some five yards ahead. That, in effect, was the end of Sydney Wooderson's half miling career. His only subsequent mark of significance was a 1:53.9 effort in 1940.

Before leaving the thirties mention must be made of four other names. John Powell, the 1932 Olympic finalist, compensated for a disappointing showing at the Berlin Games by running the race of his life a fortnight later in Stockholm. In returning 1:50.8 for 800 metres behind the world record 1:49.7 by Glenn Cunningham (USA), Powell became the second fastest British two-lapper up until that time and he finished in front of two men who were destined to become very famous indeed: Lanzi (3rd in 1:51.4) and Harbig (6th in 1:55.3). As for Godfrey Brown, his achievements have already been chronicled in the previous chapter. He, too, gained a success over Harbig, who in 1939 was to slash nearly two seconds from Wooderson's 800 metres record with a phenomenal 1:46.6, and his rare excursions over the half suggested that he could have beaten 1:50 had he specialised at the distance for a year.

Two equally tantalising might-have-beens were R. Scott and Guy Wethered. Scott was a month short of his nineteenth birthday and still a pupil at Ashby de la Zouch Grammar School when he placed third in the 1935 AAA half in what was then an unheard of time for a junior of 1:53.9. He never raced seriously again. The following spring he collapsed and was unconscious for thirty-six hours due to what was diagnosed as a 'temporary displacement of the heart' and for the next three years he ignored athletics in order to concentrate on his studies. War was declared almost immediately after he left college and by the time it was over Scott was 29 and felt too old to make a comeback. Finally, there was the 6 feet 5 inches tall Oxford University student, Wethered, who in 1939—at 19—won the 880 against Harvard and Yale in 1:52.4. In happier circumstances he might have developed into a strong challenger at the 1940 and 1944 Olympics; instead he was killed in action.

Arthur Wint, from Jamaica, was the dominant half-miler in Britain during the early post-war years. Twice, in 1948 and 1952, he finished second to Mal Whitfield (USA) in an Olympic 800 metres final, and he won the AAA title in 1946, 1950 and 1951, clocking his fastest time of 1:49.6 on this last occasion. Among native practitioners the most successful during this era were John Parlett and Roger Bannister.

Parlett, whose best 880 in 1946 was a mere 1:59.4, made his international debut against France in 1947, placing third in 1:51.2. By the following season he was being talked about as a potential Olympic medallist in view of the spectacular finishing burst he produced in the AAA Championships to win in 1:52.2 over New Zealand's Doug Harris (a 1:49.4 performer) and Wint. At Wembley, though, he tired himself with an unnecessarily fast semi-final time of 1:50.9 and in the final he was badly bumped and was never in the picture. Although his times had improved only fractionally Parlett had matured into a really formidable opponent by 1950 and he proceeded to capture the two glittering prizes on offer that season. Early in the year, at the Empire Games in Auckland, he reversed his usual tactics by leading from start to finish in his 880 yards heat (setting a personal best of 1:52.1)—a race he considered the most satisfactory of his career—and in the final, after leading through a 54.0 first lap, he entered the home straight third and kicked to victory in 1:53.1.

Parlett was soundly defeated in two high-season races, the AAA Championships and British Games, but was back in peak form for the occasion that mattered most: the European 800 metres championship in Brussels. Audun Boysen (Norway), whose best time of 1:48.7 was over $2\frac{1}{2}$ seconds faster than that of any of his rivals that season, ripped off at his usual hectic pace and was a dozen yards clear at 400 metres in 51.6. The youthful Bannister was in fourth place (53.8) with Parlett just behind. The Britons succeeded in narrowing the gap and, entering the straight, Bannister caught his man. For some seconds it looked like his race but in the last few yards Parlett flung himself ahead and in a photo finish the veteran Frenchman Marcel Hansenne was found to have snatched second position from Bannister. Parlett's winning time was 1:50.5, while Hansenne and Bannister shared an ungenerous 1:50.7 . . . personal bests by both the British runners. These three closely matched athletes clashed again two weeks later in the context of the Britain v. France match in Paris and Parlett, with a second lap of under 54 seconds, won in 1:53.5 from Bannister (1:54.0) and Hansenne (1:54.2). The following season Parlett reduced his best 880 yards time to 1:51.6 when dead-heating with Wint and recorded a 4:09.2 mile, for fourth spot on the British all-time list. Bannister's career will, of course, be covered in the chapter that follows.

The mid and late fifties were dominated by Derek Johnson, Brian Hewson and Mike Rawson—all runners of world class. The first two were brilliant juniors who always seemed bound for greatness. Johnson was only 17 when, in 1950, he won the AAA junior 440 in a record 48.8, and next year he clocked 1:55.4 for the half. Hewson, three months younger than Johnson, won the 1951 AAA junior title in 1:55.3. They met in major competition for the first time at the 1951 British Games, Johnson winning 1:56.7 to 1:57.8.

Hewson was still only 20 when in 1953 he won the first of six AAA titles and opened his international account. Johnson missed that season as he was abroad on National Service but he returned in the autumn to begin studies at Oxford. A winter's cross-country

racing increased his stamina at no cost to his natural speed and in
1954 the former boy wonder whom many had already written off
as 'burned out' emerged from the shadows to become the most
exciting half-mile star for many years. His 47.9 440 yards at Oxford
on May 6th was understandably overlooked in the turmoil surrounding Bannister's mile that evening but at the inter-county
championships a month later he was deservedly acclaimed for his
victory over Hewson in 1:50.2—a gigantic improvement compared
to his previous best of 1:52.9 and a time bettered among UK half-
milers only by Wooderson.

Johnson, whose versatility was to astonish the athletics public
for several seasons, had found his true event. He once explained his
fondness for the half-mile: 'I believe it requires all the virtues of
the other flat track events—technique, speed, strength and simple
decisive tactical ability—plus an unpredictable element of luck,
which gives it added spice.' He (1:50.7) and Hewson (1:51.2) filled
first two places in the Commonwealth Games 880 in Vancouver
and, at the European Championships in Berne, Johnson underlined
his British supremacy with a simply magnificent 800 metres clocking of 1:47.4—a full second inside Wooderson's UK and former
world record. Yet such was the standard of this race that in spite
of missing Rudolf Harbig's world record by only 0.8 second and
finishing within two yards of the Hungarian winner, Lajos Szentgali, his meagre reward was fourth position. Hewson, who had won
his heat in a championship record and personal best of 1:50.2, failed
to survive the next round.

The competition between these two became more intensive in
1955. Both broke Wooderson's record of 1:49.2 in the Britain v.
West Germany match, Johnson winning by a fifth of a second in
1:48.7; but, 12 days later against Hungary, Hewson took advantage
of Johnson's absence to defeat Szentgali in 1:48.6. Midway between
these British record performances Hewson got the better of Johnson in an 880 at Glasgow (1:49.3 to 1:49.7) but the race was won in
1:49.2 by the American Tom Courtney. Hewson also shone at
longer distances that season, his marks including a 3:59.8 mile (a
time that really meant something in 1955), 2:55.4 ¾ mile and 2:20.2
1,000 metres.

But what of Mike Rawson? A relatively late developer—his best
at 19 was only 2:03.0—he first made a name for himself in May
1956 when he beat both Johnson and Hewson in the space of a

fortnight and, in the absence of both, he went on to win the AAA title from his Birchfield clubmate Mike Farrell. As Hewson (who had lowered his 800 metres time to 1:47.5) announced his intention of going for the 1,500 metres in Melbourne Britain's Olympic trio at 800 metres was Johnson, Rawson and Farrell. Rawson was narrowly eliminated in the semi-finals but the other two qualified for the eight-man final, a pleasant surprise in Farrell's case.

The final proved to be one of the most thrilling in Olympic annals. The Americans, Courtney and Arnie Sowell, set the pace for the first lap, the position at the bell reached in 52.9 being Sowell (best time of 1:46.7), Courtney (1:46.4), Boysen (1:45.9), Johnson (1:47.4), the USA's Lon Spurrier (880 yards world record holder at 1:47.5) and Farrell (1:49.3). Courtney and Sowell entered the finishing straight level with Johnson boxed in behind in fourth place. Suddenly, with seventy metres to go, a gap appeared between the two Americans . . . and, quick as a flash, Johnson darted through into the lead! Sowell could not hold the pace, so it was left to the 6 feet 2 inches, 180 pounds Courtney to fight it out with the 5 feet 9½ inches, 146 pounds Englishman. There was absolutely nothing between them until the last ten yards, when Courtney's superior strength made itself felt. He snapped the tape first in 1:47.7 while Johnson, surely one of the most heroic losers in athletics history, was timed in 1:47.8. Then followed Boysen, Sowell, Farrell (1:49.2) and Spurrier.

From the stopwatch point of view Johnson proved even greater in 1957. In finishing second to Courtney in 1:48.5 at the London v. New York match he regained the UK 880 yards record and later in the season he lowered his 800 metres record to 1:46.9 (behind Belgium's world record holder Roger Moens and Courtney) and subsequently 1:46.6 (Courtney winning again). Not that the other British half-mile stars were content to leave it all to Johnson. Hewson defeated Sowell in a 1:49.2 half in California and both Scotland's Jim Paterson and Rawson were timed in a metric 1:47.5 behind Sowell in France. These times were fairly sensational as they represented a vast improvement over their previous best. Paterson, who never broke even 1:54 after this one outstanding season, was responsible for the most bizarre race of the year. All the top Britons were assembled at the Glasgow Rangers Sports and Paterson, seemingly carried away by the occasion, sped through the first quarter in an incredible 49.2! Inevitably he 'died' with 300 yards remaining and the race went to the outsider, Farrell, in his best time of 1:49.2 with Johnson, Hewson and Rawson all clocking 1:49.6 and placed in that order.

It was Rawson and Hewson who shared the honours in 1958. Hewson captured the European 880 yards record with 1:47.5 and both he and Rawson finished ahead of the already legendary Herb Elliott in the AAA Championships. The Australian turned the tables, though, at the Commonwealth Games, his extraordinary second lap of 50.5 (for a time of 1:49.3) proving just too sharp for Hewson. Rawson, outclassed a dozen yards in arrears, took the bronze medal in Cardiff but at the European Championships in Stockholm a month later he ran the race of his life to edge the ever present Boysen for victory in 1:47.8. He had to endure a series of traumatic experiences before the gold medal was finally his. Firstly, in his semi-final he was fouled by a Polish athlete and only a desperate lunge enabled him to qualify in fourth place. Then, in the final—another ill-mannered race—he was swept clean off the track in the stampede for the first bend! That seemed to dispose effectively of his chances but, running with uncanny judgment, he charged from fourth to first place in the final 20 yards . . . only to find himself disqualified for having left the track. Eventually, after a two hour wrangle, the jury of appeal named Rawson as champion. A below par Johnson finished seventh. A few weeks later, against France, Hewson—an equally sensational winner of the European 1,500 metres crown—beat Rawson by inches as both men clocked their fastest ever 800 metres time of 1:47.0.

Johnson took a serious crack at the longer distances in 1959, to such good effect that he topped the UK 1,500 metres rankings with 3:42.9, but shortly afterwards a serious illness forced him to quit athletics competition. The will was still there, though, and after an absence of nearly four years he made a touching and inspiring comeback in 1963, culminating in an 800 metres time of 1:50.0. That really was the end for Johnson whose fantastic range of performances included 10.0 for 100 yards, 21.9 for 220, 47.7 for 440 (and 46.2 for a 400 metres relay leg), 1:17.9 for 660 (an indoor world's best), 1:46.6 for 800 metres, 1:48.5 for 880, 2:20.4 for 1,000 metres, 3:42.9 for 1,500 metres, 4:05.0 for the mile, 9:15.0 for 2 miles, 9:16.8 for the steeplechase, 25.4 for 220 hurdles and 53.7 for 440 hurdles. Hewson's career was also terminated prematurely by a persistent leg injury that ruined his prospects for the 1960

Olympics. Rawson, however, still competes occasionally and won the AAA indoor 440 yards title as recently as 1965.

The years since 1958 have been disappointing in terms of major international championships. Not one medal came Britain's way in 1960, 1962, 1964 or 1966 and the only truly noteworthy placing was fourth by Chris Carter in the 1966 European Championships, his time of 1:46.3 constituting a UK record. Carter and his arch-rival John Boulter (co-holder of the European 880 yards record with 1:47.3 in 1967) have nevertheless made a major contribution to British half-miling history by gaining maximum points in five international matches out of seven between 1964 and 1966 and by bettering 1:48 for 800 metres on more than twenty occasions.

5

THE MILE

THE mile is undeniably the glamour event of the athletics programme, at least in English-speaking countries. Ever since the earliest days of track and field activity the mile has attracted more hullabaloo than practically all the other events put together. During the past thirty years or so this has been largely occasioned by the possibility of four minutes being broken (a relatively commonplace occurrence nowadays) but even in the days when 4:10 or 4:20 were the sought after time targets the mile was a favourite with spectators and competitors alike. Not surprisingly, the event's history is littered with outstanding personalities and achievements.

Early performances are difficult to substantiate. Among the pioneering amateurs the Irishmen N. S. Greene (4:46.0 in 1861) and George Farran (4:33.0 in 1862) are believed to have held the 'records' of their day. The best by an Englishman around this time was most probably the 4:41.0 by Percy Thornton in 1863. Professional marks are even harder to authenticate, but among times that seem likely to be genuine are 4:30.0 by James Metcalf in 1825, 4:27.0 by W. Matthews in 1849, 4:22.25 by Siah Albison in 1860, 4:20.5 by tiny (5 feet 4½ inches, 112 pounds) Edward Mills in 1863. The professional mile championship of England, staged on a 651-yard track before a 15,000 crowd in Manchester in 1865 produced a classic race with William Lang and William Richards dead-heating in 4:17.25 following quarters of 60.0, 65.5, 68.5 and 63.25. Lang won the run-off the following week in 4:22.0, twenty yards ahead of Richards. One may discount Lang's reputed 4:02.0 on a downhill track at Newmarket but, even so, thirty years were to pass before any amateur in the world was to run as fast as 4:17.

The first unpaid runner to break 4½ minutes was a long striding six-footer by the name of Walter Chinnery. This athlete, who could not even better five minutes until his twenty-second year, recorded 4:29.6 in March 1868 but although he improved to 4:29.0 later in the season the record passed quickly to Walter Gibbs, who returned 4:28.8 in April. Gibbs was obliged to retire shortly afterwards on medical advice but his record, modest as it was, survived for six years. It was broken in 1874 by Walter Slade with 4:26.0, a time he reduced to 4:24.5 the next year. Actually, Slade's London Athletic Club colleague James Scott had been credited with 4:26.5 in 1870 but experts of the day dismissed the performance as 'too absurd to need refutation'. As well as being a prolific record setter —in one five day period in 1876 he broke the world 880 yards mark three times and the 2 miles once—Slade was a fine competitor. He won the English mile title every year from 1873 to 1877 and the 4 miles also in 1874.

Last and by far the greatest of the 'Walters' of nineteenth-century miling history was Walter George, of Moseley Harriers. If Lon Myers was the outstanding short distance runner of the Victorian era then W. G. George was just as obviously the pre-eminent long distance star. The mile was merely one of several events in which he excelled, yet it is predominantly as a miler that he is remembered.

George was born at Calne, Wiltshire, on September 9th 1858. A cyclist and footballer in his younger days, he won his first mile race at the age of 19 with a time of 4:29.0 off 45 yards—equivalent to about 4:36 for the full distance. He developed at a remarkable rate for the very next season (1879) he became English champion at the mile (4:26.2) and 4 miles (20:51.8). That was the year in which *two* rival English championship meetings were staged: one organised by the Amateur Athletic Club, the other by the London Athletic Club. George's successes came at the LAC promotion.

There was no dispute in 1880, for at the inaugural AAA Championships George won both titles in 4:28.6 and 20:45.8. He rounded off that season by lowering Slade's world mile record to 4:23.2 after passing the ¾ mile in 3:14.0 and setting new 4 miles figures of 19:49.6 —over half a minute faster than Slade's previous best. Illness (he was plagued throughout his career by asthma and hay fever) held him back in 1881 and he was beaten in the AAA mile by B. R. Wise, later to become Attorney General of New South Wales, but later in the year he recovered sufficiently to produce a world 3 miles record of 14:42.8.

The 5 feet 11 inches, 136 pounds Worcester pharmacist carried all before him in 1882. He began his record spree as early as March with a 30:49.0 6 miles (he won the English cross-country title the same month); in May he ran 10 miles in 52:56.5 and in June he

slashed his mile time down to 4:19.4 after passing the $\frac{3}{4}$ mile in a
sensational 3:08.75. At the AAA Championships he won the half
(1:58.2), mile (4:32.8) and 4 miles (he ran only one lap as there
was no challenger) on July 1st and added the 10 miles (54:41.0)
two days later. At the end of July he reduced the 2 miles record
to 9:25.6 . . . but that was not all. In November he journeyed to the
United States to meet the equally celebrated Lon Myers in a series
of three races. Myers, holder of the world record at 1:55.6, won the
half-mile in 1:56.6 with George only three yards behind in a British
best of 1:57.0. One week later George levelled the score with an
easy mile win in 4:21.4 and in the decider, a three-quarter mile
event watched by a heavily wagering crowd of over 50,000, the
Englishman clinched the rubber with a 3:10.5 victory on a snow-
covered track. No doubt about it, Walter George was the world's
greatest runner.

Ill health struck again in 1883, with the result that George met
with a triple defeat at the AAA Championships, but by November
he was fit enough to improve his 10 miles mark to 52:53.0. It
was an indication of what was to follow. A contemporary described
George as 'a tall thin man with a prodigious stride, which arises
from his bringing his hips into play more than any distance runner
we have ever seen, and years of practice and training cultivated his
staying power to an extraordinary degree'. Extraordinary is certainly the word to use to describe his activities in 1884.

As in 1882 he started off with victory in the English cross-country
championship. Here, in cold facts and figures, is what followed:

    April 7th: World records at 6 miles (30:26.0) and 10 miles
(51:20.0), the latter mark surviving for twenty years.
    April 26th: World record at 2 miles (9:17.4) which lasted for nine-
teen years.
    May 17th: World records at 3 miles (14:39.0) and 4 miles
(19:39.8).
    June 21st: AAA titles at 880 (2:02.2), mile (4:18.4) and 4 miles
(20:12.8), the mile time standing as a world record for nine years.
    June 23rd: AAA 10 miles title in 54:02.0.
    July 28th: World records for 6 miles (30:21.5) and one hour (11
miles 932 yards), the latter unbeaten for twenty years.

Having achieved everything open to him in the amateur field,
George looked around for new worlds to conquer. His gaze alighted
on William Cummings, a Scottish professional who had beaten
4:20 on five occasions with a best of 4:16.2 in 1881. George applied

to the AAA for permission to race Cummings: half the gate money to be donated to the Worcester Infirmary, the other half to be handed over to Cummings. George asked nothing for himself, although he was in financial difficulties after having failed to complete his pharmaceutical studies. He would be happy to remain an amateur just as long as he was given the chance to prove himself the best miler of the day. Predictably, the AAA turned down George's request. Under no circumstances, stated the governing body, could an amateur compete with a professional. There was only one course open to George . . . he turned 'pro'.

The first clash came about at Lillie Bridge Grounds on August 31st 1885. Such was the popular appeal of the match (not to mention the opportunity of a little flutter) that 30,000 people fought their way into the stadium and it is said that George had to climb up a ladder from the coalyard next door in order to reach his dressing room at the top of the grandstand! George was in superb form, as testified by a 4:10.2 time trial, and he proceeded to burn off his tiny opponent from Paisley. He led from the start at a tremendous clip, passing the quarter in 58.2 and the half in 2:02.0. The pace slackened to 3:09.0 at ¾ mile but it was still too fierce for Cummings, who was tailed off in the final furlong. George won by over fifty yards, easing up, in 4:20.2.

Anything went in these professional encounters but George, a newcomer to the game, gave Cummings a piece of his mind after the race. Cummings' explanation of his behaviour, as recorded by F. A. M. Webster in *Athletics of Today*, went like this: 'Ah did not try t'spike thee, lad. What Ah did was to try and frighten thee by just tappin' tha heels wi'ma finger tips as tha brought foot oop behind. Ah think Ah did scare thee, but not enough to beat thee. More's t'pity!'

The red brickdust track at Lillie Bridge was the scene of the return match on August 23rd 1886. George was a clear favourite but the 11,000 spectators were afforded more of a race this time. George undertook the pacemaking and practically duplicated the speed of the first race: 58.5 at 440, 2:01.75 at 880. With a quarter-mile to go the pair were level in 3:07.75, the signal for Cummings to draw away to a six-yard lead. George's supporters were stunned, but only momentarily, for their hero quickly caught and passed the Scot, who went on to collapse some seventy yards from home. George broke the tape alone in 4:12.75, easily the fastest mile run in competition and one of the outstanding sporting exploits of last century. Just how far ahead of his time was George can be gauged by the fact that no man ran faster until Norman Taber (USA) clocked 4:12.6 in 1915 and no Briton bettered his time until Sydney Wooderson returned 4:12.7 in 1935!

Another aspect of George's pioneering work is that at the time of his death, in 1943, the Swedish milers Gunder Hagg and Arne Andersson were approaching very close to four minutes, nurtured on a system of training known as 'fartlek'. And on what did Gosta Holmer, the system's originator, base 'fartlek'? Why, on the training methods of one W. G. George. *Plus ça change, plus c'est la même chose.*

Returning to the amateur ranks, we pick up the story with William Snook. Although utterly overshadowed by clubmate George, the short and thickset Snook was nonetheless a distinguished runner in his own right. He preceded George as 2 miles record holder with 9:33.4 in 1881 and his best mile time of 4:20.0 in 1883 was only a few fractions of a second outside the record. His tally of AAA titles came to eight, including no fewer than four in 1885: the mile, 4 miles, 10 miles, and 2 miles steeplechase. Alleged to have infringed the expenses rule, he was banned by the AAA in 1887.

Our attention turns now to the Irish-American Tommy Conneff. Born in County Kildare, he emigrated to the USA in 1888, the year in which he had won the AAA title in a modest 4:31.6. 'Five feet five and a half inches of sinewy boyhood has he to recommend him', wrote *The Sporting Life* on that occasion. Five years later he broke George's world amateur mark with 4:17.8, lost it to Fred Bacon in July 1895 and regained it the following month with a time of 4:15.6. Reputed to have run 4:10 in training, Conneff's finest performance was probably his 3:02.8 ¾ mile in 1895—which stood as a world record until 1931. As a sergeant in the 7th US Cavalry he met his death in 1912, drowned in Manila Bay. Another Irish crack of the period was Dublin's George Tincler—a man once described by Walter George as 'the greatest miler I ever saw'. He was said to have bettered 4:09 in training but his greatest race was as a professional in America in 1897 when he defeated the veteran Conneff in 4:15.2, the ¾ mile being reached in 3:08.0.

Fred Bacon first came into prominence in 1893 as winner of the AAA mile in 4:22.2, a title he was to win three years running. On the last occasion, in 1895, he took fleeting possession of the record with 4:17.0 after seizing the lead 300 yards from home from Bill Lutyens. Bacon's previous best was 4:18.2 in Scotland the previous year, the same day as he ran 3 miles in 14:27.6! Bacon, who gained AAA victories also at 4 and 10 miles, later covered ¾ mile in 3:02.4 and 11 miles 1,243 yards in the hour as a professional, having been disqualified along with sprinters Charles Bradley and Alf Downer by the AAA in 1896.

Bacon's British mile record only just survived the attentions of Hugh Welsh at the 1898 AAA Championships, the Scot's time being 4:17.2. Welsh retained the title next year in a mediocre 4:25.0 with Charles Bennett, the national cross-country and 4 and 10 miles track champion, in second place. Nothing there to mark Bennett as a miler extraordinary but it was he who in 1900 was to become the first of Britain's three Olympic 1,500 metres gold medallists. Bennett, a member of Finchley Harriers, held on to his cross-country title in March 1900 over a course in excess of 10 miles, won the AAA mile in a pedestrian 4:28.2 and then led every step of the way to score a two-yard win over France's Henri Deloge in the Olympic race in Paris in 4:06.2. The metric mile was then in its infancy, for Bennett's time—although worth barely 4:25 for the full mile—was the fastest yet recorded. Another Olympic title came his way in the 5,000 metres team race, of which he was also the individual winner in 15:20.0. He wound up his career with an English ¾-mile record of 3:10.8 in September 1900.

Timewise, a rather better performer was Joe Binks, the man who disposed of Bacon's record at the 1902 AAA Championships. Binks ran a waiting race, content to follow while the first three laps were reeled off in 60.2, 66.2 and 67.6. Saving his finish until the last straight he whizzed past Lt. H. C. Hawtrey (destined to win the 5 miles race at the unofficial Olympics of 1906) to win by a couple of yards in 4:16.8. Alf Shrubb, the great distance runner, failed to finish after having led at the half distance. Although the time remained unbeaten by a British amateur until 1921, Binks considered the best performance of his career came at the 1902 Civil Service Sports when he finished third from scratch in 4:21.8 with the track under water, a gale blowing and heavy rain falling. A master 'pot hunter', Binks claimed to have won more open handicaps from scratch than any other runner, and one season he won a first prize at every distance from 100 yards to 10 miles cross-

F

country. But Joe's greatest contribution to athletics was as an organiser (the popular British Games were a brainchild of his) and correspondent for the *News of the World*—for which newspaper he covered every Olympic Games from 1908 to 1956. He did not retire until 1957, and right up until his death in 1966 (aged 91) he maintained a close interest in the sport to which he devoted all his working life.

The nearest approach to Binks' record for some years was the 4:17.8 by C. C. Henderson-Hamilton in the 1905 Oxford v. Cambridge Sports—a match best performance that was to elude such talents as Philip Baker, Arnold Strode-Jackson, Henry Stallard, Douglas Lowe, Jerry Cornes and Jack Lovelock and which finally fell in 1949 . . . to one Roger Bannister. Henderson-Hamilton was one of several distinguished athletes killed in the First World War.

Britain fielded no fewer than five of the eight finalists in the 1,500 metres at the London Olympics of 1908 but the title went to the American, Mel Sheppard, in an Olympic record equalling 4:03.4. A close second in 4:03.6 was AAA champion Harold Wilson, who had led into the final straight after making his break 300 yards out. This diminutive Yorkshireman, only 5 feet 4 inches and 115 pounds, had a few weeks earlier become the first man to break four minutes for the distance, clocking 3:59.8 in an Olympic trial race at the newly opened White City. The bronze medal went to the Oxford 'Blue' Norman Hallows in 4:04.0; in his heat he had posted an Olympic record of 4:03.4 while eliminating Italy's star, Emilio Lunghi.

The United States seemed almost certain to retain possession of the title in 1912 what with 20-year-old Abel Kiviat, who had reduced the world record to 3:55.8 the previous month, and John Paul Jones, holder of the mile record at 4:15.4, in the field. Britain's representatives in Stockholm hardly seemed to be in the same class, for neither Philip Baker (Cambridge University) nor Arnold Strode-Jackson, from 'the other place', had ever beaten 4:20 for the mile. The British squad, wrote Webster in *Athletics of Today (1929)*, 'was probably the poorest Olympic team that has ever left these shores, and the last thing we expected was to win a middle-distance event'.

The fourteen-man field in the final was headed at the bell by Kiviat, with his countrymen Norman Taber and Jones at his heels.

Jackson, a novice in this class of competition, had been running well wide all the way and was in seventh place a good half-dozen yards down on Kiviat. Baker, his chances ruined by an injured foot, was ninth. Jackson gradually worked his way into the bunch of four in pursuit of Kiviat rounding the final bend and, entering the straight, was only just behind Kiviat, Taber and Jones. The battle to the tape was one of the most thrilling in Olympic history. It looked to be Kiviat's race until, thirty yards from the end, the internationally unknown Jackson burst past to win by a clear stride. His time was 3:56.8, an Olympic and British record equal to a mile in little over 4:15. Kiviat placed second in 3:56.9, Taber was third in the same time and the plucky Baker finished sixth.

'Jacker', as he was affectionately known, was a remarkable personality. Born in 1891, the nephew of hurdling pioneer Clement Jackson, he went up to Oxford in October 1910. Rowing was the sport that attracted him most but on the advice of his uncle he took up running instead in 1911. His approach was casual, even by Oxbridge standards. His training consisted less of running than of massages, walking and golf, while he was certainly not averse to smoking and drinking. Obviously possessed of great natural ability, he won the mile against Cambridge in 1912 in 4:21.4—an event he was to win again in 1913 (4:24.2) and 1914 (4:23.2). He practically never raced outside of university meetings and never so much as entered for, let alone ran in, the AAA Championships. 'Jacker' achieved fame of another sort during the Great War. He gained the DSO and three bars (one of only seven officers to achieve that distinction), was wounded three times and became, at 27, the youngest acting brigadier in the British Army. He ultimately settled in America and became a naturalised US citizen in 1945.

Baker, later The Right Hon. Philip Noel-Baker, was also to make a name for himself in wider spheres. He served as Minister of Fuel and Power in Mr Attlee's Government and was awarded the Nobel Peace Prize in 1959. But that is jumping too far ahead, for Baker remained a top-class athlete for several years. He and Albert Hill did their country proud at the 1920 Olympics, for the two veterans (Hill was 31, Baker 30) finished first and second in the 1,500 metres. Hill, who had triumphed in the 800 metres two days earlier, won in 4:01.8 with his colleague a few yards behind in 4:02.4. Just as Baker had done all he could in his reduced state to help 'Jacker' in Stockholm so in Antwerp he sacrificed his own chance of a gold medal to ensure that Hill made Olympic history by becoming the first Briton to gain such a double.

Hill, who had tied Binks' British record of 4:16.8 in 1919, finally demolished it by fully three seconds in the 1921 AAA Championships. It was a memorable occasion, even if Hill did fall far short of his ambitious target of 4:08—4.6 seconds inside Norman Taber's world figures. Hill and his coach Sam Mussabini planned for four laps of 62 seconds each but the pressures of competition and the size of the field (22 runners!) caused an even pace schedule to be thrown to the winds. Leading all the way, with 20-year-old Hyla ('Henry') Stallard at his shoulder, Hill unreeled the first three laps in 59.6, 64.4 and 67.2. Stallard made a sustained challenge over the last furlong but Hill resisted to score by 2½ yards in 4:13.8. Stallard improved by about eight seconds in recording 4:14.2. Meanwhile, a delightfully mischievous touch was lent to the proceedings by a section of the crowd who, sensing the record was doomed, chanted for the 'benefit' of Joe Binks in the press box:

> It's going, it's going,
> His head is falling low;
> I hear those unkind voices calling
> Poor Old Joe!

Both Hill and Stallard were carried shoulder high from the track. For Hill it was a fitting climax to a career spanning no less than eighteen years; for Stallard it was merely the prelude to greater things. Stallard was woefully handicapped in the 1924 Olympic 1,500 metres by a severe foot injury sustained in a heat, although whether even at his fittest he could have held the phenomenal Paavo Nurmi is a moot point. The final found Stallard in great pain; indeed he was only semi-conscious for much of the race.

Yet so courageous a runner was he that he managed to pick up a bronze medal in the British record time of 3:55.6, fifteen yards behind the flying Finn. Not surprisingly, he collapsed as he crossed the finishing line. The newly crowned 800 metres champion, Douglas Lowe, finished an equally remarkable fourth in 3:57.0.

Cyril Ellis was Britain's next miler of international stature. His best time was 4:15.0 in 1932 although four years earlier he bettered 4:13 in a relay. He placed fifth in the 1928 Olympic final in 3:57.6 and some weeks later set a world record of 2:11.2 for the infrequently contested 1,000 yards event. Perhaps his finest competitive effort was when he scored a slow but satisfying 1,500 metres victory

in 1929 over France's Olympic silver medallist, Jules Ladoumegue
—the man who was to be the first to break 3:50 for 1,500 metres and
4:10 for the mile.

Reggie Thomas and John ('Jerry') Cornes emerged as the two
leading performers of the early thirties. Thomas, a Welsh airman,
won the 1930 AAA mile by a whopping 20-yard margin over
Cornes in 4:15.2, with future Olympic and European champion
Luigi Beccali (Italy) a similar distance behind in third place, and
went on to win by fifteen yards at the Empire Games in 4:14.0.
Thomas enjoyed a successful season in 1931, too. He had no less
than thirty yards to spare over Ellis in retaining his AAA title in
4:16.4 and during the summer he posted British records of 4:13.4
for the mile (laps of 61.0, 63.0, 65.0, 64.4), 3:55.0 for 1,500 metres
and 3:05.0 for ¾ mile. A split Achilles tendon ruined his chances
at the 1932 Olympics but he returned in 1933 to win the AAA title
in 4:14.2 and set a personal best 1,500 metres time of 3:53.6 behind
Beccali's world record breaking 3.49.0 in Milan.

Cornes excelled himself at the Los Angeles Games by gaining
the silver medal behind Beccali, his strong finishing kick drawing
him away from such celebrities as Phil Edwards (Canada), Glenn
Cunningham (USA), Eric Ny (Sweden) and, in seventh place, a certain Jack Lovelock of New Zealand. The times were 3:51.2 for
Beccali, 3:52.6 for Cornes—easily a British record and equivalent
to around 4:11 for the mile. Cornes, who was born in India, served
in Nigeria as an Assistant District Commissioner in 1933 . . . a
season that was notable for a world record by Lovelock and a
schoolboy best by Sydney Wooderson.

In the strictest sense Jack Lovelock has no place in a history of
United Kingdom athletics for he was born and raised in New
Zealand, wore the silver fern in one Empire and two Olympic
Games and never ran for Great Britain or England in an international match. However, he arrived at Oxford in October 1931 as
a 21-year-old Rhodes scholar and a mere 4:26 miler, and for the
whole of his momentous international career he was studying and
working in England. He progressed at an astonishing rate in 1932,
setting a British record (athletes from anywhere in the British
Empire were eligible in those days) of 4:12.0 in May. The 440 times
were eccentric—57.5, 64.5, 71.0, 59.0—and indicated he could run
considerably faster when he developed a keener sense of pace
judgment. Lovelock observed in his diary that it felt like 'running on

air' and concluded: 'A badly judged race, but it was 4:12'. This run, followed by another British record at ¾ mile of 3:02.2 (after passing 880 behind pacemaker Cornes in a scorching 1:57.5), elevated the frail looking medical student to the rank of a potential Olympic winner in Los Angeles. As it turned out, Lovelock was unable to sustain such brilliant form for he was beaten by Cornes (4:14.2) in the AAA Championships and finished a jaded seventh in the Olympic final in 3:57.8.

Lovelock learnt much from his experience in 1932; it was his first season in the 'big time', after all. Consequently, 1933 found him a more mature competitor. The supreme test of the season was to be the clash against the strapping American star, Bill Bonthron, and Lovelock planned his campaign accordingly. He opened his American tour by winning unpressed at Harvard in 4:12.6, just the sort of performance he needed to boost his confidence for he realised he might have to better Ladoumegue's world record of 4:09.2 to succeed against Bonthron at Princeton. He was a good prophet, for Bonthron set a hot pace to pass the ¾-mile mark in 3:08.5. Displaying the cool judgment that was to pay such handsome dividends three years later, Lovelock delayed his effort until the final straight and then rocketed past his man to win going away by seven yards. The times were sensational . . . 4:07.6 for Lovelock, 4:08.7 for Bonthron.

While Lovelock was monopolising the athletics headlines in 1933 an 18-year-old Londoner named Sydney Wooderson was just beginning to attract the attention of the sport's more perceptive followers. Young Sydney, who had finished sixth in the Public Schools mile championship in 1931 and second (4:34.4) the following year, made it third time lucky when, with a spectacular final furlong in 30.2, he defeated future internationals Denis Pell and Jack Emery in 4:29.8—a record for the meeting. Promising, certainly . . . but who could have predicted that the very next year this pint sized schoolboy would actually defeat the great Lovelock?

The occasion was the Southern Championship, held on a grass track at Guildford late in June. The massive field of twenty-eight, spread across the track in three rows, included both Lovelock, who had just lost his world record to Glenn Cunningham, and Cornes, back from Africa and raring to get back into international athletics. On paper it looked a two-horse race but fortunately athletics is rarely that cut and dried. Upsets can and frequently do occur.

Aubrey Reeve, who had not previously beaten 4:20, was the man who created the sensation at Guildford. He took everyone by surprise in unleashing a fierce kick 220 yards from home and won in 4:14.8. Lovelock, admittedly suffering from a knee injury, looked a safe enough second—until Wooderson, now Kent senior champion and a pupil of Albert Hill, stormed past just before the line. Both were credited with 4:15.2, an improvement in Wooderson's case of over twelve seconds! Truly the 5 feet 6 inches, 125 pounds Blackheath Harrier had arrived.

Interest ran high for the return match at the AAA Championships two weeks later and it too proved a remarkable race—if for the wrong reasons. The trouble was that none of the nine finalists felt prepared to cut out a reasonable pace and consequently the field shuffled reluctantly around the opening lap in 68 seconds. To the crowd's growing dismay, to put it mildly, the 'speed' dropped still lower the second time around and the half was called in a funereal 2:22.5! Cornes pepped things up a little with a 65.5 third lap but the pattern of the race was 'made' for Lovelock, now fully fit, and he produced a 58.6 last lap to win by eight yards in 4:26.6 from Wooderson (4:27.8) and Cornes. Lovelock, Wooderson, Cornes: that was the order again in the Empire Games on the same White City track the following month. This time the bell was reached in 3:12.8 and it was Wooderson who made the initial break for home. He had not the strength to see it through . . . yet . . . and Lovelock gathered him in without much trouble to win by five yards in 4:12.8. The lion hearted 19-year-old Wooderson fought back against Cornes, who had slipped into second place, to win the silver medal in a time that was unofficially recorded as 4:13.4, equalling Reggie Thomas's UK best. Cornes finished third, a yard behind, and Reeve fourth.

Pursuing his policy of one all-important race per season, Lovelock set his sights in 1935 on the much publicised 'mile of the century' at Princeton. The opposition included Bonthron and Cunningham, and a 30,000 crowd flocked to the stadium expecting both an epic race and a time around the 4:04 mark. The race was indeed a good one but a 64.9 first lap put paid to any chances of a record. Cunningham unsuccessfully atttempted to run Lovelock into the ground during the middle two laps but the pace was not severe enough and Lovelock proved much too strong in the closing stages. His time was 4:11.2. Having triumphed in the one race that mattered to him, the rest of the season became an anti-climax for Lovelock and one ought not to attribute too much importance to his subsequent defeats by Wooderson . . . though all credit to the Englishman for taking his chances. In the first clash, at the AAA, Wooderson beat Lovelock at his own game by outsprinting the master in 4:17.4. Three weeks later, before a 50,000 crowd in Glasgow, he repeated the dose in the UK record time of 4:12.7 (61.6, 65.8, 64.4, 60.9).

Surprisingly, Wooderson's record tumbled after only seventeen days. The man responsible was a Scot, Robert Graham, who had finished an unnoticed fifth in the previous year's Empire Games. Only 20, Graham was timed in 4:12.0 but although he made the Olympic team next season he never again ran as fast. Another Scot to excel in 1935 was international half-miler Hamish Stothard, who clocked a record 3:04.8 for ¾ mile.

The year of 1936 belonged, of course, to Lovelock. He planned his campaign to perfection: nothing mattered except that he should be at his zenith on August 6th, the day of the Olympic 1,500 metres final. Whether Wooderson, who again outsprinted the New Zealander in the AAA mile (in 4:15.0), could have succeeded in Berlin had he been fully fit is a moot point; as it was he was eliminated in his heat in 3:56.4, victim of an ankle injury. He ran with his leg bandaged and performed gallantly even to finish the race, for X-rays later revealed he had a cracked bone. It was a bitter blow; on the strength of his UK record of 4:10.8 in June (laps of 60.6, 64.4, 63.8, 62.0) and his victory over Lovelock he was clearly an outstanding contender for a medal. His unexpected departure from the Olympic scene—his injury having been kept secret before the race—came as a shock to British sports fans, but at least they were able to console themselves with the triumph of Lovelock, whom they considered one of their own.

The 26-year-old doctor, knowing well his capabilities, had not begun serious training until late April but by mid-June he was fit enough to run 3 miles in 14:20.2 with a 59.4 last lap and 880 yards in 1:55.0 on successive weekends. His defeat in the AAA mile discouraged him not at all, for he simply lacked an edge to his finishing speed and there was still a month in which to remedy that. His final pre-Olympic competition was a 9:03.8 2 miles in unfavourable conditions on July 25th, a British record. Clearly he was not lacking in stamina and a ¾ mile time trial in 3:01 suggested there was little remiss about his speed either. Thus he arrived in Berlin

happy in the knowledge that he was in the finest physical condition
of his life.

Only Wooderson, among the top stars, was missing from the
twelve-man final. The first five in the 1932 final were back again—
Luigi Beccali (Italy), Jerry Cornes (GB), Phil Edwards (Canada),
Glenn Cunningham (USA) and Eric Ny (Sweden)—plus such more
recently developed talents as Archie San Romani (USA) and European 800 metres champion Miklos Szabo (Hungary).

The irrepressible Jerry Cornes made the early pace but the leader
at 400 metres in 61.5 was Cunningham, with Lovelock a comfortable fourth. Ny moved ahead on the second lap to pass 800 metres
in 2:05.0, closely followed by the three favourites: Lovelock,
Cunningham and Beccali. The slowish tempo suited Lovelock perfectly; he knew his prolonged sprint was a match for anyone and
the slower the pace the earlier he would be able to launch that
finishing drive . . . with the consequent bonus of surprise. Cunningham sized up the situation and acted accordingly. He powered into
the lead and accelerated in brutal fashion, covering the half lap
from 800 to 1,000 metres in 30 seconds flat. He was still in front at the
bell, reached in 2:51.0, but Lovelock and Ny were at his shoulder.

With fully 300 metres to go the New Zealander struck; in a flash
he was six yards ahead and streaking for the tape like a man
possessed. Cunningham was the first to recover from the shock of
seeing Lovelock take off at this unprecedentedly early stage but even
though the barrel-chested Kansan produced a phenomenal turn of
speed he was unable to make any noticeable impression upon the
dainty black-clad figure with the silver fern splashed across his
singlet. Little wonder, for Lovelock was in the process of covering
that final 300 metres in 42.8, the last lap in 56.8! Never had there
been such a finish. At the tape Lovelock's lead was a secure five
yards; his time of 3:47.8 smashed Bill Bonthron's world record by
a second and was the equivalent of around 4:06 for the mile. What
a triumph for the man who, four years earlier, had written dis-
piritedly in his diary following the Los Angeles débâcle: 'I should
give a lot to re-run that race when on form.' This time he was able to
note: 'It was the most perfectly executed race of my career.' Harold
Abrahams aptly summed it up in the Official British Olympic
Report—'Lovelock won by stupendous running combined with
brilliant generalship. No matter where he was placed in the race he
seemed to be controlling it. His genius and personality were apparent

throughout. He gave the impression of supreme and unbeatable confidence.'

Cunningham clung to second place in 3:48.4, also inside the previous world figures; Beccali was third in 3:49.2; San Romani (whose son was to run a 3:57.6 mile in 1964) was fourth in 3:50.0; the eternal Edwards was fifth in 3:50.4; and in sixth place Cornes lowered his own UK best of 3:52.6, set in Los Angeles, by 1.2 seconds. This great race proved to be the Englishman's international swansong though he did continue running cross-country for Thames Hare and Hounds until 1949! It was Lovelock's last significant competition, too. In his case there was a sad postscript for the world was prematurely robbed of his medical gifts when, afflicted with double vision, he fell to his death under a subway train in Brooklyn on December 28th 1949—eight days before his fortieth birthday.

Wooderson carried all before him in 1937. He won the AAA title by twenty yards in 4:12.2, broke Cornes' 1,500 metres record with 3:51.0, defeated Szabo and San Romani at the White City, set a British ¾ mile mark of 3:00.9 and loafed to victory in the mile against Germany. The climax of a flawless season came about at Motspur Park on August 28th. The occasion was a specially framed mile handicap, a planned record attempt in fact, at his club's meeting. As was the case also in his similarly arranged half-mile the following year everything was in his favour: good weather, well prepared track and willing pacemakers. A crowd of 3,000 flocked to the University of London ground, the spectators including two past masters of the event in 78-year-old Walter George and Wooderson's own coach, Albert Hill. Reggie Thomas, destined one week later to produce a personal best 1,500 metres time of 3:53.5 in Finland, set off at a very fast clip from his mark of ten yards and drew Wooderson with him. The upright little Blackheath Harrier with the long stride raced through the opening furlong in 28.6 and covered the initial quarter in 58.6. The middle couple of laps went by in 64.0 and 64.6, leaving Wooderson 59.4 seconds to lower Cunningham's figures. It was a task just within his capabilities for he sped around in 59.2 to finish in 4:06.4. For the first time in the twentieth century an Englishman was world mile record holder.

If anything, Wooderson's 1938 campaign was even more distinguished, for he succeeded in both his main objectives: to break the world half-mile record and win the European 1,500 metres title.

Wooderson was a clear favourite for the championship in Paris, particularly since he had cut his UK record to 3:49.0 the previous month, and indeed he fulfilled all expectations by winning comfortably in 3:53.6 from Belgium's Joseph Mostert and the ageing Beccali. A few days later, in Oslo, Wooderson defeated Mostert again—this time in 3:48.7, only a tenth outside Szabo's European record. The Empire Games mile, held in Sydney in February 1938, would have been a cakewalk for the city's namesake but he chose to stay at home to prepare for his final exams as a solicitor and the race went to Welshman Jim Alford in a personal best of 4:11.6.

Wooderson began 1939 in sensational style. He won the intercounties mile in May by no less than sixty yards from Alford in 4:07.4 and the following week became the first man to break three minutes for three laps (2:59.5). The very next day he sailed on the *Normandie* bound for the USA and yet another of Princeton's 'mile of the century' epics. The race, conducted in a blaze of publicity and watched by a crowd of 28,000, resulted thus: 1, Chuck Fenske 4:11.0; 2, Glenn Cunningham 4:11.6; 3, Archie San Romani 4:11.8; 4, Blaine Rideout 4:12.0; fifth and last, Wooderson 4:13.0. A curious result. What happened to England's hero, whom Albert Hill had predicted would win in 4:03? For three and a half laps the 'slight, anaemic-looking chap who does not look capable of running round the corner without swooning' (as one American reporter described him) led at a virtual jogtrot: 64 at 440, 2:08 at the half, 3:14 at the three-quarters. The whole field was tightly packed and it was hardly surprising that an 'incident' should occur as the runners gathered themselves for the sprint to the wire.

Here is Wooderson's account of what happened, as published in *World Sports* in 1947: 'We were certainly badly bunched. That was natural enough. Rideout did not touch me as he sprinted past me into the lead, but he was so close in that I hit the rail trying to avoid him and stumbled. I ran into trouble, that was all it was. It's the luck of the game.' Fair enough, but for weeks the controversy raged on both sides of the Atlantic. British correspondents claimed their man had been fouled, while their American brethren denied any such thing. At least one accused Wooderson of impeding Rideout by blocking his path. Rideout's own version of the affair, though, was: 'Wooderson was a beaten runner when I passed him. I cut in too quickly. I'm sorry. That's the last thing I'd want to do to a whipped runner.'

Wooderson returned to England in time for the AAA Championships, and a 27.9 final furlong brought him his fifth successive title.
His time was 4:11.8 but he was surprisingly pressed by Denis Pell,
an old schoolboy rival, who finished only a step behind in 4:12.0.
Later in the season Pell defeated Rideout in a White City mile
and returned 3:50.2 for 1,500 metres, fourth fastest in the world
that year, in the match against Germany in Cologne. Unhappily,
Pell was destined to lose his life during the war, victim of a flying
accident—as was Reggie Thomas shortly after the end of hostilities.
As for Wooderson, he managed to remain fairly active on the track
throughout the war despite poor health and recorded 4:11.0 in 1940,
4:11.2 in 1941, 4:16.4 in 1942, 4:11.2 in 1943 and 4:12.8 in 1944.
This last mentioned mark was set in the 'Stalin Mile' in Manchester
in July 1944, shortly before he developed severe rheumatism. He
was in hospital for nearly four months, followed by two months
convalescence, and was told by doctors that he could never run
again. They bargained without Sydney's iron will. Within six months
of leaving hospital he was racing again and, incredibly, that same
year—1945—he went on to record the fastest 1,500 metres and mile
times of his career!

Twice, within weeks of VE Day, Wooderson tangled with the tall,
powerfully built Swede, Arne Andersson, whose 4:01.6 mile in 1944
stood as the world record until his compatriot Gunder Hagg
returned 4:01.3 twelve months later. The result of the first encounter
seemed a foregone conclusion. On the one hand there was the
steadily improving Andersson, who as a resident of a neutral power
had been able to train uninterrupted for the past six years; on the
other there was Wooderson, now in his thirty-second year and beset
by ill health and the hardships of a nation at war. Almost eight
years had elapsed since his record 4:06.4, a time which in any case
would have left him about 30 yards adrift of Andersson's 4:01.6.
The sport-starved British public flocked to the White City on August
Bank Holiday, lured primarily by this David and Goliath act . . .
and the 54,000 fans inside the stadium had much to cheer.
Andersson won, of course, but how gallant Wooderson was in
defeat. Just before the bell, reached in 3:08.2, Wooderson thrilled
his supporters by sneaking into the lead but although unable to
withstand the Swede's finish he ran brilliantly to lose by only four-
tenths of a second in 4:09.2.

Yet better was to come! The two men met again in Gothenburg

the following month and once more Andersson triumphed by the slender margin of four-tenths or three yards—only this time they were precisely five seconds faster. Yes, Wooderson clocked 4:04.2, which was 2.2 seconds inside his 1937 British record and a mark bettered in all miling history only by the three Swedes, Hagg, Andersson and Rune Persson. It was, as Guy Butler wrote in his booklet *Sydney Wooderson and Some of his Great Rivals*, 'the most remarkable performance of his running career'. Andersson set a blistering pace, passing the quarter in 58.6, the half in 2:00.1 and the three-quarters in 3:02.8. The ever game Englishman not only sustained the speed but went ahead on the final lap, trying all he knew to shake off his great opponent. He was still in front at the 1,500 metres mark in 3:48.4 (a British record) but had to concede in the finishing straight. Rune Gustafsson, a 4:04.6 performer, and Persson were left well behind. Wooderson's lap times in this, his last major race at the distance with which he is most closely associated, were 59.0, 61.5, 62.5 and 61.2.

Doug Wilson, whose best time was 4:11.4 in 1945, won the first post-war AAA mile title and continued to feature among Britain's top specialists for several seasons but it was left to Bill Nankeville to offer a serious challenge to the world's best. He won the first of four AAA Championships in 1948 (defeating Luxemburg's Josy Barthel, the man destined to score a sensational victory in the 1952 Olympic 1,500 metres, in 4:14.2) and shortly afterwards took sixth place in the twelve-man Wembley Olympic final in 3:52.6. He made notable progress in 1949, clocking 4:08.8 on a flooded track at the Championships, and in 1950 he broke Wooderson's British 1,500 metres record when returning 3:48.0 for third place in the European final in Brussels after having led into the finishing straight. Nankeville, famed for his boisterous finish, served Britain well for the next three seasons—he set personal bests of 3:46.6 and 4:07.4 in 1953 and contributed to three relay world records—but by then British miling hopes rested on the shoulders of Roger Bannister.

Indirectly, Bannister's success can be traced back to Wooderson. He was 16 when taken by his father to the great Bank Holiday meeting at the White City in 1945 and the sight of Wooderson battling against Andersson made a deep impression on him. 'Seeing Wooderson's run that day inspired me with a new interest that has continued ever since', Bannister wrote in his autobiography, *First Four Minutes*. He met with a little success in cross-country running at school and, on going up to study medicine at Exeter College, Oxford, in October 1946, he decided to train seriously for athletics. He made his miling debut in the freshmen's sports that autumn but it was an unspectacular beginning to a momentous career. Uncharacteristically, as it was to turn out, he tried to lead all the way and was beaten in the finishing sprint; his time a mediocre 4:53.

But it was not long before his awesome talent made itself felt. Although nominally the third string he won the 1947 inter-varsity race on March 22nd, the day before his eighteenth birthday, in 4:30.8 . . . 'I suddenly tapped the hidden source of energy I always suspected I possessed', he wrote. He improved to 4:24.6 that season and was invited to become a 'possible' for the following year's Olympic team but, displaying far-sightedness unusual in one so young and ambitious, he declined the offer as he felt himself unready for such a level of competition. His eyes were already trained upon the 1952 Olympic Games.

In fact Bannister did make the British Olympic team at Wembley; not as a competitor but as assistant to Evan Hunter, the *chef de mission*. The following year he developed into a miler of international significance. In March he clipped a second off his best 1948 time with 4:16.2; in June he cut his half-mile time by nearly five seconds to 1:52.7 and on an Oxford and Cambridge tour of the USA he clocked 4:11.1 (world's fastest by a 20-year-old) and 4:11.9. Already people were talking about him as a potential four minute miler.

Examinations in July 1950 left little time for intensive training, so Bannister decided to concentrate on the half-mile that season— and to good effect. He followed Arthur Wint home in the AAA Championships and, in his very first international appearance for Britain, finished a splendid third in 1:50.7 in the European 800 metres final inches behind John Parlett and the French veteran, Marcel Hansenne. In subsequent 800 metres races he defeated both his conquerors and just before the year's end, in New Zealand, he outstripped a good international field in his best mile time of 4:09.9. The significant factor was his last lap time . . . 57.1.

The mystique surrounding the lanky, long striding medical student grew throughout 1951. Almost god-like in action he seemed to epitomise the ancient Greek concept of athletic perfection. More to the point, as the Press was eager to exploit, in Bannister Britain possessed a miler capable of becoming the first man to break through the four-minute barrier. From 1951 to 1954 he was to be the greatest crowd-puller in British athletics. A remote figure inclined to recoil from the massive publicity surrounding him, he strictly rationed his appearances at the major meetings. Thus, every race of his at the White City assumed the nature of a special occasion and the crowds flocked through the turnstiles to watch.

There was a lull in miling standards in 1951 and, although he ran no faster than 4:07.8, Bannister found himself ranked first in the world—the first Briton to achieve that distinction since Wooderson (4:07.4) in 1939. Certainly he was capable of much better, for in April he covered ¾ mile in 2:56.8 (laps of 60.0, 59.7, 57.1), only a fifth of a second outside Andersson's world best and nearly three seconds faster than Wooderson's English record. Ten days later he unleashed what was then considered a prodigious last lap of 56.7 to win the 'Benjamin Franklin' mile in Philadelphia in 4:08.3, far ahead of American stars Fred Wilt and Don Gehrmann. He returned to England in time for the Whitsun British Games and proceeded to thrill a large crowd with his spectacular finish over the last 300 yards. He whipped a formidable field by thirty yards in 4:09.2 thanks to a 56.9 final quarter. He competed in only two more mile races that season, winning the Kinnaird Trophy event in 4:16.2 (defeating two other future four-minute performers in Gordon Pirie and Chris Chataway) and his first AAA title in 4:07.8. He ended the year with a 3:48.6 1,500 metres in Yugoslavia—ten yards behind the inspired local hero Andrija Otenhajmer. It was a brave effort by Bannister for he had not trained properly for five weeks and yet his time was equivalent to about 4:07 for a mile.

Bannister provoked widespread criticism in 1952 by his method of preparation for the only race that mattered to him: the Olympic 1,500 metres final in Helsinki. He decided well in advance not to run any serious mile or 1,500 metres races prior to the Games, presumably taking it for granted that his 1951 form and obvious potential would automatically win him selection for the British team—an assumption which annoyed his rivals and critics. His one mile race, a 'solo' effort at the inter-hospitals championships, took 4:10.6, but this plus an impressive victory in the AAA 880 (1:51.5) satisfied the selectors.

What was not revealed to the public until after the Games was his astonishing time trial at Motspur Park on July 16th, ten days before the Olympic final. Reeling off the laps in 58.5, 57.5 and 56.9, he covered ¾ mile in a phenomenal 2:52.9. That sort of running suggested he was capable there and then of a mile in around 3:58; like Lovelock sixteen years earlier his unwavering single-mindedness had brought him to a peak at just the right moment. But fate intervened to deny Bannister the victory that surely would have been his. At the eleventh hour the Olympic organisers decided to insert a semi-final round. Bannister's hopes were dashed. All his training had been directed towards running a well separated heat and final; now he was obliged to race on three consecutive days. He left for Helsinki a beaten man, psychologically. No longer did he believe in his own invincibility and, being a thoroughbred type of runner heavily dependent upon nervous energy, he could not hope to succeed unless his mind was attuned to victory. In the circumstances his fourth place in the British record time of 3:46.0 was no mean achievement, but that did not prevent several British newspapermen labelling him a flop. In those unenlightened days anything short of total success was usually considered total failure. The winner, significantly one of the hardest training middle-distance men of that era, was a rank outsider—Luxemburg's Josy Barthel.

Had Bannister won that race he would probably have retired but in order to compensate for his own personal disappointment he decided to extend his running career for another two years. Although reluctant to admit it, he was intrigued by the very real possibility of his becoming the first man to break four minutes. For years Gunder Hagg's world record of 4:01.3 had remained unthreatened. Suddenly, right at the end of 1952, Australia's John Landy—who had been eliminated in Bannister's heat in Helsinki—rocked the athletics world by improving at one stroke from 4:10.0 to 4:02.1! Another serious challenger for the honour arose in the spring of 1953 in the person of Wes Santee (USA), who returned 4:02.4. As for Bannister, he launched his own offensive in May 1953 when, assisted by Chataway, he put together laps of 62.3, 61.9, 61.0 and 58.4 to break Wooderson's national record with a time of 4:03.6.

The following month, amid bizarre circumstances, Bannister travelled even faster. Santee, never reluctant to blow his own trumpet, had announced that he would be breaking four minutes in the American Championships on June 27th, so Bannister and two friends, Chris Brasher and Don Macmillan, arranged in secret to try to forestall the young Kansan. Accordingly, taking advantage

History is made as Roger Bannister breaks the tape at Oxford on May 6th 1954 in 3 min. 59.4 sec.

Gordon Pirie takes the lead during the 1953 Emsley Carr Mile followed by Wes Santee (USA), Bill Nankeville, Ingvar Ericsson (Sweden) and Chris Chataway

Derek Ibbotson (left) narrowly wins the 1956 AAA 3-miles title from Chris Chataway in conditions all too familiar to the White City

of the time difference, they set about their task during the lunch break at the Surrey Schools meeting at Motspur Park. Macmillan, a gigantic Australian, towed Bannister around the first two laps in 59.6 and 60.1 before falling back but at the bell (3:01.8) Brasher, who had jogged two laps in the time that Bannister had taken to run three, was on hand to act as pacemaker and windshield for the final quarter. That last lap occupied 60.2 and thus Bannister, after passing 1,500 metres in 3:44.8, finished in a magnificent 4:02.0— 5.6 seconds faster than Santee took to win his USA title.

The time never reached the record books. It was rejected by the British Amateur Athletic Board, who issued the following statement: 'The Board, having very carefully considered the circumstances connected with this performance, regrets that, although it has no doubt that the time was accomplished, it cannot recognise the performance as a record. It has been compelled to take this action because it does not consider the event was a *bona fide* competition according to the rules. The Board wishes it to be known that whilst appreciating the public enthusiasm for record performances, and the natural and commendable desire of athletes to accomplish them, it does not regard individual record attempts as in the best interest of athletics as a whole.'

Bannister completed the season with a 4:05.2 win at the AAA Championships, a 4:07.6 anchor leg for Britain's world record breaking 4 × 1 mile relay team and a personal best 880 of 1:50.7. The most memorable miling performance of the year, though, came from Gordon Pirie. The national cross-country champion and world record holder for 6 miles, Pirie was never considered as a miler (his best was a mere 4:11.0) prior to the inaugural 'Emsley Carr' mile race at the August British Games. Pirie thought otherwise, and his self-confidence was justified . . . he outsprinted Wes Santee, no less, in 4:06.8!

And so to 1954 and the realisation by 25-year-old Bannister of the miler's dream. He and Brasher trained together all winter, with Chataway joining in at weekends; the training, on the advice of Brasher's coach Franz Stampfl, taking the form mainly of fast repetition quarters. The attempt was set for May 6th, the occasion being the annual match between Oxford University and an AAA representative team at Iffley Road. The trio had been picked *en bloc* by the AAA and it was agreed that Brasher, primarily a steeplechaser, would lead for 2½ laps, Chataway would take over and maintain a four-minute tempo for as long as possible, and then it would be up to Bannister to complete the job.

The final three weeks of preparation, as noted by Norris and Ross McWhirter, went as follows:

> April 14th: ¾ mile solo time trial in 3:02.0.
> April 15th: 880 yards solo time trial in 1:53.0.
> April 16th–19th: rock climbing with Brasher in Scotland.
> April 22nd: 10×440 yards at average of 58.9 each.
> April 24th: ¾ mile time trial with Chataway in 3:00.0.
> April 26th: ¾ mile in 3:14, 8 minutes rest, ¾ mile in 3:08.6.
> April 28th: ¾ mile solo time trial in 2:59.9.
> April 30th: 880 yards time trial in 1:54.0.
> May 1st: easy 4 miles stride; followed by rest until day of race.

Norris McWhirter, a gifted athletics writer who had long been a friend and confidant of Bannister's, was the announcer at Oxford on that historic evening of May 6th and to him fell the honour of revealing to the world that the four minute barrier had at last been breached. His exact words, brilliantly calculated to prolong the suspense and thus heighten the excitement, were: 'Ladies and gentlemen, here is the result of event number nine, the one mile. First, number forty-one, R. G. Bannister of the Amateur Athletic Association and formerly of Exeter and Merton Colleges, with a time which is a new meeting and track record and which subject to ratification will be a new English Native, British National, British All-Comers', European, British Empire and WORLD'S record. The time is THREE (at which point the rest of the announcement was lost in the roar of the 1,200 crowd) minutes, fifty-nine point four seconds.'

The record attempt, which had very nearly been called off owing to a high wind which only died down minutes before the start, was executed with admirable precision. Brasher, disregarding Bannister's mid-lap cry of 'faster', covered the opening quarter at just the right speed. He passed the post in 57.4, with Bannister showing 57.5 and Chataway 57.6. The order remained unchanged throughout the second lap; times at the half were Brasher 1:58.0, Bannister 1:58.2, Chataway 1:58.4. As Brasher began to falter so Chataway moved smoothly into the lead as arranged. The plan was working perfectly. The bell clanged with Chataway a yard ahead, 3:00.4 to 3.00.5. Bannister ('the effort was still barely perceptible') looked full of running but could he muster a last lap of 59.4? With 230 yards to go he accelerated past his gallant pacemaker. The true test had begun. 'I had a moment of mixed joy and anguish, when my mind took over', Bannister wrote in his eloquent autobiography. 'It raced well ahead of my body and drew my body compellingly forward. I felt that the moment of a lifetime had come. There was no pain, only a great unity of movement and aim. The world seemed to stand still, or did not exist. The only reality was the next two hundred yards of track under my feet. The tape meant finality—extinction perhaps.

'I felt at that moment that it was my chance to do one thing supremely well. I drove on, impelled by a combination of fear and pride. The air I breathed filled me with the spirit of the track where I had run my first race. The noise in my ears was that of the faithful Oxford crowd. Their hope and encouragement gave me greater strength. I had now turned the last bend and there were only fifty yards more.

'My body had long since exhausted all its energy, but it went on running just the same. The physical overdraft came only from greater willpower. This was the crucial moment when my legs were strong enough to carry me over the last few yards as they could never have done in previous years. With five yards to go the tape seemed almost to recede. Would I ever reach it?

'Those last few seconds seemed never-ending. The faint line of the finishing tape stood ahead as a haven of peace, after the struggle. The arms of the world were waiting to receive me if only I reached the tape without slackening my speed. If I faltered, there would be no arms to hold me and the world would be a cold, forbidding place, because I had been so close. I leapt at the tape like a man taking his last spring to save himself from the chasm that threatens to engulf him.

'My effort was over and I collapsed almost unconscious, with an arm on either side of me. It was only then that real pain overtook me. I felt like an exploded flashlight with no will to live; I just went on existing in the most passive physical state without being quite unconscious. Blood surged from my muscles and seemed to fell me. It was as if all my limbs were caught in an ever-tightening vice. I knew that I had done it before I even heard the time. I was too close to have failed, unless my legs had played strange tricks at the finish by slowing me down and not telling my tiring brain that they had done so.

'The stop-watches held the answer. The announcement came—
"Result of one mile . . . time, 3 minutes"—the rest lost in the roar of
excitement. I grabbed Brasher and Chataway, and together we
scampered round the track in a burst of spontaneous joy. We had
done it—the three of us!'

For the record, the other finishers were: 2nd, Chataway 4:07.2
(a personal best); 3rd, William Hulatt 4:16.0; 4th, Brasher (un-
timed). The other two competitors, Alan Gordon and George Dole
(an American), were prevented from finishing by the crowd which
swarmed over the track. Bannister's unofficial time at 1,500 metres
was 3:43.0, equal to the world record shared by Hagg, Lennart
Strand (Sweden) and Werner Lueg (West Germany).

Bannister had become the most widely publicised athlete in history but such is the ephemeral nature of record breaking that less
than two months later he was succeeded as world's fastest miler by
Landy who, in Finland, was timed at 3:57.9 some forty yards ahead
of the ubiquitous Chataway (4:04.4). In pushing the Australian to
the limit Chataway had himself passed the ¾ mile mark in an extraordinary 2:57.5. Landy paid this tribute: 'The record would not have
gone if it had not been for Chataway chasing me round the track.'
Bannister must have viewed the activities of his friend with somewhat mixed feelings!

Track fans the world over waited with bated breath the con-
frontation of the two fastest milers in history at the Commonwealth
Games in Vancouver. Probably no race, before or since, ever
attracted such attention; the names of Bannister, the 25-year-old
newly qualified doctor from London, and Landy, the 24-year-old
schoolmaster from Melbourne, were on everyone's lips. Norris
McWhirter summed it all up in *Athletics World*, the lively monthly
magazine he and twin brother Ross edited: 'If the United States'
pre-war promotions were "Miles of the Century" then the British
Empire Games one mile final on August 7th must be the "Mile of
the Millenium". The race between this great pair will assuredly
hinge upon the fact that Bannister possesses the most devastating
finish of any miler (witness his 53.8 last lap after a 3:13.8 bell in
his 4:07.6 mile in London on July 10th) while Landy is the greatest
pace runner ever seen (witness his throbbing third lap of an unprecedented 58.5 in his world record run).'

The race proved to be a classic. Landy, a fluent short-stepping
front runner, knew his only chance of winning was to set such a

severe pace as to drain off Bannister's legendary finishing powers.
He sped through the first quarter in 58.2, five yards ahead of the
stately, long striding Bannister (58.8) A second lap of 60.0 enabled
Landy to open up a lead of nearly ten yards, 1:58.2 to 1:59.4, but
on the crucial third circuit Bannister succeeded in narrowing the gap
to a mere yard or two: 2:58.4 against 2:58.7. Now over to Ross
McWhirter for his eye witness account of that pulsating last
lap. . . .

'The crowd by now had become almost delirious with excitement.
First it seemed as if Bannister had got the Australian just where he
wanted him. Bannister only had to turn on the famous burst and
the race was his. But no. To the delight of the Australians the gap
remained steady throughout the seventh furlong. Had Bannister
been run into the ground? Landy's white shoes flashed down the
back straight. Bannister, like a great white hoop, bowled along
after him. The English contingent had their hearts in their mouths.
Never had Roger gone so far in a mile without making that crushing strike of his. Worse still the gap opened perceptibly as the
two men approached the long home bend.

'Then you see it all unfold. Bannister raised his tempo—for all
the world like a high horse-power car building up the revs—and
in he slammed the clutch as he pulled round the Australian. Landy
—with all the natural anxiety of a man running the front race who
is nearing home—shot a nervous glance over his left and inside
shoulder. Panic! Poor John saw nothing. As his head came round
all he could see was a white giant on his starboard bow receding
in the distance towards the haven of this hell called miling.

'Bannister, reaching down into his carefully nurtured reserves
to a depth that ceases to be a merely physical operation, drew away
relentlessly. There was no ugly loss of form as the two greatest
milers in the world closed on the tape. Landy was holding on to
almost the same stride and pace that he had shown since he took
the lead—but Bannister was transported in that higher register that
Landy simply admits he does not possess. Amid deafening applause
Bannister crashed through the tape into waiting arms, while the
bemused Landy crossed the line some four yards behind, much the
less distressed.'

Bannister had run a perfect race and in registering the British
record time of 3:58.8 he had covered the laps in 58.8, 60.6, 59.3 and
60.1. As Landy explained: 'I had hoped that the pace would be so

fast that he would crack. He didn't. When you get a man in that sort of situation and he doesn't crack, you do.' What a supreme competitor Bannister was. Three weeks later, at the European Championships in Berne, he fairly toyed with a talent-laden field to win the 1,500 metres in 3:43.8, the final 200 metres taking just 25 seconds. Bannister, who had completed five seasons without defeat in a mile race, never competed again. In December 1954 he announced his retirement on the grounds that his work as a doctor left him insufficient time to train seriously.

The void created by Bannister's absence was partially filled in 1955 by the joint efforts of Chataway and Brian Hewson, both of whom were timed in 3:59.8 at the White City at Whitsun in a race won by Hungary's Laszlo Tabori in 3:59.0. By the time of the Melbourne Olympics in 1956 Britain's hopes in the 1,500 metres were pinned on Ken Wood, a former cyclist who had not taken up running until the end of 1951, when he was 21. An ungainly mover, particularly in relation to the graceful Hewson, Wood was blessed with immense stamina (he was a cross-country international and held the British 2 miles record of 8:34.8) and possessed a formidable 'kick'. His times were not remarkable, but his competitive record was. He had slammed Tabori and his equally distinguished country-man Istvan Roszavolgyi in a 3:43.4 1,500 metres at Whitsun (with a sub-54 last lap), outsprinted Hewson in the AAA mile, and defeated the redoubtable Stanislav Jungwirth over four laps in the Britain v. Czechoslovakia match. Wood, however, was never a major factor in the Olympic final and placed ninth in 3:44.8. Hew-son, who led into the finishing straight before tying up under pressure, was fifth in 3:42.6 and Ian Boyd was eighth in 3:43.0. The title went to Irishman Ron Delany in 3:41.2. Britain's fastest miler in 1956 was none of these; it was 5,000 metres bronze medallist Derek Ibbotson, who had created a sensation reminiscent of Pirie in 1953 by entering the 'Emsley Carr' Mile—merely because his fiancée wanted an extra ticket for the after-match banquet—and winning in 3:59.4! His previous best had stood at 4:07.0 but this was no flash in the pan, as events in 1957 were to prove.

Ibbotson, variously described as the Gay Cavalier of Athletics, the Clown Prince of the Track and the Four Minute Smiler, quickly developed into one of the most popular figures in the sport. The crowds delighted in his swashbuckling manner of running and his infectious sense of fun. To this day—and he is still competing with distinction although now it is as a coach for Longwood Harriers that he performs his most valuable services—he retains a special place in the public's affection.

Born near Huddersfield on June 17th 1932, Ibbotson joined Longwood in 1947 and soon established himself as a potential star. He won the 1949 Yorkshire junior mile title and the following winter placed sixth in the English youths' cross-country championship. While still only 19 he finished fifth in the 1952 inter-county 3 miles in 14:21.4 and improved the following week to 14:09.4. As his best mile time was only 4:19.2 his future seemed certain to revolve around the 3 miles. A coal mine accident caused him to miss the whole of the 1953 track season but he resumed his climb to the top the following year. An indication of his possibilities was provided in the 1954 AAA 3 miles. That memorable race was won by Freddie Green by a foot or two from Chataway, with both caught in the world record time of 13:32.2. For nearly two miles Ibbotson held the searing pace before being dropped; he finished eighth in a personal best of 14:03.2.

The turning point in his track career was reached shortly before the end of 1954 when he was called up for National Service in the RAF. He found he was able to train more assiduously than in the past and his running benefited correspondingly. The breakthrough occurred in Manchester in May 1955. Gordon Pirie was attempting the British 2,000 metres record and, as expected, cut out a throbbing pace. All his opponents were dropped . . . all that is except for Ibbotson, who near the end of the fourth lap even had the effrontery to take the lead and was timed at the mile post in 4:08.8. This was some ten seconds inside his previous best and there was still another 427 yards to cover! Pirie overtook his fellow Yorkshireman 200 yards from the tape and went on to win in a record 5:09.8 but it was Ibbotson, who finished in a fine 5:12.8, who attracted most attention. The following week Ibbotson slashed nearly half a minute off his best 3 miles time in winning the inter-county title in 13:34.6, only 8.2 seconds away from the world record held by Vladimir Kuts (USSR). One celebrated coach was so impressed that he declared Ibbotson was the strongest runner he had ever seen and predicted he would be the first man to crack 13 minutes. Two days later he finished third in the 6 miles in a world class 28:52.0.

Further evidence of his tremendous stamina was his third place in the 1956 national cross-country championship. On the track he continued to make splendid progress, setting a personal best mile time of 4:07.0 in the RAF Championships and defeating Chataway by inches for his first AAA 3 miles title in 13.32.6. He won against Czechoslovakia in 13:28.2, covering the last lap in a whirlwind 57.8, and two days afterwards came the 'Emsley Carr' mile explosion in which he became Britain's fourth and the world's ninth four-minute miler with lap times of 59.8, 61.0, 61.8 and 56.8. Ian Boyd finished second thirty yards behind in 4:03.2, while the Olympic 1,500 metres champion-to-be Ron Delany (admittedly not at his fittest) was third in 4:06.4. Ibbotson was chosen only for the 5,000 metres at Melbourne and he gained the bronze medal in his fastest time of 13:54.4 behind Kuts and Pirie.

Ibbotson's exciting 1957 campaign got off to a curious start. In March, six days after filling sixth position in the 'National', he was involved in a most puzzling indoor mile race in Manchester. Hewson set a tremendous pace before blowing up, leaving Ken Wood to run out the winner in 3:37.4. Obviously the distance was incorrect but if, as some suggest, the runners covered one lap (128 yards) too few it means Wood's performance was worth inside 3:39 for 1,500 metres at a time when the world outdoor record stood at 3:40.5! Alas, this is one of the unsolved mysteries of athletics. The following month Ibbotson returned to the same track and beat Hewson, 4:07.0 to 4:07.2. This pair represented Britain in a widely heralded mile race in Los Angeles in May. Australian Merv Lincoln won in 4:01.0 from Hewson (4:01.4), Tabori (4:01.6) and Ibbotson (4:02.1). The very next night 'Ibbo' gained revenge over Lincoln in 4:06.4 while Hewson defeated the highly rated Arnie Sowell (USA) in a 1:49.2 half.

The first of Ibbotson's two great days in 1957 was June 15th. In the morning his wife Madeline, herself an international half-miler, gave birth to their first child and in Glasgow that afternoon Derek celebrated with a European record of 3:58.4—second only to Landy's world standard. It was an exceptional run for it was extremely hot, the track was dusty, he was unpressed over the last 660 yards . . . and for good measure he had been spiked early in the race. His lap times were 58.0, 60.3, 61.5 and 58.6. Imagine the sensation, therefore, when Britain's athletics idol was ignominiously eliminated in his mile heat at the AAA Championships on July 12th. He arrived at the stadium too late to warm up properly and found himself unable either to win the heat or—next best thing—

qualify as one of the six fastest losers. It was a temporary lapse;
next day he reassured his public by winning the 3 miles in a UK
record of 13:20.8.

THE highspot of Ibbotson's career took place on the same track
six days later. Here is how I described the event in a booklet entitled
The Ibbotson Story:

'The occasion was the invitation mile race on the first day of the
memorable London v. New York match. The huge crowd (plus
several million televiewers) were treated to one shattering performance after another and by the time the mile came on at 8 p.m.
the spectators were in a high pitch of excitement.

'The line-up was dazzling. There was Derek, holder of the European mile record at 3:58.4; Stanislav Jungwirth (Czechoslovakia),
who only a few days earlier had set an incredible world 1,500 metres
record of 3:38.1; Ron Delany (Ireland), the Olympic 1,500 metres
champion whose best mile time was 3:59.0; Stefan Lewandowski
(Poland), who had run the metric equivalent of about 4:02; Ken
Wood, with a best of 4:00.6; Alan Gordon, a 4:06.2 man; and Mike
Blagrove, essentially a half miler but with a 4:07.1 mile to his credit.

'Track and weather conditions were just about as perfect as they
can be in England. Straight in front from the gun went diminutive
Blagrove, who fairly streaked around the opening bend followed
by the ungainly Jungwirth, a zestful looking Derek, and the unorthodox high stepping Delany. The order remained virtually
unchanged throughout the first lap which occupied the sensationally
short period of 55.3 seconds. A second lap of just over a minute
followed and Blagrove reached the half mile in 1:55.8, with Jungwirth, Derek and Delany packed close behind.

'Some 150 yards later Blagrove, who had selflessly run himself
out, dropped sharply away and Jungwirth shrugged into the lead.
The tempo dropped abruptly and the bell tolled for the Czech in
exactly three minutes. Derek was half a stride away, and he in turn
was followed by Lewandowski, Gordon and Delany, with Wood
running comfortably at the rear. A world record was a distinct
possibility—but by whom? It was still anybody's race.

'Jungwirth continued plodding along in the van until the beginning of the back straight. Derek made a sudden strike for leadership,
dropped back for an instant, and then accelerated strongly past the
Czech star. There was still fully 300 yards to go and Derek's move
was a bold gamble. But Derek's judgment was not at fault and to

tumultuous cheering he strode powerfully around the eighth and final bend and was never seriously challenged in the finishing straight.

'Derek had won the greatest (mass) mile race in history and moreover his time of 3:57.2 was the fastest ever recorded. It was a complete triumph for the lad from Yorkshire. He had run the distance faster than any other man on earth; he had defeated the most formidable opposition that the world could offer; he had run a perfect tactical race. The full result was: 1, Ibbotson 3:57.2 (world record); 2, Delany 3:58.8 (Irish record); 3, Jungwirth 3:59.1 (Czech record); 4, Wood 3:59.3 (personal best); 5, Lewandowski 4:00.6 (Polish record); 6, Gordon 4:03.4 (personal best). Blagrove did not finish. Derek's time at 1,500 metres of 3:41.9 was a British best performance.'

The rest of the season was necessarily anti-climactic for Ibbotson, even though he beat four minutes again in Finland. Too much racing (over seventy events!) and travel took their toll and he lost several races he ought to have won. Indeed, he was never to recapture his most sparkling form in the seasons that followed but although he never again bettered four minutes his popularity remained undimmed.

The British miling ascendancy in 1958 passed to Brian Hewson. The European half-mile record holder was, to his dismay, chosen for the 1,500 metres instead of the 800 at the European Championships in spite of having flopped in the Commonwealth Games mile. The selectors came under fire but, happily for them, Hewson justified their foresight. He set a UK record of 3:41.1 in his heat, while in the final he hung inconspicuously in midfield (he was seventh of twelve entering the home straight) until in the closing stages he produced an astounding burst out in the fourth lane to surge past Dan Waern (Sweden) and Delany and win by a yard in 3:41.9. In succeeding weeks he just missed the world 1,000 metres record with 2:19.2 and set other personal bests of 3:58.9 for the mile and 1:47.0 for 800 metres.

British miling went through a lean period in the next few seasons. Between 1959 and 1963 only Pirie, Stan Taylor, Mike Berisford and Bruce Tulloh managed to beat the increasingly less formidable time barrier and results at the 1960 Olympics, 1962 European Championships and Commonwealth Games were very discouraging. The 'new wave' emerged in 1964, led by Alan Simpson,

who produced a UK 1,500 metres record of 3:39.1 and finished
fourth in the Olympic final barely a yard behind the silver medallist.
John Whetton was eighth in the same race, after recording 3:39.9
in his semi-final.

Simpson, a talented but erratic performer, bettered Ibbotson's
3:57.2 three times in 1965, with a best of 3:55.7 (59.0, 60.6, 59.4,
56.7). Just how devalued the once magical four-minute mark had
become was emphasised by the fact that during 1965 eight Britons
clocked 3:59.9 or better a total of fourteen times. Mike Wiggs,
holder of the UK 3 miles and 5,000 metres records, recorded 3:57.5
while both Whetton and Andy Green were timed in 3:57.7. Neill
Duggan, while a student in the USA, moved into second place on
the British all-time list in 1966 with 3:56.1 but again it was Simpson
who came closest to major honours: he was second in the Commonwealth Games and fourth in the European Championships. Although
deposed as AAA champion Simpson remained Britain's most
successful miler in 1967 and by the end of the season had bettered
four minutes no fewer than eleven times in his career.

6

LONGER DISTANCES

BY comparison with the performances accredited to leading professionals of the day, the pioneer amateur distance runners were of a modest standard. The first to approach 10 minutes for 2 miles was Richard Webster, who as Baron Alverstone later became Lord Chief Justice of England, but his time of 10:05.0 at the 1865 Cambridge University Sports was small beer beside 9:11.5 by the Manchester innkeeper William Lang (known as the 'Crow Catcher') in August 1863. Lang's record was certainly a remarkable one for it remained unsurpassed by amateur and professional alike for almost forty years. On the way he passed the mile mark in 4:27, which was faster than the best amateur time then on record! Earlier in the year, Lang had set a 10 miles record of 52:36 and twice defeated the celebrated North American-Indian runner, Luke Bennett or 'Deerfoot' as he was better known.

Even Lang met his match in the 'pro' 10 miles championship in May 1863. Eight thousand spectators surrounded the 260-yard track at London's Hackney Wick for the race and, other than those who wagered on the wrong man, none could have been disappointed by what was offered them. The 'Gateshead Clipper', Jack White, all 5 feet 2½ inches and 108 pounds of him, set off at an incredible pace for those days. He zipped past the mile in 4:40, 2 miles in 9:39, 3 miles in a world's best of 14:36 (at which stage an unwell 'Deerfoot' retired, having already been lapped), 4 miles in 19:36, 5 miles in 24:40 and 6 miles, with Lang abreast, in 29:50—a time that withstood all assaults until Paavo Nurmi clocked 29:41.2 in 1921! White, probably the least known of history's great distance runners, covered the next mile in a murderous 4:55. Result: Lang retired exhausted and White was content to shuffle through the remainder of the race to win in 52:14.

The amateurs progressed quite rapidly but even as the 1880 season got under way the top marks were still far short of Lang's and White's. The best 2 miles stood at 9:42.0 by the famous miler Walter Slade in 1876; the 3 miles figure was 14:46.0 in 1877 by

James Gibb, whose other claim to fame was that he introduced 'ping-pong' into this country; at 4 miles it was 20:22.0 by Slade in 1875; and at 6 and 10 miles 36-year-old James Warburton had recorded 31:12.5 and 54:06.5 respectively in 1879—reputedly entertaining the crowd by performing cartwheels during the course of the longer race!

It was left to Walter George to elevate the records to a truly honourable level. His great year was 1884, during which he set world amateur bests of 4:18.4 for the mile, 9:17.4 for 2 miles, 14:39.0 for 3 miles, 19:39.8 for 4 miles, 30:21.5 for 6 miles, 51:20.0 for 10 miles and 11 miles 932 yards in the hour. It is said that he ran 10 miles in 49:29 and 12 miles in 59:29 in training. The first of that imposing tally of records to fall was the 3 miles mark, for in 1889 James Kibblewhite clocked 14:29.6 . . . though this was ten seconds slower than the 'pro' record set by the Scot, Peter Cannon, the previous season. Kibblewhite was also a successful championship competitor, garnering six AAA titles in the 1–10 miles range between 1889 and 1892, including a triple (1, 4, 10 miles) in 1890.

One of Kibblewhite's keenest rivals was Sid Thomas, whose career at or near the top spanned the period from 1887 to 1895. This pupil of the great Jack White won five AAA titles at 4 and 10 miles (the 3 and 6 miles did not receive championship status until 1932) and posted world records of 30:17.8 for 6 miles in 1892 and 14:24.0 for 3 miles in 1893. The 3 miles record was notable in that the first and last laps were covered in only 64.6 and 64.8 respectively. E. C. Willers, who was to lower George's 4 miles figures to 19:33.8 the following week, finished five yards behind. Another record that fell to Thomas was that for 15 miles which he covered in 1:22:15.4 in 1892.

The last outstanding British distance runners of the nineteenth century were Fred Bacon, an ephemeral holder of the world mile record, George Crossland and Harry Watkins. As a professional in 1897—both he and Crossland were suspended permanently by the AAA in 1896 for accepting appearance money—Bacon covered 11 miles 1,243 yards in the hour after passing 6 miles in 30:28.4 and 10 miles in 51:11.0. Crossland's most notable exploits were covering 20 miles in 1:51:54 in 1894 and running 4 miles (less 36 yards) in 19:28.6 in 1896. The best effort by Watkins was as a professional in 1899 when, racing past 6 miles in 30:21.0 and 10 miles in 51:05.2, he notched up 11 miles 1,286 yards in the hour—a distance that remained unbeaten throughout the world until 1913 and in Britain until as late as 1953.

To this list of prominent nineteenth-century distance stars could be added the name of Charles Bennett, winner of the AAA 4 miles from 1897 to 1899 and champion also at 10 miles in the latter year. His greatest triumphs were reserved for the 1900 Olympic Games in Paris where he finished first in both the 1,500 metres (4:06.2) and the 5,000 metres team race (15:20.0). In the longer race, a curious affair altogether, he led Great Britain to victory over France (the only other nation to field a team), winning by twenty-five yards from John Rimmer, with Sidney Robinson sixth and Alfred Tysoe seventh. The other 'British' team member, Australian Stan Rowley (an 'even-timer' who had finished third in the 60 metres sprint!) dropped out after 3,500 metres. Apparently the French officials insisted on all starters having to complete the distance, or else the team in question would suffer disqualification. So Rowley, acting under orders from the British team management, dropped to a walk after the first lap in order, to quote *The Field's* correspondent, 'to prove the absurdity of the French regulation of insisting on counting the full number of starters'. Fortunately the farce was brought to an end after seven laps of the 500 metres track when Rowley was permitted by the judge to stop. So much for the boiling cauldron of Olympic competition, 1900 style.

That first year of the new century was significant also for the AAA Championships debut of young Alfred Shrubb. No more than a novice, he did well to fill third place in the 4 miles some 115 yards behind Rimmer (20:11.0) but only twenty-five yards down on Bennett, the second man. The foundation of a momentous career was laid.

Alf Shrubb, who was born at Slinfold (Sussex) on December 12th 1878, could thank a stack of blazing straw for his introduction to athletics. One evening he heard the clanging of a firebell and, together with a member of Horsham Blue Star Harriers who happened to be passing, he ran three miles to the scene of the fire. The athlete was impressed by the running of his companion—who was dressed in his working clothes and heavy boots—and persuaded him to join the local club. That was in 1898. Shrubb, a small man (5 feet 6½ inches, 118 pounds) with a short, shuffling stride, was endowed with unusual powers of endurance, perhaps attributable to his habit as a boy of following foxhunts on foot. Improvement came swiftly and in order to further his career Shrubb joined South London Harriers in September 1900.

The first major honour to come his way was the English cross-country title in March 1901, and the following month he defeated Rimmer for the 10 miles track title in 53:32. A second AAA Championship (4 miles in 20:01.8) followed in July. He succeeded in the same races in 1902, and in the autumn started his record collection with English standards of 6:47.6 for 1½ miles and 19:31.6 for 4 miles. Earlier, he had broken all known records for 15 miles when he clocked 1:20:15.8 but on that occasion he had to play second fiddle to the 5 feet 4 inches tall Fred Appleby (1:20:04.6). In 1903 Shrubb demonstrated his versatility by, on the one hand, winning the English and inaugural International cross-country championships and, on the other, defeating British record holder Joe Binks for the AAA mile crown in 4:24.0. He also retained his longer distance titles but his supreme achievements that year were world records at 2 (9:11.0) and 3 (14:17.6) miles within the space of nine days.

His exploits in 1904 overshadowed all that had preceded; without reservation Shrubb established himself as the greatest distance runner the world had so far encountered. Here, in bare figures, is a catalogue of his most outstanding successes:

March 5th: won fourth consecutive English cross-country title.
March 26th: won second consecutive International cross-country title.
April 9th: won fourth consecutive AAA 10 miles title.
May 12th: set world 5 miles record of 24:33.4.
June 11th: set world 2 miles record of 9:09.6, which survived until 1926, the 880 yards splits being 2:06.0, 2:21.0, 2:31.4 and 2:11.2. Note the first and last half-miles totalled 4:17.2—only just outside the the British mile record!
June 13th: set world 4 miles record of 19:23.4, which survived until 1924.
July 2nd: won AAA mile in 4:22.0 (first and last laps totalled 2:01.4) and fourth consecutive 4 miles title in 19:56.8 1¼ hours later.
August 27th: set world 3 miles record of 14:17.2, which survived until 1922.
November 5th: set world records of 29:59.4 for 6 miles, 31:02.4 for 10,000 metres, 35:04.6 for 7 miles, 40:16.0 for 8 miles, 45:27.6 for 9 miles, 50:40.6 for 10 miles (which survived until 1928), 56:23.4 for 11 miles, and 11 miles 1,137 yards in the hour. He began the race at an incredible rate, covering the first quarter in 64.8 and the half in 2:14.2!

This last race, at Glasgow's Ibrox Park on Guy Fawkes Day, was Shrubb's masterpiece for during its course he blew up every available world mark from 6 miles onwards. The event was a sealed handicap, with Shrubb's 13 'opponents' receiving starts of between one and six minutes. Conditions were far from ideal: the track was sodden and a lively wind was blowing. But nothing could hold back the 25-year-old Sussex tobacconist. Inspired, as he related afterwards, by the skirl of bagpipes he began lapping runners after a couple of miles and caught the last of his rivals before the final mile. Once the 10 miles record was secure (that was the one he coveted, having twice failed to beat George's figures) Shrubb was content to slacken off and thus the professional Harry Watkins' distance of 11 miles 1,286 yards eluded him. At the conclusion of $11\frac{3}{4}$ miles (reached in 60:32.2) Shrubb was hoisted shoulder high from the track and, to a heartfelt rendering of 'Will Ye No Come Back Again', carried in triumph to the pavilion.

As Britain was unable to send a team to the Games in St Louis that year Shrubb was deprived of the chance of Olympic immortality. Admittedly the 5,000 and 10,000 metres did not enter the programme until 1912 but it is possible that Shrubb would have won the 1,500 metres which went to James Lightbody (USA) in 4:05.4. As for the 4 miles team race, Shrubb could have been expected to lap the American winner, A. L. Newton (21:17.8).

The Glasgow triumph proved to be Shrubb's last great race as an amateur for after spending several months away touring Australasia he was declared a professional by the AAA in October 1905. He continued to race as a 'pro' into his forties but never quite recaptured the former spark. That's not to say he didn't put up many notable performances. On one occasion he defeated Canadian Billy Sherring, winner of the unofficial Olympic marathon of 1906, in a 15 mile race by a margin of six laps—enabling him to make his way back to the dressing room, pick up his camera and return in time to snap his rival finishing. Another time he raced a horse over 10 miles and lost by a mere 15 yards in 52:20. From 1920 to 1926 he served as Oxford University's coach and in 1928 he emigrated to Canada where he spent the rest of his life. The AAA made a pleasant, if somewhat belated, gesture by reinstating him in his 75th year and five years later, in 1958, he donned vest and shorts once more to run the last leg of a relay celebrating the centenary of the Canadian town he lived in. He died on April 23rd 1964.

Chris Brasher takes the water jump ahead of German rivals Heinz Laufer and Friedrich Janke at the White City. Laufer went on to win in 8 min. 55.8 sec. but two months later Brasher became Olympic champion in 8 min. 41.2 sec.

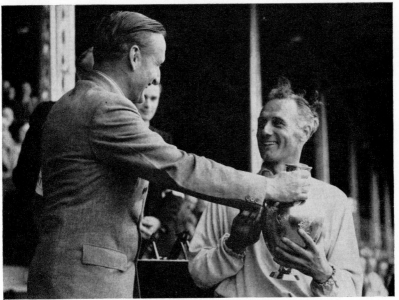

Lord Burghley presents a trophy to fellow all-time hurdling great, Don Finlay

(left) Jim Peters on the way to his first AAA marathon success, in 1951.
(right) Ken Matthews, Olympic 20 kilometres walk champion in 1964

Not least of Shrubb's legacies to future generations of runners was his dedication towards training. Montague Shearman, in his book *Athletics*, set out the training schedule used by a successful four-miler in the nineteenth century. It went like this: Monday—2 miles slowly; Tuesday—one mile; Wednesday—3 miles; Thursday —one mile, faster; Friday—$\frac{2}{3}$ mile steady fast pace; Saturday—2 miles steady fast pace; Sunday—brisk walk of 6–10 miles. That represented a weekly mileage of twenty or less.

Shrubb's training was much more demanding, as he relates in his book *Running and Cross-Country*: 'I have never trained but in one fashion, and that is to rise at 7 a.m. and after going through ten minutes free exercise dress quickly and get out of doors for a brisk 2 miles walk before breakfast, going about $4\frac{1}{2}$ miles per hour pace. After breakfast, and sufficient time for digestion, I run 4–5 miles on the track. This distance is increased to 8 miles once or twice each week. Lunch at 1 p.m. and back to the track at 3 p.m., taking 3 miles continuous run the first week each afternoon, 8 to 10 miles the second week, and 2 miles fast continuous runs daily the third week. Thereafter, vary the afternoon runs at top speed from 2 miles to 4, 5, 6, 8 and 10 miles steady runs.' His warmup consisted of jogging 880 yards wearing heavy boots—'it gave me more spring after putting on light racing shoes'.

With the halcyon days of Alf Shrubb over, amateur distance running in Britain settled down to a rather undistinguished level which was to persist until after the Second World War. Capable runners there were but for more than forty years there was no one worthy of being mentioned in the same breath as Shrubb.

Two odd Olympic races, held for the first and last time at the 1908 Games at the White City, were dominated by British runners. The 5 miles went to Emil Voigt (he was born in Manchester of German parents) in 25:11.2, while in the 3 miles team race Britain scored the lowest possible total of six points. The individual winner in 14:39.6 was 29-year-old Joe Deakin, who had placed no higher than ninth in the AAA 4 miles. Incredibly, Deakin is *still* an active athlete some sixty years later; he competes each Boxing Day in the Surrey Athletic Club cross-country handicap.

The 5,000 and 10,000 metres events entered the Olympic schedule in 1912 and, nearly 200 yards behind the world record smashers Hannes Kolehmainen (Finland) and Jean Bouin (France), George Hutson gained the 5,000 metres bronze medal in 15:07.6. Only a

H

few months after winning his third consecutive AAA 4 miles title in 1914 Hutson died on the battlefield. Britain's first and only Olympic 10,000 metres medal was earned in 1920 by the little-known Scot, James Wilson, who was the reigning International cross-country champion. He kept up with Paavo Nurmi (Finland) and Joseph Guillemot (France) until the last lap and finished third, only five seconds behind champion Nurmi, in 31:50.8.

At last, in 1936, Shrubb's British records began falling. The first to go was the 10 miles mark which William Eaton reduced to 50:30.8. Only nine days later Eaton set a 6 miles standard of 29:51.4, which James Burns improved to 29:45.0 later in the season. Burns also recorded 30:58.2 for 10,000 metres for fifth place in the Olympics, while Peter Ward covered 3 miles in 14:15.8. The following year, in Finland, Ward accomplished a world class performance of 14:31.6 for 5,000 metres after passing 3 miles in 14:02.0. He finished only four yards behind Taisto Maki, who was destined to set several world records in the next two years, and ahead of Olympic 10,000 metres champion Ilmari Salminen. It was, however, Ward's fellow Cambridge 'Blue' Jack Emery who emerged as the top man in 1938. He took the International cross-country championship, won the AAA 3 miles, gained fourth place in the European 5,000 metres, broke Shrubb's 2 miles record with 9:07.6 and ran a swift 3:53.4 for 1,500 metres. Emery retained his national title in 1939 in 14:08.0., after covering the final half-mile in 2:08, and lowered his 2 miles time to 9:03.4, but the war put an end to his promising career.

Sydney Wooderson, already prominently featured in the previous two chapters, looms large also in this one. The former world record smasher at 800 metres, 880 yards and mile decided to move up to the 3 miles and 5,000 metres in his final track season, 1946. He made his debut in the AAA Championships and led nearly all the way to win from the Dutch star, Willy Slijkhuis, in the British record time of 13:53.2. His last lap of 59.0 was considered quite phenomenal by contemporary observers. After winning against France in 13:57.0 all was ready for the European Championships in Oslo. The opposition was indeed formidable but Wooderson, only a week short of his thirty-second birthday and racing at 5,000 metres for the very first time, was quietly confident.

He ignored the stampede at the start and gradually worked his way through the field, sure of his own pace judgment. He was eighth after the first lap, sixth after three laps and fourth after six. On the eighth lap Viljo Heino (Finland), holder of four world records, Gaston Reiff (Belgium), Slijkhuis and Wooderson—in that order—detached themselves from the rest. The titanic struggle was just beginning. With 1,000 metres to run, Reiff fell back and Heino was feeling the effects of his 10,000 metres victory the previous evening. The Dutchman took the lead for the first time in the race with Wooderson at his heels. It was now a two-man race and Slijkhuis, that AAA defeat fresh in his memory, tried everything to drop his opponent. The pace got faster and faster, the crowd more and more frantic, but the position remained the same. Then, with half a lap remaining, Wooderson struck. Slijkhuis was power-less to resist and by the finish, having sped around the final 400 metres in 61.6, Wooderson was over thirty yards ahead. His time was as brilliant as the manner of his victory. Only Gunder Hagg (13:58.2) had ever run faster than his 14:08.6; it was a cool 23 seconds inside Ward's British record and was the equivalent of about 13:40 for 3 miles. Trailing in his wake Slijkhuis recorded 14:14.0, Evert Nyberg (Sweden) 14:23.2, Heino 14:24.4, an inter-nationally unknown Czech by the name of Emil Zatopek 14:25.8 and Reiff (who was to become Olympic champion in 1948) 14:45.8.

Wooderson raced on the track only once more. He set out to break 9 minutes for 2 miles on his favourite Motspur Park Track but, following a 4:26.6 first mile, he developed Achilles tendon trouble and was slowed down to 9:12.8. Even this was not quite the end . . . two years later he won the English 9 miles cross-country title! What an amazing athlete he was.

The next few seasons saw Britain's distance runners fall far short of foreign standards but by the time of the 1950 European Cham-pionships an internationally respectable figure had arisen in the person of Dr Frank Aaron, the national cross-country champion and AAA 6 miles winner in a British record of 29:33.6. A veteran of sixteen years competition (as a cross-country runner he was Northern youths' champion back in 1937 and the winner of an international junior race in Paris in 1940) Aaron ran grittily in the Brussels 10,000 metres. He was second to the by now legendary Zatopek with three laps to go, then came the fiasco. 'Jimmy' Green, editor of *Athletics Weekly*, described it thus: 'The lap recorders got into a fearful muddle and gave the leading runners behind Zatopek the idea that they had only one lap to go instead of two.

Alain Mimoun (France) went away and finished strongly—as he thought—only to find he had a further lap to go. The same happened to the next half-dozen runners and many ran off the track only to be pushed back to complete the race. We had the spectacle of completely exhausted runners staggering around the track for places. Mimoun managed to keep his position and Aaron, after losing many places, ran himself right out to gain fourth place and then collapsed.' Aaron's compensation for missing a medal in these unfortunate circumstances was a British record of 30:31.6.

Aaron encountered some unforeseen opposition in the inter-counties cross-country race in January 1951. A tall, almost painfully thin, youngster in a Surrey vest set off at a scorching pace and it took Aaron a mile and a half to catch him. The impetuous youth, who created even greater astonishment by stubbornly holding on to second place to the finish, was one Douglas Alistair Gordon Pirie—running in his first important senior championship. Only 19 (he was born in Leeds on February 10th 1931), Pirie, the son of a Scottish cross-country international, could already look back on eight years of racing. His first substantial success came in 1947, the year his elder brother Peter won the English youths' cross-country title, when on the sacred White City cinders he won the National Air Training Corps mile championship in 4:42.0. In 1948 he improved to 4:33.6, placed third in the AAA junior mile, ran 6 miles (heresy by a 17-year-old in those days) in 33:40 . . . and high jumped 5 feet 4 inches.

The really significant event of 1948 for Pirie, though, was the Olympic Games. Up in the Wembley stands he watched mesmerised as Zatopek methodically killed off his rivals in the 10,000 metres. Thirteen years later Pirie was to reminisce in his autobiography *Running Wild*: 'This tremendous dynamo of a man sparked off something inside me and I went home to start on the road to emulate Zatopek. I missed the other days at the Olympics for I was concerned only in running to be a great champion like Zatopek.'

That 10,000 metres shaped Pirie's destiny. He became obsessed with the desire to reach Zatopek's standard and raise the rather dismal level of distance running then prevalent in Britain. He punished himself unmercifully in training but the dream of becoming the British Zatopek sustained him through all the physical hardship and mental anguish. The immediate results, in 1949, were unspectacular but in January 1950 he won his first meaningful title,

the Southern junior cross-country. During the summer he slashed
his mile best to 4:19.8 (behind a certain Chris Chataway) as well
as running 3 miles in 15:02.6 but still he was not satisfied with his
rate of progress. 'I had to make a decision which would determine
whether I was to become a champion or not. The question was had
I trained too much or not enough? I slept on the problem and
woke next morning with the decision already clear in my mind.
My training would become harder.'

Drawing inspiration from a photo of Zatopek pinned to his locker,
Pirie stepped up his workouts. Not content merely with covering
an unheard of (in Britain anyway) mileage he further tortured himself by running up to eight miles at a time wearing heavy Army
boots. He was criticised by many 'experts' who glibly predicted he
would burn himself out, but he persevered with his spartan regimen
and in 1951 began to reap the rewards. He lined up for the AAA
6 miles with a 4:14.4 mile and 14:21.2 3 miles behind him; 29
minutes and 32 seconds later he snapped the tape—champion and
British record holder. Second in 29:50.0 was the equally youthful
Walter Hesketh. Next day Pirie, never one to rest on his laurels,
went for the 3 miles and placed a creditable fourth in 14:12.0. The
race was won by the narrowest of margins by Roy Beckett from
Chataway in 14:02.6. Suddenly Britain was brimming over with
distance running talent. Beckett and Hesketh (who went on three
weeks later to beat Pirie in the record 6 miles time of 29:13.8) did
not continue in athletics long enough to fulfil their promise but
Pirie and Chataway, so different in outlook, background and appearance, were to blossom into two of the world's greatest runners.

Whereas Pirie epitomised the dedicated clubman (Alf Shrubb's
club, South London Harriers), Chataway was the archetypal casual
public school and Oxbridge athlete. Pirie was dark, tall and lean
(6 feet 2 inches, 144 pounds); Chataway was red-headed, of medium
height and stocky (5 feet 9 inches, 152 pounds). Pirie loved to run
away from his opposition early in the race; Chataway preferred to
sit in and bank on his fiery finish.

Chataway, ten days the elder, made his debut in national competition at the 1948 Public Schools Championships and finished
third in the mile. A few months later he, too, was an enthralled
spectator at the Olympics, the race that captured his imagination
being the 5,000 metres struggle between Reiff and Zatopek. At the
1949 schools meeting he improved from 4:42.0 to 4:27.2 in second

place and maintained the rapid advance in 1950, during his National Service in the Army, when he captured the inter-services mile in 4:15.6 . . . with Pirie, of the RAF, third. He attracted much wider notice in 1951. Now an Oxford undergraduate he clocked 4:12.0 for the mile and in his first international race, at the Whitsun British Games, he missed Emery's British record of 9:03.4 by only four-tenths in winning the 2 miles. Later in the month he made a fairly inauspicious 5,000 metres debut in Paris, finishing a distant third in 14:47.8 behind Reiff and Mimoun. His next major event was the AAA 3 miles but, despite a 57.6 last lap and a time of 14:02.6, the verdict went to Beckett.

Pirie and Chataway trained for the Olympics in their own way: Pirie for between two and four hours every day, Chataway for half an hour three or four days a week! The results by both were impressive. Chataway broke Roger Bannister's inter-varsity mile record with 4:10.2, set a British 2 miles mark of 8:55.6 and won the AAA 3 miles in 13:59.6; Pirie relieved Wooderson of his national 3 miles record with 13:44.8 and regained the 6 miles record from Hesketh with 28:55.6 in the AAA Championships. As was to be so often the case, Pirie drew the best out of his rivals in those record runs: Frank Sando clocked 13:48.0 and 29:05.2, Fred Norris returned 29:00.6.

Few seriously expected the young British stars to defeat men like Zatopek, Mimoun and Germany's Herbert Schade at the Olympics but, for the first time in many years, there was a possibility of a medal. It was not to be. In the 10,000 metres Pirie stayed with his Czech god for only two-thirds of the distance before falling back to finish seventh; the British hero in fact was Sando, who placed fifth in a record 29:51.8 in spite of losing a shoe in the third lap. Four days later, in the 5,000, Chataway made an audacious bid for victory. At the bell, Schade led from Chataway. Mimoun and Zatopek, all in a bunch, with Pirie trailing well behind in fifth spot. With 300 metres to go Chataway accelerated into the lead and passed 3 miles in an estimated 13:43 but on the crown of the last bend, just after the other three had swept past, the exhausted Englishman tripped over the raised track kerb and went sprawling. But for the accident he would certainly have been an easy fourth; as it was he finished fifth in 14:18.0. Pirie, unaware of what had happened, pipped him for fourth just before the line.

Chataway, preoccupied by examinations, did not compete much

in 1953. He progressed to 4:08.4 and 8:49.6 but this was little compared to Pirie's exploits during the year. From January, when he
beat Reiff over the country in Belgium, to October, when he wound
up his track season with a world's best 4 miles time of 18:35.6, it
was records and victories all the way. In cold figures he took part
in thirty-two individual races ranging from 800 to 10,000 metres,
won twenty-seven of them and set world records for 6 miles
(28:19.4) and 4 × 1,500 metres relay, unofficial world bests for 4
miles (18:45.2 and 18:35.6) and 5 miles (23:34.2), and British records
at 1½ miles (6:35.8 twice), 3,000 metres (8:19.2 twice, 8:11.4 and
8:11.0), 2 miles (8:47.8 and 8:47.4), 3 miles (13:41.8, 13:36.4 and
13:34.0), 5,000 metres (14:02.6), 4 miles (19:04.0, 18:45.2 and
18:35.6), 5 miles (23:56.2 and 23:34.2), 6 miles (28:47.4 and 28:19.4)
and 10,000 metres (29:17.2). Add to that the first of three successive
English cross-country titles and a rapturously acclaimed mile win
over the highly touted Wes Santee (USA) in 4:06.8. Not since the
days of George and Shrubb had Britain seen the likes.

Even Zatopek, it seemed, would have his hands full in 1954,
especially as Pirie announced his intention of running 13:50 for
5,000 and 28:50 for 10,000 metres at the European Championships.
The world records then stood at 13:58.2 and 29:01.6. He was looking as good as his word when, in June 1954, he set personal bests of
1:53.0 for 880 yards and 4:05.2 for the mile, but a cracked bone in
his left foot kept him out of the big races. British hopes switched to
Chataway who in the early season had only just missed Reiff's world
2 miles record with a resounding 8:41.0, the second fastest time
ever, and had helped both Roger Bannister and John Landy to their
mile records. Gunder Hagg's world 3 miles mark of 13:32.4 dating
from 1942 seemed particularly vulnerable and, sure enough, Chataway clipped off a fifth of a second in the AAA Championships . . .
only to find himself second, as in 1951, in the same time as the
winner!

The astonishing new champion was 27-year-old Freddie Green,
a protégé of Jack Emery. During a long career—he was Midland
junior mile titlist in 1944—he had gained a few successes, like
winning the inter-county 3 miles in 1951, but it was not until 1953
that he began to show his true paces. No faster than 14:04.0 the
previous year he recorded 13:46.0 for 3 miles for second in the
AAA Championships less than twenty yards behind Pirie. He
represented Britain in the 5,000 metres three times in 1953, finish-

ing second to Pirie in two races and winning the third. Nevertheless, there was little warning of his explosion in the 1954 AAA Championships. It was a remarkable race throughout, for the first of the great Kenyan distance runners, Nyandika Maiyoro, ripped off an unprecedented opening mile of 4:23.4, 45 yards ahead of Chataway and Green who were timed in 4:29.6. They caught him shortly before 2 miles (9:01.6) and although Chataway looked a certain winner when he launched his finishing drive 300 yards from the tape it was Green who proved the stronger. The 6 miles title went to Peter Driver in 28:34.8 with twelve men bettering 29½ minutes, a time that would have constituted a British record only three years earlier.

Further evidence of the impressive depth in the country's distance-running standards came at the Commonwealth Games in Vancouver when England gained a clean sweep of the medals in the 3 and 6 miles. Chataway won the 3 miles in 13:35.2 ahead of Green (13:37.2) and Sando (13:37.4); while in the 6 miles the first three were Driver (29:09.4), Sando and marathon star Jim Peters. Success was harder to come by at the European Championships a few weeks later. Driver was almost lapped by Zatopek in the 10,000 metres, finishing sixth, but the ever reliable Sando excelled himself by clocking a personal best of 29:27.6 for the bronze medal. Zatopek, who had set a world record of 13:57.2 earlier in the season, was co-favourite with Chataway for the 5,000 metres. Indeed they waged a fine race, with the Englishman coming out on top in 14:08.8 . . . the trouble was that Vladimir Kuts (USSR) snapped the tape some ninety yards ahead in a record 13.56.6!

It was a classic case of under-rating the opposition. Kuts had shot into prominence in August 1953 when he had led from the start to the last lap of a 5,000 metres race against Zatopek—at one stage being over 40 yards ahead—eventually finishing second in 14:04.0. He established a reputation as a front runner lacking in pace judgment who could be relied upon to 'blow up' in the closing stages. This must have been the short-sighted attitude adopted by Zatopek and Chataway in Berne, for although Kuts' early pace was swift it was not ridiculously fast and yet his opponents allowed him to slip clean away. By the time Zatopek and Chataway realised that the muscular Soviet sailor was not going to crack it was too late to remedy the situation and, somewhat sheepishly, they had to settle for battling out the silver medal. No fewer than four of the fifteen finalists dropped out during this bizarre race, among them Green.

Revenge, total and sweet, was exacted by Chataway forty-five days later during the London v. Moscow floodlit meeting at the White City on October 13th. This match, which featured the first appearance in London of a Soviet team, generated immense interest and represented the high-water mark of popular support for athletics in Britain. A crowd of 40,000 flocked to the stadium and an estimated audience of 15 million watched the proceedings on television. The star turn, of course, was the 5,000 metres. The four-man field included Peter Driver and Vladimir Okorokov but there were eyes only for 23-year-old Christopher John Chataway and 27-year-old Vladimir Pyotrovich Kuts.

The race was run at a scorching pace as Kuts tried his utmost to break the spirit and body of his rival. He could have been forgiven for feeling that his sixth lap of 62.4 would have settled the hash of any opponent but Chataway, inspired by the tumultuous roaring of the crowd, stayed with him. The atmosphere was electric as the bell sounded, with Kuts remaining just a stride ahead. Chataway usually struck with 300 yards to go and the crowd waited expectantly; nothing happened. It was obvious now that he was being stretched to the very limit in simply sticking to Kuts's hip. Still there was no change as the heroic pair swung into the short finishing straight. 'Was a man who has never bettered 3:58 for 1,500 metres going to outkick a 3:45.4 man who had trailed him all the way?' wrote Norris McWhirter. 'The crowd was on its feet, millions of armchair televiewers went white at the knuckles. The moment was symbolic. Could a spare-time amateur businessman who trains 35 miles a week live with a full-time "State" athlete who trains 135 miles a week in this waging of "total" sport? As if impelled by the roar of the delirious crowd Chataway switched over to the super-human. With sheer savagery he struck late but decisively and with consummate if desperate timing surged past his quarry five tantalising yards before he could claim the asylum of the tape. In a blizzard of flash-bulbs Chataway found himself being embraced by Roger Bannister, now not only a friend but a fellow immortal in the history of the track.'

The race was the thing but the times also were an occasion for rejoicing. Chataway had sliced no less than five seconds from the world record with 13:51.6 (Kuts 13:51.8) while at the 3 miles post both had clipped Kuts's record of 13:27.4: Kuts 13:27.0, Chataway 13:27.1. Kuts, however, had the last word in 1954. Ten days afterwards, in Prague, he beat Zatopek by nearly half a lap in 13:51.2.

Chataway returned the compliment in July 1955 by regaining the 3 miles record with 13:23.2 in a race in which he was assisted by new star Derek Ibbotson. Pirie made a welcome return to top-class competition, defeating Zatopek in three races out of four, setting a personal best 3 miles time of 13:29.8 and recording such diverse performances as 6:26.0 for 1½ miles (a world's best) and 22 miles 278 yards in two hours—behind Joe Lancaster's world's best of 22 miles 418 yards. But Pirie met with several reverses, too: notably being left over half a lap behind by Kuts in a 10,000 metres in Moscow. The year's most consistent British six-miler was Ken Norris, who followed up his AAA win (a race best remembered for Pirie's collapse, apparently due to dehydration, one lap from the end) with sound performances in all his internationals. In addition, Norris—who as a junior ran no faster than 16:47—recorded 13:29.8 for 3 miles inches behind Sando.

Back in 1953, when the world 5,000 metres record stood at 13:58.2, Pirie claimed that one day he would run 13:40, a time that then appeared to be in the realm of science-fiction. But Pirie knew better than most that man had only just begun to scratch the surface in distance running and wasn't in the least surprised when in 1955 Sandor Iharos (Hungary) was timed at 13:40.6. Pirie, of course, was not satisfied with just being proved a good prophet: he wanted that record for himself. By 1956 he was ready. Stronger and faster than ever following the introduction of weight training into his preparations Pirie quickly snapped into top form. His first *coup* occurred on a rain-sodden track at Bergen on June 9th. Not only did he remove 3.8 seconds from Iharos's record (and no less than 25.8 seconds from his previous best) with a staggering 13:36.8 but he also defeated Kuts (13:39.6) by twenty yards into the bargain.

Kuts, fresh from a national 3,000 metres record four days earlier, cut out a torrid pace from the outset yet was quite unable to drop Pirie. An idea of how standards had rocketed in the space of a couple of years can be gauged from the intermediate times: 1,000 metres was passed in 2:36.0 (compared to 2:41.4 in the Chataway v. Kuts duel in 1954), 2,000 metres in 5:22.0 (5:31.5), 3,000 metres in 8:09.0 (8:16.4) and 4,000 metres in 10:57.0 (11:09.8). With 300 yards remaining, Pirie unleashed an extraordinary burst of speed;

his final 300 metres in fact occupied a mere 41.2 seconds. But for a lack of foresight by the officials Pirie would undoubtedly have cracked the 3 miles record on the way; as it was he must have clocked somewhere around 13:13. Pirie revealed in his book that he had intended leading throughout but that the first lap was so fast (60 seconds) that he decided to dictate the race from behind. 'Every straight I ran to Kuts's shoulder to hustle him along to a greater speed', he wrote. 'At no time did I allow him to slacken to gather energy for a burst. We pelted along, Kuts leading and I moving to his shoulder continually for that 12½ laps bash . . . I was unaware that it was a world record because the intermediate times were only called to Kuts in Russian by Russians or in Norwegian to the spectators. Had I really belted that last straight my time could have been three or four seconds better. I was elated and could not sleep a wink all night, for I had achieved one of my greatest ambitions— that of capturing the 5,000 metres world record.'

Three days later, at Trondheim, Pirie was rewarded with another world record after a fine 3,000 metres race with Jerzy Chromik (Poland), holder of the world steeplechase record. Pirie kicked home in 7:55.6 to equal Iharos's mark although his actual time was 7:55.5. Even that was not all: in Amsterdam on June 24th he defeated the East German, Klaus Richtzenhain (destined to win the Olympic silver medal in Melbourne), over 1,500 metres in a personal best of 3:43.7. What a week!

Pirie's next target was Zatopek's 10,000 metres record of 28:54.2 but a soft track, high wind and lack of opposition conspired against him and, after a 14:20.4 first 5,000 metres, he finished in a UK record tying 29:17.2. A leg injury kept him out of the AAA Championships and in his absence Ibbotson won the 3 miles from Chataway (13:32.6 for both) and Ken Norris the 6 miles in a national record of 28:13.6. Pirie returned to action with personal bests of 4:02.2 for the mile and 8:42.6 for 2 miles and a second trip to Scandinavia in September found him back to his superlative early season form. Taking on the great Hungarian trio of Sandor Iharos, Laszlo Tabori and Istvan Rozsavolgyi over 3,000 metres at Malmo he beat the lot in a world record 7:52.8—a race Pirie believes to be the best he ever ran. Incidentally, on the morning of the race he did fifty bursts over 100 yards!

It's easy to be wise after the event but Pirie, whose last significant race prior to the Olympics was a personal best 1,500 metres of

3:43.4, might have succeeded in the Melbourne 5,000 metres had he concentrated on that event alone. Instead, he went first for the 10,000 metres and fell between two stools. On paper Kuts, the world record holder at 28:30.4, was over three-quarters of a minute faster than Pirie. A less uncompromising athlete might, in the circumstances, have aimed for a fairly 'safe' silver medal but Pirie, and all credit to him, wanted the gold or nothing. A glance at the result (1st Kuts 28:45.6, 8th Pirie 29:49.6) suggests that Pirie failed utterly, yet the truth is that he came agonisingly close to winning.

Kuts and Pirie dropped the field after nine laps and such was the tempo at which their epic struggle was conducted that the 5,000 metres mark was passed in 14:06.8, just a fifth of a second slower than Zatopek's Olympic record! Kuts tortured his rival with a series of bursts. Pirie takes over the story: 'He was deliberately doing this fast-slow to put me off my rhythm. I was so tired that I couldn't lead to stop him doing it. He tried desperately to shake me off, sometimes running in the third lane . . . I thought that with four laps to go I had passed the danger point and that it was only to be a matter of covering this last short distance before the gold medal was mine. This was not taking Kuts's strength into account. He put in another phenomenal burst after forcing me to take the lead momentarily. I broke with only 3½ laps left and Kuts's flagging spirit was renewed . . . I staggered the last three laps at about walking pace. I was utterly exhausted, like a punch-drunk boxer, but I was still determined to cross the finishing line.'

Kuts later admitted he was at breaking point himself when he inflicted the burst that finally caused his rival to crack. Had Pirie responded once more Kuts would have been the one to give up— that's how close it was. Fifth in the race was Ken Norris. Three days later all three British representatives, Pirie, Chataway and Ibbotson, qualified for the 5,000 metres final. Kuts, seemingly none the worse for his earlier exertions, led all the way in the final to win by eighty yards in 13:39.6 from Pirie (13:50.6) and Ibbotson (personal best of 13:54.4). Chataway, fourth at 4,000 metres in 11:03.0, paid the penalty for too casual a preparation and stomach cramp caused him to fall away to eleventh place in this his last race.

Honours in 1957 were shared by Ibbotson, who won the AAA 3 miles in a UK record of 13:20.8 six days before his world mile record, and George Knight, who set a national 10,000 metres mark of 29:06.4. The next season threw up some fine talent—notably

Stan Eldon, who posted UK records of 28:05.0 for 6 miles and 29:02.8 for 10,000 metres and clocked 13:22.4 for 3 miles, and Peter Clark, with times of 8:37.6 (2 miles), 13:25.0 (3 miles) and 13:53.8 (5,000 metres). Both gained fourth places in the European Championships: Clark in the 5,000 and Eldon in the 10,000. Ibbotson had a poor season and Pirie, bronze medallist in the European 5,000 metres, was only moderately successful.

Eldon, an inveterate front runner, enjoyed another good campaign in 1959 with some resounding international victories and a series of fine times including 13:47.8 for 5,000 metres. Meanwhile, over the longer track distances, Fred Norris reigned supreme. This veteran, who did not take up running until he was 27, had in 1956 become the first Briton to run 10 miles inside 50 minutes and cover over 12 miles in the hour. He improved in 1958 to 48:47.8 and 12 miles 515 yards as well as setting world's bests of 1:43.55.4 for 20 miles and 22 miles 1,610 yards in two hours. His best performance in 1959 was 48:32.4 for 10 miles.

Once again, in 1960, it was Gordon Pirie, now 29, upon whom Britain's Olympic hopes rested. His chances had never looked better. At the Whitsun British Games he had scored a magnificent double by defeating world 2,000 metres record holder Rozsavolgyi in a 3:44.1 1,500 metres and repeating the treatment in the 3,000 metres (7:57.2). Obviously his speed was as good as ever and so too was his stamina judging by his personal best 6 miles time of 28:09.6 in winning his first AAA title for seven years. He looked quite unbeatable in his final major race prior to the Games, the 5,000 metres against France. Covering the last lap in an astonishing 54.6 Pirie won in 13:51.6. Unhappily, the Rome Olympics proved a fiasco for Pirie. The victim apparently of inadequate acclimatisation to the heat he failed even to reach the final as he ambled home in a pathetic 14:43.6. He came back in the 10,000 metres with a personal best but even that sufficed only for tenth place. Finishing immediately ahead were team-mates John Merriman in a UK record of 28:52.6 and Martin Hyman. It was scant consolation when, a fortnight later, Pirie belatedly achieved one of his most nagging ambitions by running a mile in 3:59.9.

It was thought that Pirie would retire at the end of the 1960 season but he decided to continue for one more year—'to ram it down the selectors' throats that they took us to Rome too late'. This final fling resulted in Pirie becoming AAA 3 miles champion again, breaking Bruce Tulloh's British record of 13:17.2 by eight-tenths (though Tulloh regained it the following month with a European mark of 13:12.0), coming close to his world 3,000 metres record with 7:54.8 and setting a lifetime best of 3:42.5 for 1,500 metres. On the debit side he was convincingly beaten by Olympic champion Murray Halberg (New Zealand) over 5,000 metres and was last in the Britain v. Hungary race at the same distance. Pirie closed his eventful and, for the most part, brilliant career with a 5,000 metres victory in the match between England and the Russian Federal Republic, followed by a well deserved lap of honour around the same White City oval that 14 years earlier had been the scene of his first big track race. Pirie, who then turned professional, has since made his mark as a coach—his most notable protégée being the world's fastest woman miler, Anne Smith. Incidentally, a poll conducted by *Athletics Weekly* in December 1965 to determine its readers' views as to the greatest athletes of all time resulted in Pirie being voted first among Britons with 36 per cent, followed by Roger Bannister (19 per cent), Derek Ibbotson (9 per cent) and Douglas Lowe (6 per cent).

The outstanding achievement of 1961 came from Basil Heatley, the National and International cross-country champion. He shattered Zatopek's world record for 10 miles by all of 25 seconds with a superb 47:47.0. Another record: a UK 6 miles mark of 27:54.4 by even-pace specialist Martin Hyman. It was Hyman's Portsmouth clubmate, Tulloh, who monopolised attention in 1962. He started the year on a sensational note for in New Zealand in January, within the space of three days, he broke Ken Wood's UK 2 miles record with 8:34.0 and hacked over five seconds from his fastest mile time in recording 3:59.3 behind world record breaker Peter Snell. He confirmed his outstanding range and ability at the Whitsun British Games by winning the 3 miles on the Saturday in 13:20.2 and the 6 miles on the Monday in 27:57.4, which at that date constituted the swiftest distance double within 48 hours in all athletics history. Two more scintillating runs followed: a 29:01.4 10,000 metres, with the second half completed in 14:21.4, and victory in the AAA 3 miles (13:16.0) over the amazing 18-year-old Canadian Bruce Kidd. His one reverse prior to the European 5,000 metres title race in Belgrade was an inches defeat by Poland's Kazimierz Zimny, although even then Tulloh equalled his best 5,000 metres time of 13:52.8.

Taking heed of the fact that Zimny could outsprint him over 200 metres Tulloh decided to make an early break in the big race, rather in the manner of Halberg in Rome. The ruse paid off. He startled the opposition by scuttling away (in bare feet as usual) on the penultimate lap, built up a ten-yard lead and clung tenaciously to it all the way to the tape. The overall time of 14:00.6 may have been unexceptional but his speed in the latter stages was fantastic: last 400 metres in 57.4, last 800 metres in 1:59.8, last mile in around 4:12! Earlier in the Championships Roy Fowler, the AAA 6 miles champion and co-holder with Mike Bullivant of the UK record of 27:49.8, snatched the bronze medal in the 10,000 metres inches ahead of Hyman. The Commonwealth Games late in the year provided less satisfaction. A weary Tulloh was beaten into fourth place in the 3 miles, while Welshman John Merriman (third) finished ahead of England's quartet in the 6 miles.

The revelation of 1963 was bearded Don Taylor, a runner whose persistent Achilles tendon trouble forced him to average only 30–35 miles a week in training—about a third of the mileage undertaken by most of his rivals. Taylor's best 6 miles prior to that season had been a mediocre 31:15.4 yet in the match against West Germany he won the 10,000 metres by half a lap in the UK record time of 28:52.4 and the following month displayed unexpected speed in returning 7:58.2 for 3,000 metres. Injury prevented his ever regaining such sparkling form in later seasons.

In view of her formidable strength in depth, Britain's total flop in the Tokyo Olympic 10,000 metres in 1964 was as inexplicable as it was disappointing. On paper, Bullivant (who had set a European record of 27:26.6 in winning the AAA 6 miles) and Ron Hill (27:27.0) were the two fastest performers in the world but in a race won in the comparable time of 28:24.4 Hill finished eighteenth and Bullivant twenty-first. The 5,000 metres provided little comfort. Only Mike Wiggs reached the final and he suffered the mortifying experience of tripping over on the second lap. Pluckily he picked himself up and shot off in pursuit but only a superman could have overcome such a handicap and Wiggs finished eleventh. Mel Batty, the man who had kicked off the season in such brilliant style by reducing Heatley's world 10 miles record to 47:26.8, succumbed to injuries and did not even get to Tokyo.

Wiggs in 1965 was reminiscent of his former adviser, Pirie, in his great years of 1953 and 1956. Three times he bettered four minutes for the mile although that distance was now only a side-line. Over 3 miles and its metric equivalent he was in a class above his closest British rivals and with times of 13:08.6 (3 miles) and 13:33.0 (5,000 metres) he established UK records that would have constituted world records only the previous year. It was an eventful season all round. Derek Graham, probably the greatest Northern Irish runner of all time, broke the UK 2 miles record with 8:33.8; Irish-born Jim Hogan (28:50.0) and Mike Freary (28:37.2) improved upon the national 10,000 metres standard; while both Hill (15 miles in 1:12:48.2 and 25,000 metres in 1:15:22.6) and Tim Johnston (30,000 metres in 1:32:34.6) set official world records. The previous holders were Emil Zatopek (1:14:01.0 and 1:16:36.4 in 1955) and Scotsman Jim Alder (1:34:01.8 in 1964). Also well worthy of mention was the 13:16.4 3 miles by 30-year-old Bill Wilkinson, an even-time sprinter way back in 1952 who had taken to three-miling only in 1963; and one-hour distances of 12 miles 758 yards by Freary and 12 miles 742 yards by Hill.

With Wiggs racing only a handful of times the three-miling supremacy in 1966 passed to Graham (fourth in the European 5,000 metres) and an exciting young discovery by the name of Allan Rushmer, who tied Wiggs' 3 miles record of 13:08.6 in placing third at the Commonwealth Games and was fifth in the European 10,000 metres in 28:37.8. Tulloh made a brilliant comeback as a six-miler with a European record of 27:23.8 in the AAA Championships; Freary cut the national 10,000 metres figures to 28:26.0; and Hogan followed up his success in the European marathon by setting a world 30,000 metres record of 1:32:25.4. Other noteworthy achieve-ments during the year were Wilkinson's 13:39.6 5,000; 3 miles times of 13:12.2 by the Scot, Ian McCafferty, and 13:12.4 by Dick Taylor at the Commonwealth Games; and 6 miles clockings of 27:24.8 by Fowler and 27:26.0 by Hill.

The standard of six-miling declined in 1967 but there was never such richness at two and three miles. McCafferty held the 2 miles record at 8:33.2 for less than three weeks before Taylor got to work with 8:30.2. He did, however, retain possession for the season of the UK 3 miles record with 13:06.4 although the most successful competitor of the year was Rushmer, whose best was 13:09.2. Taylor's best was 13:11.4 and all three of these young men should improve sufficiently to join the hallowed ranks of those who have broken 13 minutes for the distance. To keep the British times in perspective it must be pointed out that the Australian Ron Clarke holds the world record of 12:50.4 and has run 6 miles in 26:47.0.

7

THE MARATHON

IT is a popular misconception that the marathon race owes its origins to the ancient Olympic Games. The event was in fact contested for the first time at the inaugural Olympics of the modern era in 1896. At the suggestion of a Frenchman, M. Michel Bréal, the organisers arranged as a climax to the festivities a race from the plains of Marathon to the gleaming marble stadium in Athens, in commemoration of Pheidippides' legendary feat of 2,386 years earlier. The distance was 40 kilometres (24 miles 1,504 yards) and, amid great rejoicing, the race was won by a Greek, Spyridon Louis, in 2:58:50. The next two Olympic marathon champions were Michel Theato (France) and English-born Thomas Hicks (USA).

The rather odd distance (26 miles 385 yards or 42,195 metres) that has come to be accepted as the standard length of a marathon race was a legacy of the 1908 Games. The course from Windsor Castle to the entrance of the White City Stadium measured exactly 26 miles but in order that the runners might finish opposite the royal box an extra 385 yards were tacked on. This race, like several other marathons to follow, is remembered chiefly for a gallant loser. Few recall the winner's name—it was John Hayes (USA) in 2:55:18.4—but every athletics fan has heard of Dorando Pietri, the Italian who entered the stadium first, collapsed on the track, was helped across the line and subsequently disqualified.

British runners, who had expected to dominate the proceedings, made the pace for half the distance before dropping out of the reckoning. The highest placed home entrant turned out to be W. T. Clarke . . . twelfth in 3:16:08.6. Still, in those days anyone who could complete a marathon, regardless of position or time, was regarded as something of a physical phenomenon. The organisers, for their part, took pains to provide as much comfort as possible for the runners. 'Refreshments en route', proclaimed the instructions to competitors: 'The Oxo Company have been appointed official caterers and will supply the following free of charge to competitors: Oxo Athletes Flask, containing Oxo for immediate use; Oxo hot and cold; Oxo and soda, rice pudding, raisins, bananas, soda and milk.' Just as well the announcement ended . . . 'Stimulants will be available in cases of collapse.'

Next year the Polytechnic Harriers in collaboration with the proprietors of the *Sporting Life* started the annual Windsor to Stamford Bridge (or Chiswick in more recent years) race. The first winner was Fred Barrett in 2:42:31, over twelve minutes faster than Hayes' Olympic time. Harry Green, who was successful in the 1910 race, made amends for his disappointing showing at the 1912 Olympics (13th) by recording an excellent 2:38:16.2 in a *track* race at Stamford Bridge in 1913. Another unsuccessful contender at the Stockholm Games, Edgar Lloyd, went on to make his name at ultra-long distances, his numerous records including 50 miles in 6:13:58 in 1913.

The first Briton to place among the first six in an Olympic marathon was Irish-born Sam Ferris, who finished fifth (2:52:26) in 1924. Ferris remains one of the great names in British road running history; he won the Polytechnic marathon eight times between 1925 and 1933, was AAA champion from 1925 to 1927 and competed in two more Olympics. He came eighth (2:37:41) in 1928, only 4 minutes 44 seconds behind the winner; while in 1932 he recorded 2:31:55 to finish second a mere nineteen seconds after Argentina's Juan Zabala. Ferris may have forfeited the gold medal in Los Angeles through being over cautious in the early stages. He was over four minutes down on Zabala at the halfway turning point and was still no higher than sixth after twenty miles. Then he began to move. With 4½ miles to go he was fourth (at which stage the Scot, Duncan Wright, was leading Zabala by a minute) and less than two miles later he had moved into second position, behind Zabala. Ferris was closing all the way to the tape, looking unbelievably fresh, and was little more than 100 yards in arrears at the end. The winner, on the other hand, finished in a state of collapse.

Wright, who had defeated Ferris by half a mile in the 1930 Empire Games, lost ground in the closing stages but his fourth position, in 2:32:41, was a magnificent effort. This was for Wright, as for Ferris, his third and finest Olympic performance. Back in 1924, running with his feet bandaged, he was in fifth place close behind the leaders at seventeen miles. The bandages, however, created more trouble than they were worth and he sat down to remove them . . . developed cramp . . . and was forced to retire.

The other outstanding figure during the Ferris-Wright era was Harry Payne, who did not begin his running career until the age of 27. Ten years later, in 1929, he won the AAA title over the Windsor to Stamford Bridge course in a splendid 2:30:57.6—the fastest on record. He judged his effort admirably. Fourth at ten miles in 58:05, he took over the lead at seventeen miles, was 1¾ minutes ahead of Ferris at twenty miles (1:55:06) and proceeded to win by over eight minutes. The previous year, in capturing the AAA title, he had clocked 2:34:34 but had finished only thirteenth (2:42:29) in the Olympics.

Scotland's marathon running tradition, founded by Dunkie Wright, was maintained by his Maryhill clubmate Donald McNab Robertson—six times AAA champion between 1932 and 1939. He seemed to make a habit of being involved in desperately close finishes. In 1932 he defeated Wright by 1.4 seconds in 2:34:32.6 and in 1936 he prevailed over Ernie Harper by 1.2 seconds in 2:35:02.4, but the biter was bit in the 1946 AAA title race when Squire Yarrow (at the age of 40, two months the elder) edged him by just one-fifth of a second in 2:43:14.4! Imagine flogging oneself for over 26 miles only to lose by a few inches. Robertson showed up well in the 1936 Olympics to take seventh in 2:37:06.2 after passing three men in the last four miles but Britain's hero in Berlin was 34-year-old Harper, a man who could look back over a dozen years of international competition. He had won the AAA 10 miles track title in 1923, finished fourth in the following year's notorious Olympic cross-country race (won by Paavo Nurmi) and lifted the International cross-country championship in 1926. At the 1928 Olympics he had come in twenty-first in 2:45:44 after having reached the halfway point sixth. His most recent notable exploit was setting a world two hours track record of 20 miles 1,604 yards in 1933.

This grand veteran surpassed all reasonable expectations by matching Japan's Kitei Son stride for stride for mile after mile. Even though the pair ignored the fast start by defending champion Zabala—he was over a minute ahead of them at six miles—their pace was a cracking one. At the halfway mark Zabala was timed in 1:11:29, Son and Harper in 1:12:19. Zabala fell victim to his own impetuosity and was overhauled just before 17½ miles. Harper continued to run his heart out but in Son he was facing the greatest marathoner the world had yet produced. Inevitably the Korean-born Japanese representative drew away, to win in 2:29:19.2, but Harper worked wonders to remain within half a mile of him. His time was 2:31:23.2.

Another silver medal came Britain's way two years later at the European Championships, with Yarrow clocking 2:39:03, and yet another at the 1948 Olympics. The recipient on this latter occasion was Tom Richards, a Welshman who had first made ripples in the pool of marathon racing by taking fourth place in the 1939 Polytechnic race in 2:50:26.4. Richards improved considerably after the war but was persistently overshadowed by Jack Holden. It was Holden, winner of the 1948 AAA title in 2:36:44.6 (Richards was second in 2:38:03), who was considered Britain's golden hope at the Olympics but he fell victim to the bane of all road runners . . . blisters. In order to guard against sore feet he had pickled his feet in potassium permanganate but when blisters developed under the leather-like outer skin he had no alternative but to drop out. Holden was not the only poignant figure, for Etienne Gailly (Belgium) experienced the mortification of reaching Wembley Stadium first but in such an exhausted state that two men overtook him during the lap of the track. Delfo Cabrera (Argentina), a worthy successor to Zabala, won in 2:34:51.6 with Richards, who finished very fast à la Ferris in 1932, sixteen seconds behind. Richards continued in competition for many years, setting a personal best of 2:29:59 in 1954 (at the age of 44), but without ever again featuring prominently on the international scene.

It was different in Jack Holden's case. Three years Richards' senior, he it was who kept the flag flying proudly. Born at Bilston (Staffs) on March 13th 1907, Holden joined Tipton Harriers in 1925. Within four years he was an English cross-country international and during the thirties he built up the most distinguished record in cross-country history: national champion in 1938 and 1939; international champion in 1933, 1934, 1935 and 1939. He was also a useful track runner—three times AAA 6 miles titlist—though not reckoned in world class.

As he was 38 when the war ended it might have been thought that Holden's running days were long over but in 1946 he decided to take up marathoning. He made a successful debut by taking the Midland title in 2:46:34 but the selectors overlooked him when picking the team for the European Championships. Just to show them the error of their ways he completed the season with two great runs. He triumphed in the South London Harriers 30 miles road race in 3:02:09 and in a track race over the same distance at the White City (120 laps!) he recorded a world's best of 3:00:16.4, his time at the marathon point *en route* being 2:36:39.4. The European title, meanwhile, went to Meikko Hietanen (Finland) in 2:24:55 but the course was about 1¼ miles (say seven minutes) short. Yarrow was seventh in 2:30:40.

Holden gained the first of four consecutive AAA titles in 1947 as he outdistanced Richards by half a mile in 2:33:20.2, and followed with the fastest '30' on record—2:59:47. He was, however, surprisingly beaten by a little known Luxemburger, C. Heirend, in Czechoslovakia's classic Kosice marathon. Holden's first international success materialised at Enschede (Netherlands) in 1949 but his winning time of 2:20:52 was extremely flattering, but the course was three kilometres or about 11 minutes under distance.

His great season was 1950 when, aged 43, he proved himself the world's number one marathoner by winning five races out of five including the British Empire and European Championships. He began in February with the Empire Games in Auckland. He won by over four minutes in 2:32:57, a performance all the more remarkable in that he ran the last ten miles barefoot after discarding his sodden shoes . . . and was even attacked by a Great Dane a couple of miles from the end. Next came the Midland (2:38:23.6), Polytechnic (2:33:07) and AAA (personal best of 2:31:03.4) races, and as a grand finale he seized the European crown in 2:32:13.2. As he was presented to the 19-year-old Prince Baudouin of Belgium this astonishing runner was able to remark: 'Glad to meet you, sir. Met your father and grandfather before you!'

Holden made his farewell in 1951. He attained a new level of excellence by winning the Finchley 20 miles road race in a record 1:50:48, 1½ minutes ahead of 1948 Olympic 10,000 metres representative Jim Peters, but in the Windsor to Chiswick race two months later Peters, making a spectacular marathon debut, ran Holden into the ground and set a UK best time of 2:29:24 in the process. Holden displayed his usual aggressiveness; he led by thirty seconds at 15 miles but in attempting to stay with Peters over the final few miles he ran himself to a standstill. *Le roi est mort, vive le roi.*

The new king of the marathon brought a fresh approach to the event. Just as Emil Zatopek revolutionised track running standards by his training methods and racing performances so Jim Peters revised all concepts of how to run a marathon. With very rare exceptions, the marathoner of the pre-Peters era was basically a 'plodder', a man with highly developed qualities of persistence and courage but quite lacking in speed. Two and a half hours, which had first been approached by Hannes Kolehmainen (Finland) as long ago as 1920, remained the magical figure throughout three decades of marathon running. Peters and his coach, 'Johnny' Johnston (an Olympic 5,000 metres finalist in 1928), came to realise that, given a suitable preparation, 2 hours 20 minutes was a definite possibility. That they succeeded in translating theories into deeds assures them of an important place in the history of athletic progress.

Peters, a Londoner born on October 24th 1918, had considered retiring after the disappointment of being lapped in the Olympic 10,000 metres. At the age of 29 he could look back on a certain measure of success as a track runner—AAA champion at 6 miles in 1946 and 10 miles in 1947—and although his times were nowhere near world class he had at least achieved his ambition of representing his country. Johnston pleaded with him to train for the next Olympic marathon. Peters was reluctant, for he knew the demands that would be made on his time and body, but after continual persuasion from Johnston and such stars of the past as Sam Ferris and Harry Payne he decided, towards the end of 1949, to give it a try. The following May he entered his first long distance road race, the Essex '20', and won it in the moderate time of 1:59:50.

He stayed away from serious competition for the rest of the season and athletics followers could have been pardoned for believing that Jim Peters had retired once and for all. In reality, he was steadily increasing the severity of his training, running (by accepted marathon standards) relatively short distances at only slightly under racing speed. The outcome of training every day, which few athletes attempted at that time, was that his weekly mileage was no less than that achieved by more traditional methods . . . and the tempo was infinitely faster. In other words, quality had been introduced with no reduction in quantity. By the spring of 1951 Peters was almost ready to shake the road running world. The first step was the Wigmore '15', which he won in 1:26:55. Later in April he finished second to Holden in the Finchley '20' in 1:52:24. The final tune-up prior to the start of his marathon career was the Essex '20' in May.

Here he revealed for the first time his amazing capabilities as he led right from the start to win in the unprecedented time of 1:47:08. No man had ever run the distance that fast and a remeasurement showed the course to be 600 yards short; nevertheless the time was worth about 1:49 for a full 20 miles. The revolution was under way.

It was thus amid much interest and speculation that Peters made his marathon debut in the Polytechnic race from Windsor to Chiswick in June 1951. Good twenty-milers before now had come unstuck over those torturous last six miles and 385 yards. Did Peters have what it takes? Jack Holden, for one, was soon to find out. Peters passed the ageing champion before 20 miles, which point he reached in 1:52:05, and stormed away to win by five minutes from another 'first-timer', pre-war 5,000 metres international Stan Cox, in 2:29:24. First to congratulate Peters at the finish was the race referee, Harry Payne, whose British 'record' of 2:30:57.6 set in 1929 had at last been broken. A few weeks later Peters won the AAA title in 2:31:42.

Much faster over the shorter distances than ever before as a result of his enlightened training methods, Peters filled fourth place in the 1952 National cross-country championship (he had never previously finished higher than forty-sixth) and represented England. Back on the road he was untouchable, covering the Finchley '20' in 1:49:39 and an accurately measured Essex '20' in 1:48:33. These times were judged phenomenal but it was in the combined AAA/Polytechnic marathon that he really left the athletics world gasping. The wide difference in courses makes accurate comparison of marathon performances difficult but up until June 14th 1952 the fastest ever recorded over 26 miles 385 yards was 2:26:07 by the Korean, Choi Yoon Chil, in 1951. What a sensation, therefore, when Peters snapped the tape in the Polytechnic Stadium, Chiswick, just 2:20:42.2 after leaving Windsor! Almost as incredible was the time of Stan Cox, another 'Johnny' Johnston protégé, in second place (2:21:42), while Geoff Iden was third in 2:26:53.8. 'Short course' was the first thought of the sceptics but the distance was found to be 260 yards over the standard!

Peters and Cox travelled to Helsinki the following month as favourites for the Olympic gold and silver medals, regardless of the announced intention of Emil Zatopek to contest the marathon as well as the 5,000 and 10,000 metres. Alas, neither was able to finish the race, which the incredible Zatopek won by 2½ minutes in

2:23:03.2 to complete a treble that may never be emulated. Seemingly carried away by the occasion, Peters opened up a 100 yards lead while speeding through the first ten kilometres in 31:55—faster than the time he achieved in the track race at Wembley four years earlier. He was caught shortly before ten miles and just after the halfway mark, while in third place, he developed severe cramp in his left leg. He gallantly hobbled on until eventually collapsing after nineteen miles. Meanwhile Cox, suffering from pains all down his left side, had blacked out four miles earlier while in sixth position.

Peters did his best to erase the memory of this blow during a 1953 season that rivalled that of Gordon Pirie's for sustained brilliance. He won all four of his marathons: the 'Poly' (159 yards over distance this time) in a world's best of 2:18:40.2, the AAA in 2:22:29, the Enschede race in 2:19:22 and the Turku event in another world's fastest of 2:18:34.8—$1\frac{1}{4}$ miles ahead of Finland's sub-2:20 performer, Veikko Karvonen. In addition Peters, whose best 6 miles prior to his marathon career had been 30:07, recorded 29:01.8 for third place on the British all-time list and succeeded in removing Walter George's 69-year-old English native one hour record with 11 miles 986 yards on a blazing hot afternoon.

For Peters, as for Roger Bannister, 1954 was the important year. The year in which to compensate for Olympic disappointment by winning Commonwealth and European titles. Four marathon races were scheduled. In the first, the Boston (USA) classic, he was runner-up to Karvonen in 2:22:40, but in the AAA event over his favourite Windsor to Chiswick route he lowered the world's best yet again with the stupendous time of 2:17:39.4. On the way he passed 10 miles in 52:53, 15 miles in 1:18:35 and 20 miles in 1:44:25. His perpetual shadow, Stan Cox, was second in 2:23:08.

Having just set a personal best 6 miles time of 28:57.8, Peters made his way to Vancouver for the Commonwealth Games in good spirits. He ran well there for the bronze medal in the 6 miles and all seemed ready for his first major title. The afternoon of the marathon was hot and humid, the long distance runner's nightmare, for even in normal weather the marathoner sweats profusely and can lose several pounds in bodyweight. It was obviously prudent to move off at a relatively modest pace in order to guard against the body becoming overheated and dehydrated but Peters, by nature, was a man who refused to compromise. He would not hold himself back and at 20 miles, reached in 1:48, he was quarter of a mile ahead of Cox with the rest of the field almost literally miles behind. Disaster struck both men practically simultaneously. Sunstroke caused Cox to run straight into a steel lamp-post less than two miles from the stadium, while just a few minutes later the cruel conditions took their toll of Peters. A good quarter of an hour in front of the next survivor, Peters entered the stadium in a groggy manner and proceeded to horrify the crowd (which had thrilled to the greatest mile duel in history only minutes earlier) for the next eleven minutes as he repeatedly fell over while attempting to cover the last few hundred yards of track. The agony came to an end, at least for the spectators, just 200 yards from the mirage of the finishing tape when officials, unable to stand by helplessly any longer, carried him off. Peters, who had intended running in the European Championships eighteen days later, never raced again. Indeed he was lucky to stay alive and to this day he is still afflicted by headaches and giddiness from that ordeal in the sun. The winner, by the way, was Scotland's Joe McGhee in 2:39:36 but just as the 1908 Olympic marathon will for ever be remembered for the name of the loser, Dorando Pietri, so Vancouver will always be associated with Jim Peters. And, like his Italian predecessor, he was singled out by royalty. He later received a special gold medal from the Duke of Edinburgh, who had watched his agony, inscribed: 'To J. Peters as a token of admiration for a most gallant marathon runner'.

Sam Ferris wrote in *Athletics Weekly*: 'Jim has got himself to such a state of fitness by his rigorous routine and made his recovery rate abnormal, but there must be a limit to human endurance and I think Jim has reached the stage when he has trained his body to stand so much that it is apt to go past these limits—which appears to have been the case at Vancouver. This could have happened to Jim before, and I have often said it would if he got a day hot enough and didn't moderate his pace to meet the conditions.' Such are the problems of men who seek to revolutionise athletic performances.

Cox resumed active competition but never became Britain's number one. That distinction went in successive seasons to Bob McMinnis (1955), Ron Clark (2:20:15.8 in the 1956 'Poly' but a non-finisher at the Olympics) and Eddie Kirkup (1957). Fred Norris, third in the European Championships, and Peter Wilkinson, third in the Commonwealth Games and fourth in the European, did well in 1958 but one had to wait until 1960 before any Briton joined Peters in the sub-2:20 class. That year three men did the trick—Irish born Denis O'Gorman (2:18:15.6), Arthur Keily (2:19:06), and Fred Norris (2:19:08)—but results at the Rome Olympics were poor.

The 1960 season did, however, see the rise to prominence of the man who in 1962 was to follow in Holden's footsteps by winning both the European and Commonwealth titles. His name: Brian Kilby. Self coached and only 22, he made a distinguished debut by finishing second in the Poly marathon (2:22:53) and won his place on the Olympic team by virtue of his AAA win (the first of five) in 2:22:44.8. Inexperience held him down to twenty-ninth place in Rome, a race won by the previously unknown Ethiopian, Abebe Bikila, in a world's best of 2:15:16.2. Two years and some ten thousand training miles later Kilby gained the first half of his double, taking the European gold medal in 2:23:18.8 after leading for the last seven miles. Later in the year he achieved an even more comfortable (if that term can ever be applied to marathon running) success in the Commonwealth Games and registered his best time of 2:21:17. Having proved his worth competitively, Kilby knuckled down to the task of recording some super-fast times in 1963. In the Welsh open event at Port Talbot in July he was timed at 2:14:43, the fastest by a European and surpassed only by the 2:14:28 the previous month by the Essex-based American 'Buddy' Edelen from Windsor to Chiswick. Kilby went on to win the AAA title in 2:16:45.

The big man in the all-important year of 1964 was not Kilby, however, but Basil Heatley, his Coventry Godiva clubmate. Heatley, aged 30, had been Midland marathon champion in 1956 (2:36:55.2) and 1957 (2:32:01) at a time when his best track marks were merely 13:59.8 for 3 miles and 29:07.8 for 6 miles. By 1962 he had progressed to 13:30.0 and 28:03.0 but although he had achieved outstanding successes as a cross-country runner (International champion in 1961) and was holder of the world 10 miles track record at 47:47.0 he found himself unable to make the British team for the season's two major meetings. He decided, with the Olympics in mind, to add another string to his bow by returning to the marathon and in 1963, after six years away from the event, he turned in a highly promising 2:19:56. That same year he improved his track times to 13:22.8 and 27:57.0, but any doubts as to his true vocation must have been dispelled in June 1964 when he covered the Windsor to Chiswick course in the world's fastest time of 2:13:55. Content to pass 10 miles in 51:20, a full minute behind the leaders (who included Ron Hill, credited with a world's best 20 miles road time of 1:40:55 two weeks earlier), Heatley passed Hill for the lead shortly before 20 miles (1:42:05 against 1:42:10) and came home 100 yards ahead. Hill, the UK 6 miles record holder, also bettered all known performances by returning 2:14:12, while Scotland's Jim Alder made his mark with a time of 2:17:46.

The selectors promptly named Heatley and Hill to the Olympic team with one vacancy to be filled after the AAA Championship in August. Juan Taylor, yet another Godiva Harrier, won the Welsh open race in 2:15:37 but the only way he could win selection for Tokyo was to defeat Kilby for the AAA title. The race, appropriately held in Coventry, was made even more murderous by the very warm weather. In the knowledge that there was no consolation prize for the loser the two men ground out a blistering pace, passing 10 miles together in 50:23. Eventually Taylor found he could not sustain the inhuman speed and at 15 miles Kilby was twenty seconds ahead in 1:16:20, quarter of a minute faster than the corresponding intermediate time in the much 'easier' Poly race. Kilby himself inevitably had to slacken off drastically and, his feet bleeding, he was reduced to a final time of 2:23:01. Taylor failed to finish. This grim race exacted a considerable physical and psychological toll from Kilby and it says much for his ability and temperament that he was able to finish fourth in the Olympic race in 2:17:02.4. Heatley ran with characteristic steadiness and, although outclassed by the incredible Abebe Bikila (2:12:11.2), he proved himself the second best marathoner in the world. He passed Japan's Kokichi Tsuburaya on the stadium lap and made sure of his silver medal by sprinting the final 200 metres in an extraordinary 32.3 seconds. Hill, who had dropped out of the 1962 European race, again met with misfortune and was placed nineteenth.

Coventry Godiva's magnificent marathon record was strengthened in 1965 when, in spite of Heatley's retirement from major events, the club supplied the first three finishers in the AAA title race: Bill Adcocks (2:16:50), Kilby (2:17:34) and Taylor (2:18:57). The following year Adcocks very nearly won the Commonwealth title in Kingston by reason of officials' incompetence. The marshals who should have been at the stadium entrance to guide the runners were absent—presumably lured from their posts by the prospect of catching sight of the arriving royal party—and consequently bewildered and fatigued athletes were left to fend for themselves. Jim Alder, representing Scotland, held a fifty-yard lead over Adcocks approaching the stadium and chose what was probably intended as the correct route, while Adcocks unwittingly took a short cut with the result that he appeared on the track ahead of an astonished Alder. Fortunately justice prevailed and Alder, much the stronger of the two, was able to overtake his rival and win by twenty yards in 2:22:07.8. This was remarkable running for even though the race started at 5.30 a.m. the temperature was well into the eighties with a high level of humidity. Among the non-finishers was defending champion Kilby.

As the European Championship took place only twenty-four days later the Kingston marathoners were unable to 'double' but such is the perpetual strength in this event that any one of the trio of Graham Taylor, Ron Hill and Jim Hogan stood a fine chance of succeeding Kilby. Taylor, only 21, had in June become the youngest ever AAA marathon champion (2:19:04) and was holder of the world's best 20 miles road time of 1:39:08; Hill was still the second fastest European marathoner of all time; and Hogan, who in Ireland's colours had held second place in the Tokyo marathon for over twenty miles before dropping out, was quietly determined to make his debut for Great Britain a memorable one. And Hogan it was who triumphed. Running with masterly judgment he made his break about eight miles from the end and finished well clear in 2:20:04.6, 37.6 seconds outside the personal best he recorded when placing second in the AAA event. Unhappily both Hill and Taylor, well placed for the first half of the race, came to grief. Hill, bothered by a stomach upset, finished twelfth six minutes behind Hogan, while Taylor displayed outstanding courage in finishing at all after his legs 'died' on him at eighteen miles.

Notwithstanding the championships won by Taylor, Alder and Hogan, the fastest British marathoner of 1966 and indeed of all time was the 33-year-old Scot, Alastair Wood. The fourth placer in the 1962 European Championship was timed in 2:13:45, ten seconds inside Heatley's figures, on the Inverness to Forres course. The performance was at first dismissed as suspect but the distance covered was later found to be correct. Alder had the best 1967 time (2:14:44.8), in a race won by Lancashire-born Derek Clayton (Australia) in a record 2:09:36.4.

8

THE STEEPLECHASE

STEEPLECHASING, minus the horse that is, can be traced back to that traditional home of lost causes, Oxford, in 1850. An undergraduate of Exeter College, Halifax Wyatt by name, was discussing with friends the college steeplechase in which his horse had fallen. 'Sooner than ride such a brute again', he joked, 'I'd run across two miles of country on foot.' 'Well, why not?' came the reply. And so, later in the year, a two miles steeplechase involving twenty-four fences, was staged over marshy farmland. First of the twenty-four competitors was, appropriately, Mr Wyatt.

A track steeplechase was introduced into the English championship programme in 1879 and three years later the great Walter George tried his hand. Although he had already won the 880 yards, mile and 4 miles (but he ran only a nominal lap since there were no other contestants) that same afternoon he was leading by the proverbial street when he cut his foot while negotiating the water jump and was obliged to retire. 'W.G.' never tried it again but in 1894 his younger brother, A. B. George, won the title. Two steeplechasing events were put on at the 1900 Olympics. The 2,500 metres went to George Orton (USA), who outsprinted pace-setter Sidney Robinson, but British runners cleaned up in the 4,000 metres next day: John Rimmer was first, 1,500 metres champion Charles Bennett second and Robinson third. Considering the course included stone fences, hurdles, a water jump and 'other obstacles', it is most unlikely the distances covered were really as advertised. Orton's time of 7:34.4 represents 9:05.3 pace for what was later to become the standardised 3,000 metres event while Rimmer was timed in 12:58.4—which is 9:43.8 speed. Nine and a half minutes for 3,000 metres was not beaten until 1928.

There was no official British team at the 1904 Olympics where Irishman John Daly took second place in the 2,500 metres about 100 yards behind James Lightbody (USA) after holding a long lead at the mile mark. The previous month Daly had lost in the AAA

Championships to Arthur Russell. The latter's turn came at the 1908 Olympics when he carried off the 3,200 metres (22 yards under 2 miles) title in 10:47.8, one second ahead of International cross-country champion Arthur Robertson. For some reason or other, Russell's conqueror in the AAA race, Reg Noakes, was not selected for the Games. Noakes, incidentally, was a founder member and honorary secretary of Birmingham's Sparkhill Harriers, the club that over half a century later was to produce the fastest steeplechaser in British history . . . Maurice Herriott.

The next Olympic steeplechase took place in 1920, at 3,000 metres for the first time, and Britain's already considerable tradition was boosted still further by the ludicrously easy victory of 29-year-old Percy Hodge. He led from the second lap and at the end was nearly 100 yards clear of his closest rival. The time was 10:00.4. Although Hodge has been described as ungainly in terms of style he was obviously a smooth and assured hurdler. He used to delight crowds by running over a flight of hurdles while balancing a bottle of beer on a tray and never spilling a drop! The very nature of steeplechasing demands grit, ruggedness and coolness under pressure, and these were qualities possessed in abundance by Hodge. For example, in the 1920 AAA 2 miles steeplechase (the English distance was standardised in 1913 but there was no rule governing the number of hurdles per lap until 1931) Hodge was spiked at the water jump on the second lap, causing the heel of his shoe to be ripped off. He stopped, removed the shoe, adjusted it, laced it up again and set off . . . 100 yards behind the leaders. Quite unruffled he moved swiftly through the field and went on to win by sixty yards. In the following AAA Championships he gained his third consecutive title in a championship best of 10:57.2 in spite of his stomach being bandaged up.

Another gallant runner was Evelyn Montague who, while in third place, hurt his knee taking the water jump with two laps to go in the 1924 Olympic final. He struggled on gamely to finish sixth, the winner in a world's best of 9:33.6 being Finland's Ville Ritola. 'Monty', as he was known, became a most distinguished journalist—as also did two other outstanding steeplechasers in Vernon Morgan (bronze medallist at the 1930 Empire Games) and Chris Brasher, of whom more anon.

The first Briton to crack ten minutes for the metric event was Jack Webster, the International cross-country champion of 1925.

He clocked 9:57.6 in 1927 but his 2 miles time of 10:30.6 at the 1924 English native or 'closed' championships was worth inside 9:50. Those English, as distinct from AAA or 'open' championships, were staged only from 1923 to 1925. A big improvement was effected by H. W. Townend with 9:40.2 in 1929. George Bailey, the 1930 Empire champion, progressed to 9:34.0 in the match against France in 1931 but that race was won by Tom Evenson in 9:27.4, which was only 5.6 seconds outside the world's best.

Evenson, like so many of the important names in British steeple-chasing, was an exceptional cross-country runner and there is of course an affinity between these two branches of athletics. Evenson was International champion in 1930 and also a fine flat runner, winner of the 5,000 metres against Germany in 1931 in a British best of 14:54.8. Evenson tuned up for the 1932 Olympics with a 10:13.8 2 miles victory (over Bailey, 10:14.8) in the AAA Championships and ran brilliantly in Los Angeles. He won his heat in an Olympic record of 9:18.8, which stood as a UK best until 1950, and in the final he collected the silver medal behind Finland's Volmari Iso-Hollo. This was the famous race in which, due to an official's error, an extra lap of 460 metres was run! At the actual 3,000 metres mark Joe McCluskey (USA) was second and Evenson third but the Briton snatched second place during the gratuitous lap. His time was 10:46.0. Bailey, who had been up with Iso-Hollo and Evenson until two laps from the end, finished fifth.

Top man in Britain in 1934 was S. G. Scarsbrook, Empire Games 2 miles winner in 10:23.4 ahead of Evenson and Bailey and credited with a metric 9:29.2 against France. The following season Bailey posted a personal best 2 miles mark of 10:14.2, four-tenths of a second slower than Evenson's UK record. For the next fifteen years steeplechasing languished as one of Britain's 'Cinderella' events, attracting only mediocre flat-runners who saw a possible short cut to championship honours and international representation and treated by spectators as something of a music hall turn.

The rot was stopped in 1950 thanks to Welshman John Disley and the foresight of AAA National Coach Geoff Dyson. Their partnership began in 1946 after Dyson watched Disley, then 17, win his first ever track race: 3 miles in 15:32.4. Dyson immediately sensed the steeplechasing possibilities ('I was informed that when I grew up I would run the steeplechase', Disley recalls) but it was not until the autumn of 1949 that Disley embarked upon serious training for the event. His début in June 1950, a UK 3,000 metres best of 9:18.4, was the first step on the road towards world class. Next month he confirmed his talent by clocking 10:05.4, beating another Evenson record, twenty yards behind Yugoslavia's redoubtable Petar Segedin in the AAA 2 miles.

Disley and Dyson were criticised in some quarters after this race for, running to a strict time schedule, Disley allowed Segedin to build up a lead of as much as fifty yards only to close the gap dramatically in the last couple of laps. Despite his near novice status Disley was already being hailed as a prospective medallist at the forthcoming European Championships but a foot injury ruined his chances and he limped home thirteenth. Segedin won the silver medal in 9:07.4. Foot and ankle trouble continued to hinder Disley's progress in 1951 but in his final race of the season he unleashed a fearsome last lap to leave the Swedish stars Curt Soderberg and Tore Sjostrand (the Olympic champion) floundering well behind. The time was a record 9:11.6, which was a good deal better than his fastest 2 miles time of 10:04.0 achieved behind Segedin in the AAA Championships.

Disley made gigantic strides in 1952, accomplishing more than one had dared hope for. In fact his first steeplechase race of the Olympic season resulted in a crushing defeat, 9:26.2 against Chris Brasher's 9:17.4, but this was perfectly understandable since only the previous week he had set a record time of 7 hours 24 minutes in a 25 miles mountain race across Snowdonia's 14 peaks of over 3,000 feet! At the AAA Championships Disley scored by 120 yards in the dazzling time of 9:44.0, easily the fastest 2 miles time on record and equivalent to under the magical nine minutes for 3,000 metres. Outclassed though he was, Brasher also had the satisfaction of beating Segedin and clocking 10:03.6. A few weeks later, in Helsinki, both reached the 12-man Olympic final. Disley won his heat in 8:59.4 and Brasher finished fourth in his in 9:03.2, also way inside the former British record of 9:11.6.

The final was far and away the greatest steeplechase race up to that time. Prior to 1951 only one man had ever beaten nine minutes for the 1 mile 1,521 yards course with its twenty-eight hurdles and seven water jumps but in Helsinki the seventh finisher was timed in 8:56.2 with the winner, Horace Ashenfelter (USA), setting a world record of 8:45.4. Vladimir Kazantsev (USSR), the previous record holder at 8:48.6, was second in 8:51.6 and John Disley was third in

K

8:51.8. Disley, who apart from McDonald Bailey was the only member of the British men's team to gain a medal, admits that a misjudgment cost him the silver award. He told *The Times* correspondent: 'I unwisely had my eye on the German, Gude, as the potential winner, and followed him until I found myself seventh with two laps to go. Then Dyson shouted at me from the edge of the track, and I woke up and began to chase the leaders. I had been running in a vacuum, without reminding myself all the time that there wouldn't be the same chance for another four years. And that's what you *have* to do in any Olympic final.' Disley worked his way up to third by the bell, well behind the two leaders, and almost caught Kazantsev on the line. His time, almost twenty seconds inside his pre-Olympic fastest, hoisted him to fourth place on the all-time world list. As for Brasher, he displayed the fortitude befitting one of the country's foremost mountaineers by limping home eleventh after crashing into a hurdle on the second lap.

Neither Disley nor Brasher recaptured Helsinki form during the next two seasons but the years were not wasted for both succeeded in improving their flat speed and both were largely responsible for persuading the AAA to scrap the meaningless 2 miles steeplechase in favour of the internationally recognised 3,000 metres. Ironically, the inaugural AAA 3,000 metres steeplechase in 1954, the first metric event in the long history of the championships, was won by neither. The race went to Ken Johnson in 9:00.8, with Brasher fourth and Disley a non-runner through injury.

The 1955 season was a vintage one for British steeplechasing in general and Disley in particular. At the AAA Championship Disley summoned up a phenomenal last lap of 61.5 to win in 8:56.6 from Brasher (8:59.4) and a swiftly improving Eric Shirley (9:03.4), and went on to win all four of his international match races. He returned 8:52.2 against West Germany ahead of Brasher (8:56.0); 8:55.4 against Hungary in front of Shirley (8:56.2) and European champion Sandor Rozsnyoi; a superb UK record of 8:44.2, only three seconds outside the world record, against the USSR with Brasher also excelling with 8:49.2; and 9:06.4 against Czechoslovakia a couple of yards clear of Brasher. Later in the autumn, at two White City floodlit meetings, two more of the world's greatest exponents fell victim. First Finland's Pentti Karvonen, an 8:45.4 performer, finished well behind Disley (8:48.8) and Shirley (8:49.8), and in the second meeting Poland's world record holder at 8:40.2,

Jerzy Chromik, was shunted into fourth place by the British trio. The tall and supple Shirley, a greater natural talent than his two colleagues but often lacking their tenacity, came into his own on that foggy night to win in a sizzling 8:47.6. Disley followed in 8:50.0 and Brasher showed 8:52.6.

What a magnificent season, and what glowing prospects Britain possessed for the following year's Olympics in the tried and tested Disley and the largely untapped potential of Shirley. Brasher, a good man to have in support but no prospective champion it seemed, would make a solid third string. That was still the picture at the 1956 AAA Championships where Shirley, a 3:47.0 1,500 metres performer, outsprinted Disley with 8:51.6 to 8:53.4. Brasher finished far behind in 9:02.6 and for a while it looked as though he might be omitted from the team for Melbourne but in the match against Czechoslovakia he won his ticket by registering a personal best of 8:47.2 close behind Disley's 8:46.6. However, the final test before departure was not a happy one: Brasher tripped headlong into the water early in the race and finished a bedraggled fifth in 9:09.4, Shirley fell heavily and dropped out, and Disley—the winner in 8:57.2—was short of training following an illness.

More hopeful news came from Australia fifteen days before the steeplechase final was scheduled: Brasher slashed nearly thirteen seconds off his best 2 miles flat time with an all-comers' record of 8:45.6. For the first time there was an indication that Brasher, re-united with his coach Franz Stampfl and obviously enjoying the best form of his long career, might yet fare best of the three. The results of the Olympic heats were vastly encouraging. Disley virtually dead-heated for first in his race in the very fast time of 8:46.6, Shirley won his in 8:52.6 and Brasher, visibly conserving energy, clocked 8:53.8 for a safe fourth. Three Britons in a ten-man final while no other nation had more than one representative . . . it made quite a contrast to Wembley in 1948 when none of the three British runners survived his heat or even bettered 9:40 for the distance!

Zdzislaw Krzyszkowiak (Poland) did not start; the personal best times of the other nine finalists were, in descending order: world record holder Sandor Rozsnyoi (Hungary) 8:35.6, Semyon Rzhish-chin (USSR) 8:39.8, Ernst Larsen (Norway) 8:42.4, John Disley 8:44.2, Chris Brasher 8:47.2, 'Deacon' Jones (USA) 8:47.4, Eric Shirley 8:47.6, Heinz Laufer (Germany) 8:48.4 and Neil Robbins (Australia) 8:55.4. Larsen started fast and at 1,000 metres was about ten yards clear, with Shirley fourth, Disley fifth and Brasher seventh. By 2,000 metres Brasher had worked his way through to third behind Larsen and Rzhishchin, with Shirley fifth and Disley sixth. Shirley, a bundle of nerves, dropped out of contention but at the bell five men were in with a chance of ultimate success. The order was Rzhishchin, Rozsnyoi, Brasher, Larsen and Disley. As the Russian flagged so Rozsnyoi, Brasher and Larsen challenged for the leadership. The Hungarian showed ahead briefly but, four barriers from home, Brasher launched his attack. Taking his rivals completely by surprise he quickly opened up a gap which stretched to fifteen yards by the finish. Brasher, for so many years little more than an honest plodder, was Olympic champion! He had succeeded where his infinitely more glamorous and famous colleagues, Roger Bannister and Chris Chataway, had failed.

Or had he? The result of the steeplechase, boomed the public address system: 'First, Rozsnyoi'. Brasher, it transpired, had been disqualified 'for interference in the last lap'; more explicitly for obstructing Larsen over the fourth hurdle from home. The Norwegian immediately rallied to Brasher's cause. 'Whatever happened,' he said, 'there was no need for disqualification. Brasher and I both tried to pass Rozsnyoi on the outside together when our elbows touched. It would be shocking to take the gold medal off Brasher.' An appeal was lodged and, three nerve-racking hours after Brasher snapped the tape, the jury's verdict was announced. 'After hearing the evidence of all those concerned, including the two athletes affected, the jury decided unanimously to allow the appeal and Brasher is therefore placed first. The jury consider that Brasher and Larsen came into contact with each other but that it was unintentional and both athletes stated that it did not affect their running.'

The final result, then, was: 1st Brasher in 8:41.2, a UK and Olympic record; 2nd Rozsnyoi in 8:43.6; 3rd Larsen in 8:44.0. Disley was sixth in 8:44.6, only a fraction outside his best time, and Shirley eighth in 8:57.0. For Brasher it was a triumphant finale to an otherwise unexceptional career. There cannot be many other Olympic champions who never won either a national title or an international match event!

Brasher, who was born in British Guiana on August 21st 1928, achieved his first significant success at the 1951 International Student Games in Luxemburg when he finished second in the 1,500 metres (3:54.0) behind the Grand Duchy's Olympic champion-to-be, Josy

Barthel, and won the 5,000 metres in a remarkably slow 15:07.6. That was also the year he began steeplechasing, clocking 9:21.8. He improved upon that by over eighteen seconds at the Helsinki Olympics and reached the final but his first three appearances for Britain in international matches were hardly indicative of a potential Olympic gold medallist. He was last each time, in 9:27.4, 9:46.0 and 9:33.0. By 1955, then a vastly improved runner on the flat, he was ready to explore the sub-nine minute regions. Thanks to his background of fast interval work while training with Bannister and Chataway he was able to develop a useful turn of speed to complement the rugged qualities nurtured by his mountaineering exploits. It was this fusion of talents that enabled him to unleash a searing final kilometre of 2:47.2 (i.e. 8:21.6 speed) in the Melbourne final. His coach told him shortly before the Games that he was capable of 8:29—a time yet to be achieved by a Briton—but Brasher was content to end his career there and then. 'Well done the old scrubber', read the telegram he received from his training companions at Chelsea . . . and that just about sums it up.

Disley and Shirley continued to dominate the domestic scene for the next two seasons but without ever regaining their best form. In 1959 they had to bow to youthful Maurice Herriott who, the previous year, had become the world's first 18-year-old steeplechaser to break nine minutes. During 1959 Herriott won the first of his eight AAA senior titles and recorded 8:48.6 less than ten yards behind Krzyszkowiak, who was to break the world record and win the Olympic title the following season. Herriott himself missed the Games when he fell over a hurdle in an Olympic team selection race but in 1961 he came very close to Brasher's record with 8:42.0. Misfortune struck again in 1962; he was obliged to withdraw from the European final because of a knee injury sustained in his heat. That season was notable for two new sub-8:50 performers in Dave Chapman (8:46.4) and 4:00.1 miler Brian Hall (8:49.8).

It was in 1963 that Herriott was first partnered internationally by the man destined to be his eternal second-string, Ernie Pomfret. This pair have established an enviable record in dual matches. In twelve consecutive internationals between August 1963 and June 1966 Herriott won ten times and scored 55 out of a possible 60 points, his times ranging from 8:32.8 to 8:47.4 with six marks inside 8:40. Pomfret's times varied from 8:39.0 to 8:54.6 with nine at 8:50 or better. Herriott, consistency personified, chipped away relentlessly at the UK record. He returned 8:40.4, 8:36.6, 8:36.2 and 8:35.4 in 1963, 8:33.0 and 8:32.4 in 1964. The last two performances, heat and final, were established at the Tokyo Olympics. The smooth hurdling Herriott surpassed himself there by taking second place behind Belgian world record holder Gaston Roelants, yet (shades of Disley in 1950 and 1952) he came in for criticism by those who thought he lost a gold medal by allowing Roelants to open up a fifty yards lead by the bell. Herriott snatched back forty of those yards during the last lap. Pomfret did well to reach the final, in which he placed tenth.

Herriott produced a cluster of very fast times throughout 1966 but, competitively, was less successful than in some previous seasons. He was fourth in the Commonwealth Games (8:33.2), a remarkable effort considering he had to be taken unconscious to hospital suffering from scorched lungs and dehydration, and eighth (8:37.0) in the European Championships. Pomfret was sixth and English-born John Linaker (Scotland) seventh, both in 8:41.6, at Kingston; and Pomfret clocked one second faster in placing twelfth in the European race. In 1967, for the first time, three Britons bettered 8:40 . . . Herriott 8:33.0, John Jackson (a tremendously fast flat runner with a 7:53.4 3,000 metres to his credit) 8:36.4 and Pomfret 8:37.0. Jackson, in winning the inter-county title, became the first Briton to defeat Herriott since 1960 but Herriott triumphed again in the AAA Championships. By winning for the seventh year running, Herriott equalled a 'record' held by Dennis Horgan (shot-put champion from 1893 to 1899), Don Finlay (120 yards hurdles, 1932–38), Bert Cooper (2 miles walk, 1932–38) and Harry Whittle (440 yards hurdles, 1947–53).

9

THE HURDLES

120 Yards Hurdles

HURDLING, as an activity in the Eton school sports, dates back
to 1843. More specifically the 120 yards or 'high' hurdles event was
introduced at the Oxford University sports of 1864. The barriers
in those early days—crude sheep hurdles rigidly staked in the
ground—were sufficiently fearsome as to discourage contact; consequently the hurdling pioneers used an ungainly bent-leg clearance
style in order to make sure of sailing safely over each obstacle. The
times, therefore, were very slow by modern standards but the 16.0
mark recorded by 19-year-old Clement Jackson in 1865, the year
before the height of the ten hurdles was standardised at 3 feet
6 inches, must have been a fine performance since it was not bettered
anywhere in the world for twenty-six years. A muscle injury prematurely ended the active career of the Indian-born Jackson in
1868 . . . 'I spiked a hidden oyster shell when going full bat in a
hurdle handicap after the seven-leagued legs of W. G. Grace. From
that day forth I have never run again, never tasted an oyster and
never spoken to W.G. the Great!' he related. Jackson helped found
the AAA in 1880, served as its honorary treasurer until 1910 and
his name is still commemorated by the cup presented each year to
the best British performer at the AAA Championships.

Although his name does not appear in the record books the next
significant figure was Arthur Croome, an Oxford student who in
1886 was credited with being the first man to lead over the hurdles
with a straight leg. As one historian put it: 'His style of fencing,
which was then peculiar to himself, compensated for his moderate
pace on the flat, and has since been generally adopted by successive
record breakers.' Croome himself explained: 'Men who look nice
when running over sticks take their fences in the wrong way.' He
was in fact the first real *hurdler* and in training was reputed to
have clocked 15.6.

The first 'Briton' to duck under 16 seconds officially was the

Dubliner, Dan Bulger, with 15.8 in 1892. This time was equalled in 1895 by Godfrey Shaw but he almost certainly ran faster when finishing less than a yard behind the world record of 15.4 set by Stephen Chase (USA) in the New York AC v. London AC match later in the season. It was not the custom then, or for many years afterwards, for place times to be taken. Shaw enjoyed a lengthy career. He was third in the AAA Championships in 1886, champion of New Zealand (he lived there from 1886–1891) in 1887 and AAA titlist from 1893 to 1896, his time on the last occasion being a wind-aided 15.6. Shaw also recorded 15.6 in an exhibition in 1892 but one had to wait until 1907 for the first legitimate 15.6, by Kenneth Powell. It should be noted, though, that in 1902 G. R. Garnier finished only six inches behind in a race won by an American in 15.6.

Powell, who placed in the first three at the AAA every year from 1909 to 1914 without ever winning, was killed in the First World War—as was his arch-rival and successor as British record holder, Gerard Anderson. The latter's time of 15.2 in 1912, only a fifth of a second slower than the world record, established him as one of the favourites for the Olympic 110 metres (120.2 yards) title in Stockholm but he fell in his semi-final. The gold medal went to Fred Kelly (USA) in 15.1 with Powell fifth.

Anderson's British record remained unscathed for more than a decade. Eventually in 1923 and 1925 it was matched by Fred Gaby and finally, in 1926, Gaby clipped a tenth off. Gaby had a lengthy and honourable career as a high hurdler. He was not blessed with much natural athletic talent, for as a sprinter he was no faster than 10.5 for 100 yards, but thanks to that celebrated trainer Sam Mussabini he developed into world class 'over the sticks'. He was already 24 when in 1919 Mussabini persuaded him to take up hurdling. Three years later he won the first of five AAA titles. His success in the 1927 Championships was one of his finest, for he defeated George Weightman-Smith (South Africa) and Sten Pettersson (Sweden), both shortly to become official world record holders at 110 metres, with Lord Burghley fourth. Gaby's time against a breeze and on wet, slippery turf was a personal best of 14.9. The previous month Lord Burghley had set a British mark of 14.8.

Perhaps Gaby's greatest yet most frustrating season was 1928, when he was 33. At the AAA he followed up a 15.0 heat by finishing two yards down on Syd Atkinson (14.7), the South African

destined three weeks later to win the Olympic gold. Gaby placed
sixth in the final at Amsterdam but it was a few days afterwards,
at the British Empire v. USA match, that he showed his true worth.
He took over for the third leg of the 4×120 yards hurdles relay
six or seven yards down on Steve Anderson, the Olympic silver
medallist and co-holder of the world record at 14.4. Clearly it was
an impossible situation, yet Gaby made up ground all the way and
had almost caught his man when he crashed into the final hurdle.
Even that was not the end of his career for in 1930 he collected the
bronze medal at the first Empire Games. His very best performance,
though, does not appear in any record book. It occurred in 1926
when he failed by a foot to win a 120 yards hurdles race in 17.6—
with himself having started twenty-two yards behind the line. The
ever vigilant Harold Abrahams timed him at just inside 14.4 for the
actual 120 yards hurdling section from a flying start.

Lord Burghley, of course, is best known as a quarter-mile hurdler
but his achievements in the shorter race were considerable. In 1927
he became the first Briton to crack 15 seconds (14.8) and in 1930
he clocked 14.5, only a tenth outside the world record. Later that
season he won the Empire title in 14.6 and in 1932 he placed fifth
in the Olympic final . . . but more of the 'peerless peer' in the
second part of this chapter.

While Gaby and Lord Burghley were dominating the hurdling
scene in 1928 a lad of barely 19, Don Finlay by name, was just
beginning to make himself known in the services sports world. He
won his first RAF title that year in 16.0 and next season placed third
in the AAA final some eight yards behind Lord Burghley's 15.4.
This resulted in his being selected as reserve for the British team
to meet France but it was actually as a long jumper in that match
that he made his debut. His entry into the international arena he
was to grace for the next twenty years was hardly indicative of what
was to come, for he finished sixth and last with a dismal 20 feet
$9\frac{1}{4}$ inches. He first bettered 15 seconds, hallmark of the international
class hurdler, in 1931 when he ran Lord Burghley (14.8) to half a
yard in the AAA Championships. The following year he rounded
into top form at just the right moment. Early in the season he was
beaten for the Southern title in 15.3 by Roly Harper but he went
on to win his first AAA crown in 14.9 and surpassed himself by
taking the bronze medal in 14.8 at the Los Angeles Olympics
behind the Americans George Saling and Percy Beard. At first he

was placed fourth, with third awarded to Jack Keller (USA), but after examination of the photo finish print the positions were transposed for the first time in Olympic history. Lord Burghley was fifth and Harper achieved a personal best performance of 14.9 in his heat.

Finlay reigned supreme in Europe for the remainder of the thirties. Between 1933 and 1939 he lost only nine races, three of them to the only Briton who ever got the better of him during this period, John Thornton. He won the AAA title seven years running and would probably have made it eight had not a strain kept him out in 1939 and who knows how many but for the outbreak of war. He won at the 1934 Empire Games in one of his slowest times, 15.2; otherwise he was almost invariably inside 15 seconds. It was not until the 1936 Olympics, though, that he managed to dislodge Lord Burghley as British record holder. As in Los Angeles four years earlier the supreme challenge of Olympic competition in Berlin drew the best out of Finlay. He won his semi-final in 14.5, tying the UK record for the slightly shorter 120 yards event, and in the final the same day he burst through spectacularly in the closing stages to move from third to second in a time of 14.4 He finished two yards behind Forrest Towns (USA), who three weeks later was to stagger everyone by hacking the world record down from 14.1 to 13.7. Thornton also excelled in the Olympic final to finish fifth.

Thornton accomplished his best performances in 1937 as he beat Finlay in the match against Germany in 14.6 and finished ahead of the USA 14.2 performer Leroy Kirkpatrick in his fastest time of 14.5. Finlay's fastest run came in 1937, too, but he was deprived of a magnificent European record of 14.1 in Stockholm because of alleged wind-assistance. There was no wind gauge in operation, however, and a photo taken of the finish shows a flag drooping limply. In this race Finlay beat Sweden's Haakan Lidman, whose best at that time was 14.3, by seven yards! Only the previous month Finlay had a 14.2 nullified in similar circumstances. He experienced further bad luck in the 1938 AAA Championships when, under the rules then in force, he was credited with 14.4 although the watches registered 14.29, 14.31 and 14.31. Finlay triumphed over Lidman in the European Championships, this time officially lowering the UK record to 14.3, while the ever reliable Thornton was fourth. Thornton paid the supreme sacrifice during the war but

Finlay, a much decorated RAF fighter pilot, survived and in 1947—at the age of 38—embarked upon the most astonishing comeback in athletics history.

But before dealing with the latter part of Finlay's career mention should be made of a Surrey Athletic Club colleague named Geoff Dyson who, although only 5 feet 8½ inches tall, clocked 14.8 behind Finlay in 1938. He was a good all-round athlete but it was as a coach that he made such a valuable contribution to British athletics history. He was appointed the AAA's first professional national coach in 1947 and was largely responsible for the post-war transformation of the training habits of British athletes. 'I believe', he wrote, 'that athletes are made in the winter. It is an all-the-year-round sport. With our weather and wretched training conditions this makes it tough on the British athlete, and perhaps the main task of the British coach is to keep the athlete going and in good heart at a time when the British public is thinking of soccer, filling in football pools and toasting crumpets over a huge fire!' This dynamic man was employed primarily to instruct lesser coaches and schoolteachers but he also found time to gather around himself a small but highly successful band of personal pupils. As proof of his great and varied coaching talents he developed champions in a variety of events. He transformed Maureen Gardner (whom he later married) from a good sprinter into a superb hurdler who was beaten only by inches in the 1948 Olympics; John Disley from a raw three-miler into an Olympic steeplechase bronze medallist; Shirley Cawley from a 17 feet 10 inches long jumper into an Olympic third-placer; Arthur Rowe from the novice stage into Europe's greatest shot-putter; and others like pole vaulter and decathlete Geoff Elliott who reached the fringe of world class. Dyson resigned from his post following a bitter dispute in 1961 but his pioneering work has been successfully continued by such former colleagues as John Le Masurier (the seventh ranking British 440 yards hurdler in 1939) and Denis Watts (AAA long and triple jump champion just after the war).

Now back to Finlay. He twice clocked 14.6 in 1947 and the following year not only made the Olympic team but was honoured in being selected to pronounce the Olympic Oath on behalf of all the competitors. Unfortunately, while leading in his heat he struck the final hurdle and fell. That ought to have spelled *finis* to his career but this remarkable man carried on and in 1949 defied the evidence of his birth certificate by winning the AAA title on a flooded track in 14.6, defeating the future world record holder Dick Attlesey (USA) in 14.5 and climaxing his twenty-year international career with an official British 120 yards record of 14.4 against France—the second fastest by a European that year! His international match record was almost perfect: between 1931 and 1949 he competed in the high hurdles for Britain in sixteen matches and only twice was he beaten—by Lord Burghley against Italy in 1931 and by Thornton against Germany in 1937. Yet even this was not quite the end for he took fourth place in the 1950 Empire Games in 14.7 and in 1951, aged 42, clocked 14.9 in the inter-services championships.

Finlay's heir, himself destined to remain in the top bracket for a dozen years, was Peter Hildreth, son of an Indian Olympic 200 metres representative. He had won his first hurdles race in 1940, at the age of 12, and ten years later he burst into prominence by winning the AAA title and placing third in the European Championships. For many years Hildreth's regular partner in the British team was Jack Parker and in European competition they were almost infallible. In fifteen international matches between 1951 and 1956 they notched up thirteen victories (Parker nine, Hildreth four) and twelve second places (Parker two, Hildreth ten). Timewise, there was little between them: Parker clocked 14.3 in 1955 and Hildreth recorded the same time in 1957, 1958, 1959 and 1960. Parker finished second in the 1954 European Championships, Hildreth fourth in 1958.

It was another Parker, first name Mike, who in 1961 became the first Briton to record an official 14.2 but just six days later Bob Birrell—whose brother Joe had won the 1948 AAA title while still a schoolboy—was timed at 14 seconds flat. Mike Parker achieved the coveted 13.9 in 1963, a UK record since equalled by Dave Hemery in 1966 (he won the Commonwealth title from Parker a few weeks later) and 19-year-old Alan Pascoe in 1967.

440 Yards Hurdles

Although a 440 yards race over twelve flights of hurdles was staged at the 1860 Oxford University sports and a metric version of the event (ten flights of 3 feet 0 inch hurdles) received Olympic recognition in 1900 it was not until 1914 that the AAA granted it national championship status. The winning time then and on the next occasion in 1919 was a dismal 59.8 but this was far below the standard achieved many years earlier by Godfrey Shaw, the AAA 120 yards hurdles champion from 1893 to 1896. Shaw sliced 1.8 seconds off the best known time of 59.0 by another Englishman, S. Morris, in 1886 when he recorded 57.2 for 442 yards on the Isle of Man in 1891. This stood as the world's fastest until Gerard Anderson, another brilliant high hurdler, returned 56.8 in 1910. Two years earlier, at the London Olympics, Leonard Tremeer (third in the AAA 100 yards way back in 1897) gained the bronze medal but unfortunately for Anderson the 400 metres hurdles was omitted from the 1912 Olympic programme.

F. J. Blackett, of the London Fire Brigade, was the next Briton to reach an Olympic final, in 1924, but he finished last and adding insult to injury was disqualified under the rule that operated from about 1919 to 1935 for knocking down three or more hurdles. Blackett, who set a national record of 56.0 in an AAA semi-final in 1925, came to be dwarfed by the giant talent of Lord Burghley (David Cecil), the first and only Englishman to win an Olympic hurdles title.

Born at the ancestral home near Stamford on February 9th 1905, Lord Burghley was educated at Eton but failed to make his mark on those famous playing fields. Injury prevented his gaining a 'Blue' in his first year at Cambridge but he developed sufficiently as a high hurdler in the summer of 1924 to place fourth in the AAA Championships and qualify, at the age of 19, for the first of his three Olympic trips. His was not a particularly stately debut, for he rammed into a hurdle and tumbled over in his heat. Next season he afforded a clearer view of his capabilities. After gaining a double against Oxford with 15.8 for 120 yards and a British record of 24.8 for 220 yards, Harold Abrahams noted: 'He has a great future as a hurdler if he continues to train assiduously.' That he did, by the relatively undemanding standards of his era, and in 1926 he scored his first major triumph when, in the British record time of 55.0, he defeated Tom Livingstone-Learmonth for the national title.

These two finished first and second again in 1927, Lord Burghley's time being 54.2 and his rival's 55.2. The winning mark was not only a British record but, thanks to time zoning, stood equal to the world record for a few hours—until John Gibson (USA) reeled off a remarkable 52.6 in Nebraska the same afternoon! Earlier in the season Lord Burghley had set a national high hurdles record of 14.8 and the week after the championships he reduced his low (220 yards) hurdles time to 24.7 to become the first man to hold all three British hurdling records. In 1928, for the third year running, Lord Burghley won the AAA crown in record time (54.0), once again followed home by Livingstone-Learmonth. Both rose splendidly to the occasion three weeks later at the Amsterdam Olympics. Lord Burghley qualified comfortably for the final by placing third in a semi won by the world record holder Morgan Taylor (USA) in 53.4 while 'L-L' took the other semi in a lifetime best of 54.0, eliminating John Gibson among others.

The two Britons, drawn in the outside lanes in the final, dashed off at a fast pace and led for six flights. Livingstone-Learmonth was unable to hold such speed and faded away to fifth in 54.2 but his colleague, who entered the home straight just ahead of Taylor and Frank Cuhel, was locked in mortal combat with the American pair. Deliberately chopping his stride in order to make sure of clearing the last hurdle cleanly Lord Burghley withstood the assault to snap the tape a yard to the good in his best time of 53.4. It was the first time the USA had failed to win this particular Olympic title and the hero of the hour was carried off the track shoulder high by the three British 800 metres representatives who were awaiting the start of their semi-finals. Lord Burghley delighted the 41,000 crowd at Stamford Bridge for the post-Olympic British Empire v. USA match by competing in the 4 × 2 laps steeplechase; hand vaulting the water jump he anchored his team to victory with a 1:58.2 stint. There was an unhappy ending to 1928, though, with the untimely death in the Sudan of Tom Livingstone–Learmonth.

Lord Burghley was well beaten in the 1929 AAA by his great Italian rival Luigi Facelli but gained revenge in the following year's championships when after a thrilling struggle he prevailed by inches in the British record time of 53.8. A surprisingly close third in 54.0, equal to the old record, was D. M. L. Neame. The latter placed third again at the Empire Games behind Lord Burghley (54.4) and R. Leigh-Wood. Earlier in the season Lord Burghley had approached the world 120 yards hurdles record by a tenth with 14.5 and had run 220 yards hurdles in an estimated 24.3, a step behind Irishman Bob Tisdall. Another prominent performer in 1930 was Joe Simpson, who clocked 54.2 in winning the World Student Games 400 metres in Germany. He joined the Metropolitan Police shortly afterwards and, as Sir Joseph Simpson, attained the rank of Commissioner.

A poor season in 1931 was quickly forgotten as Lord Burghley rounded into top form in defence of his Olympic laurels. Again, in Los Angeles, he displayed his fearsome competitive ability in cutting no less than 1.2 seconds from his British 400 metres record with 52.2 but such was the standard that even this dazzling time sufficed for 'only' fourth place. The winner, in one of the most astonishing breakthroughs in Olympic history, was Bob Tisdall, clad in the green of Ireland.

Born of Irish parents in Ceylon, Tisdall began hurdling at Shrewsbury when 14. By the time he went up to Cambridge in the autumn of 1928 he was already a fine all-rounder and there he established himself as one of the university's most distinguished athletes. The ever perceptive F. A. M. Webster wrote, after watching Tisdall return times of 15.8 and 25.1 in the freshmen's trials: 'He was entirely without style but, if he can be taught to step over his fences with a straight leg, I think he will prove probably the fastest hurdler Great Britain or any country has yet produced.'

Tisdall's greatest day as an undergraduate came in the match against Oxford in March 1931 when, in the space of thirty-five chilly minutes, he won the high hurdles in 15.5, the shot with 40 feet 8 inches, the long jump with 23 feet 0½ inch and the quarter in 51.0. His extraordinary quarter-mile hurdling career began with a 400 metres win in 55.0 on the magnet shaped Athens track in 1930. His next attempt, at 440 yards, was in Dublin on June 3rd 1932 and he won in 56.2. Fifteen days later, on the same track, he won the Irish Olympic 440 yards trial in 54.2. And that was the full extent of his experience when he lined up for his Olympic heat on July 31st 1932!

As Tisdall related in his book, *The Young Athlete*, the loss of sleep incurred during the two-week journey to Los Angeles left him in a poor physical state. With less than a fortnight to go before the competition he found himself to be eight pounds under his racing weight of 165 pounds and too weak even to complete a 400 metres hurdles practice run! For over a week he spent fifteen hours a day in bed and ran not a step in a desperate attempt to recuperate from his weariness. Three days before the heats he began jogging barefoot on grass. The unorthodox preparation paid off; as he walked on to the track he was almost literally bursting with pent-up energy and he cruised to victory in his heat in 54.8. Two hours later he exerted himself to such good effect that he won his semi-final in 52.8. Next day, in the final, he ran like a dream—taking fifteen fluent strides between each hurdle—and led all the way. As no one was close as he approached the final barrier he decided to aim for safety by leaping higher than necessary. But fatigue caused him to misjudge the clearance and he knocked down the hurdle with the calf of his leading leg. He managed to preserve his balance and scramble on to victory by a yard or two but the mishap cost him a world record of 51.7 since a rule in force until 1938 decreed that the tumbling of a hurdle automatically debarred a record. Tisdall later finished a creditable eighth in the decathlon . . . and that concluded his meteoric international career.

Lord Burghley, now the sixth Marquess of Exeter, retired from active competition at the end of 1933 but has continued to make a massive contribution to British and international athletics ever since as an administrator. His absence left a void in the event which has never quite been filled. His immediate successors were Alan Hunter, Scotland's 1934 Empire titlist, and Ralph Brown (Godfrey's elder brother), third in that race after winning the AAA championship, but neither ever bettered 55 seconds. In fact no British quarter hurdler approached world class until the rise of Harry Whittle after the war. Whittle, who placed seventh in the 1948 Olympic long jump, was neither a stylish hurdler nor particularly swift on the flat: his best 440 yards time was 50.2 whereas Lord Burghley was timed in 46.7 for his 400 metres relay leg at the 1932 Olympics. Yet Whittle's ruggedness proved ideal for what has been termed the 'mankiller' event. He won the AAA title seven years running from 1947 to 1953, broke Lord Burghley's British 440 yards record with 53.7 in 1949 and ended up with a best time of 52.7 in 1953. He failed by bare inches to reach the Olympic final in 1948, was third in the 1950 European and fifth in the 1952 Olympics. His closest rivals were David Gracie, a Scot, and Angus Scott (English despite the name), who recorded 52.3 and 52.4 respectively for 400 metres in 1952.

Lord Burghley's 52.2 400 metres timing survived as the national record until Harry Kane, in only his second season at the event, was credited with 51.8 for 440 yards only four yards behind Yuriy Lituyev's world record of 51.3 in the memorable London v. Moscow match of 1954. Although he was then only 21 this proved to be

Kane's greatest race; he was never again to run as fast and in finishing second he defeated the newly crowned European champion, Anatoliy Yulin. Earlier in the year Kane had gained the silver medal at the Commonwealth Games. Late in his career Kane made several attempts to regain his best form, the nearest approach being in 1962 when he won the inter-county title in 52.2.

Tom Farrell could fairly claim to be Europe's number one in 1957 . . . even though he was obliged to perform his repetition sprints on the pavement as there was no track in his home city of Liverpool! Farrell notched up victories in all of his international match races, including a win over Lituyev in the UK 400 metres record of 51.1, with Kane third in 51.7. Farrell was not the same man in 1958 and, while Lituyev won the European title in 51.1, he placed fourth in 52.0. Sixth was Chris Goudge, the new UK 440 yards record holder at 51.6. In 1960 Farrell divided his attention between the hurdles (he set a 400 metres record of 51.0) and the 800 metres, for which he clocked an impressive 1:48.3 at Whitsun. He decided to go for the 800 metres at the Olympics after winning the AAA half in 1:49.3 but failed to reach the semi-finals.

Chris Surety was the next top-liner with a record equalling 51.0 400 metres in 1961 but injuries ruined his career after 1962 and it was left to John Cooper to challenge the world's best. Cooper, a triple jump specialist between 1956 and 1959, took up quarter hurdling in 1960 and recorded 56.5. His results next season proved he had found his true event for he made the British team and clocked 52.0 for 400 metres, a time that he shaved by a tenth in 1962. Cooper made fine progress during 1963; he won five of his six international races, including a British 400 metres best of 50.5 in Volgograd on the occasion of Britain's brilliant victory over the Russian Federal Republic by 112 points to 99.

At the end of 1963 Cooper made it known that his target was to win the gold medal at the following year's Olympics. At the time this seemed unrealistic as eight men had registered between 49.3 and 50.4 in 1963 but Cooper's self-confidence proved to be not entirely misplaced. Having trained very hard with Robbie Brightwell all winter he emerged in 1964 as a vastly improved flat runner. His best 440 yards in 1963 had been 48.6, yet in August 1964 he held Olympic champion-to-be Mike Larrabee (USA) with an heroic 400 metres relay leg of 45.9. Over the hurdles he showed good form at the AAA with a British record of 51.1 but even his

L

400 metres time of 50.6 against Poland ranked him only equal tenth among the candidates bidding for Olympic honours in Tokyo. Fortunately, statistics count for little in the cut and thrust of Olympic competition. Some athletes are so petrified by the grandeur of the occasion that they find themselves mentally and physically drained and consequently unable to produce their best form; others draw inspiration from the supreme challenge. Cooper belongs to the latter group. He struck a resounding psychological blow by winning his heat, unpressed, in the fastest time of the round—50.5; and took his semi-final in 50.4 for a new UK record. In the final he unleashed a searing sprint over the run-in to overtake European champion Salvatore Morale (Italy) for second place four yards behind world record holder Rex Cawley (USA). Cooper's time was purely incidental in the circumstances; another UK record of 50.1. Later in the Games he contributed a typically gutsy leg of 45.6 to help Britain take second place in the 4 × 400 metres relay.

Cooper looked certain to become Britain's first man under 50 seconds but in 1965, understandably, he did not possess the same burning zeal and ran no faster than 50.9 for 400 metres; he missed 1966 through injury and was only a pale shadow of his former self when attempting a comeback in 1967. During Cooper's absence from the scene in 1966 the 5 feet 6 inches tall Peter Warden, who clocked 50.7 for 400 metres and obtained the bronze medal at the Commonwealth Games, and John Sherwood, AAA winner in a record equalling 51.1, filled in admirably. Sherwood matured into a world class competitor in 1967, winning the AAA title again in a UK record of 50.9, clocking 50.2 for 400 metres and losing only to the world's number one, Ron Whitney (USA). Like Cooper, he also showed tremendous pace on the flat with a best 400 metres relay leg of 45.6. With Andy Todd (19), a 14.3 high hurdler, setting a European junior 400 metres record of 51.1 the future in this event looks assured.

10

THE JUMPS

High Jump

T H E early history of British, indeed world, high jumping is dominated by the name of the Hon. Marshall Jones Brooks. When Brooks
went up to Oxford in the autumn of 1873 the best authenticated
jump on record was 5 feet 10¼ inches by Tom Davin, of Tipperary.
Brooks, only 19 at the time, quickly disposed of that by clearing
5 feet 11 inches to win the 1874 English title; the same year he
gained an international cap at rugby. Injury prevented his competing
in 1875, when fellow Oxonian Michael Glazebrook also jumped
5 feet 11 inches, but in his final competitive season of 1876 Brooks
reigned supreme.

The 6 feet tall Oxford University Athletic Club president became
the first amateur to master six feet in competition (Tom Davin is
said to have done so in training) when, off sodden cinders at
Marston on March 17th, he went over a bar measured at
6 feet 0⅛ inch. Exactly three weeks later the large crowd gathered
at Lillie Bridge for the annual 'Battle of the Blues' was privileged
to witness one of the great sporting feats of the age, for Brooks
cleared 6 feet 2½ inches from the grass take-off. The spectators rose
to him as, displaying rare showmanship, he walked back *under* the
bar. Brooks' brief and brilliant career came to an end three days
later with the regaining of the English title with one disdainful
leap over 6 feet 0 inch—complete with top hat, the story goes.
Montague Shearman, in his classic work *Athletics*, described
Brooks' style: 'He took very little run and in fact almost walked up
to the bar, springing straight over it with his legs tucked up high
and well in front of him, and invariably looked, when his legs were
once over, as if his body would fall crashing on to the bar; but he
nearly always managed to jerk his body forward again and to alight
upon his toes.'

Brooks' successor as holder of the world's best was Tom Davin's
younger brother Patrick Davin. This powerfully built six-footer

jumped 6 feet 2¾ inches in 1880 and three years later made further history by long jumping 23 feet 2 inches to become the first and only man ever to lead the world in both specialities. Pat Davin had made his first appearance as a high jumper in the 1876 Irish Championships and within a few weeks was competing in the world's first international match: Ireland against England in Dublin. The visitors won the encounter by nine events to four but the Davin brothers did the Emerald Isle proud by tying for first in the high jump. Incidentally, yet another brother, Maurice (who was 16 years older than Pat), won the hammer on this historic occasion and became the star of the show when, to the crowd's appreciation, he carried three of the heaviest members of the English team . . . one on his back and one on each shoulder, 46 stones in all! Pat jumped 6 feet 1½ inches off soft ground at Kilkenny in 1879, a fairly remarkable effort since he landed 17 feet 5 inches away from the point of take-off. Next year he displayed the versatility common to most of the great Irish stars of his time by winning five Irish titles in one day—100 yards (10.2), high jump (5 feet 11 inches), long jump (22 feet 8 inches), 120 yards hurdles and shot. One week after clearing 6 feet 4¼ inches in practice he achieved his record 6 feet 2¾ inches in his native Carrick-on-Suir.

Except for a share by George Rowdon, of Devon, the British Isles high jump record was held by one Irishman after another throughout the next three decades. After Davin there was Murty O'Brien, 6 feet 2¾ inches in 1893; James Ryan, 6 feet 3⅛ inches in 1893, 6 feet 3½ inches and 6 feet 4½ inches in 1895; Pat Leahy, 6 feet 4¾ inches in 1898; and Tim Carroll, 6 feet 5 inches in 1913.

Rowdon, a small and lightly built man possessing prodigious spring, equalled Davin's 6 feet 2¾ inches in 1889 and thus disposed of Brooks' famous English record. This was only 1¼ inches below the world record held by the 5 feet 6½ inches American, William Byrd Page—with whom Rowdon had tied for the 1887 AAA championship. His greatest jump, though, came about on August 6th 1890. Competing at an Army meeting at Haytor Camp in Devon, Rowdon soared over 6 feet 5⅜ inches—well above the world's best of 6 feet 4¾ inches set the previous year by Irish-American J. Fitzpatrick. Although a spirit level was used to test the level of the ground and the height was measured from the centre of the bar (as witnessed by several Army officers and NCOs) the AAA refused to ratify the performance owing to suspicions of sloping ground. This height was not to be bettered by an Englishman for 59 long years, which speaks volumes for his ability if less for that of his successors. Rowdon later cashed in on his abnormal springing powers by touring the music halls with a leaping act.

Returning to the Irish masters of the event, one finds that the AAA cup travelled westwards over the sea no fewer than eleven times between 1893 and 1908, the man responsible for the last four victories being Pat Leahy's younger brother, Con. The greatest of all Irish jumpers was the 5 feet 8¼ inches tall Michael Sweeney, but he played no direct part in the history of British athletics as he was taken to the United States at the age of eight. Sweeney, pioneer of the Eastern cut-off style, accomplished his world's best of 6 feet 5⅝ inches—which stood until 1912—in the eventful match between New York AC and London AC at Manhattan Field in 1895.

Had they competed, either Sweeney or James Ryan would almost certainly have become the first Olympic high jump champion in 1896; in their absence Ellery Clark (USA) won with 5 feet 11¼ inches. The 1900 gold medal went to Irving Baxter (USA) at a more respectable 6 feet 2¾ inches with unofficial European record holder Pat Leahy finding 5 feet 10⅛ inches good enough for the silver medal. Con Leahy was responsible for the only other Olympic medal Britain has ever gained in this event as he tied for second with 6 feet 2 inches. On this occasion Pat Leahy failed to reach the eight-man final. Of the two brothers Con proved to be the better competitor: he defeated a strong field in the unofficial Olympic Games of 1906 (remarkably, 5 feet 9 inches sufficed) and the following year he became the only Briton to win the American title. His best mark was 6 feet 4½ inches in 1904, a quarter-inch less than Pat's 1898 record. Incidentally, another two members of the Leahy clan made their marks as jumpers: Joe long jumped 23 feet 1½ inches in 1903 (Pat's best was 23 feet 11 inches, Con's 23 feet 8 inches) and Tim high jumped 6 feet 3 inches in 1910. What a family!

Tim Carroll, last of Ireland's outstanding high jumpers, never did himself justice in major competition and for many years British high jumping *was* Benjamin Howard Baker. His first success was winning the 1910 AAA title and in 1912 he qualified for the Olympic final by clearing 6 feet 0 inch—only to fail at the opening height of 5 feet 8⅞ inches. Howard Baker served as a lieutenant in the Royal Navy during the 1914–18 war and came back a vastly improved athlete. He broke the English record with 6 feet $3\frac{1}{4}$ inches at the 1920 AAA Championships, a height that would have gained the silver medal at the following month's Olympics where, in fact, Baker placed sixth with 6 feet $0\frac{7}{8}$ inch. Some measure of consolation came shortly after the Games when he defeated the newly crowned champion, Richmond Landon (USA), with an English record of 6 feet $3\frac{1}{2}$ inches. Next season, aged 29, he climaxed his long career by improving to 6 feet 5 inches from a grass take-off at Huddersfield to match Carroll's British and European best and miss the world record of Ed Beeson (USA) by only $2\frac{1}{4}$ inches. Quite apart from his high jumping successes, the 6 feet 3 inches, 196 pounds Baker was an English international goalkeeper, a first class water polo player, Northern champion in the 120 yards hurdles and discus, and one of the country's leading long and triple jumpers.

On his departure British high jumping plunged into mediocrity. Practically thirty years were to elapse before the emergence of the next world class performer. There was no lack of promising jumpers but not one developed to the requisite standard. While the American-monopolised world record evolved to 6 feet $10\frac{1}{4}$ inches by 1937 and Finland's Kalevi Kotkas raised the European record to 6 feet $8\frac{3}{8}$ inches in 1936 no Briton seriously challenged Baker's domestic record of 6 feet 5 inches.

Harry Simmons, an Eastern cut-off exponent, appeared to stand on the threshold of a brilliant career when, aged 17 and the youngest athletics competitor from any nation, he finished equal eleventh out of 35 at the 1928 Olympics with 6 feet $0\frac{1}{2}$ inch. But he progressed no higher than 6 feet 2 inches and a knee injury cut short his career. Even more precocious was Bill Land, who not only gained his international colours in 1931 at the age of 16 but made his debut for England a winning one as he jumped 6 feet 1 inch against Italy. The following weekend he tied for first place against Germany with a lifetime best of 6 feet $2\frac{3}{4}$ inches. Land went on to win the 1932 AAA title but placed no better than equal sixth (at 6 feet 0 inch.) in the 1934 Empire Games. Afterwards he concentrated on the javelin, with which in 1935 he set a UK record of 191 feet 7 inches. Later still he turned to the discus, which he threw 145 feet $9\frac{1}{2}$ inches in 1949 at the age of 34! The top height achieved during the thirties, in fact, was 6 feet $3\frac{3}{4}$ inches in 1938 by J. H. Dodd, the previous season's AAA pole vault champion. Dodd never competed internationally but a contemporary of his

who did so in 1937 (a discreet veil will be lowered over his performances!) was Arthur Gold, current honorary secretary of the
British Amateur Athletic Board. His personal best was 6 feet
2$\frac{7}{8}$ inches.

No sooner was the war over than British athletics found itself
blessed with a rare high jumping talent in the 6 feet 6 inches tall
person of Alan Paterson. When only 14 he had jumped 5 feet 4
inches using a simple scissors; two years later, by then a Western
roller, he was up to 5 feet 11 inches. In 1945 the Glasgow schoolboy
raised the Scottish record to 6 feet 2$\frac{1}{2}$ inches and 6 feet 3 inches and
people began to talk of him as a prospect for the 1948 Olympics,
yet so swift was his development that as early as June 1946, three
days before his 18th birthday, he relieved Baker of the UK record
with a leap of 6 feet 5$\frac{1}{2}$ inches. In July he reached the classic two
metres (6 feet 6$\frac{3}{4}$ inches), a world class mark in those days, and in
August he carried off the silver medal at the European Championships. After clearing 6 feet 5$\frac{1}{4}$ inches he was leading his only remaining rival, Anton Bolinder, because of fewer failures but to Paterson's chagrin the Swede succeeded with his final attempt at 6 feet
6$\frac{3}{8}$ inches.

Paterson continued to improve in 1947 and at the Glasgow
Rangers Sports he rolled over the magnificent height of 6 feet 7$\frac{1}{2}$
inches, second best ever by a European, in placing second—on the
fewer failures rule—to the world's number one that year, Bill Vessie
(USA). Although he was only 19 at the time that jump, only 3$\frac{1}{2}$
inches below the world record, proved to be Paterson's ceiling.
Nevertheless, he remained consistent at the 6 feet 6 inches–6 feet
7 inches level for several seasons and made up for a below-par
showing at the Wembley Olympics (he tied for seventh at 6 feet
2$\frac{7}{8}$ inches with the title won at a modest 6 feet 6 inches) by winning
the European crown in 1950 at 6 feet 5$\frac{1}{4}$ inches to become the first
Briton to win a field event. Earlier in the year he had tied for second
in the Empire Games at 6 feet 5 inches, an inch below Olympic
winner John Winter (Australia). Paterson later emigrated to Canada
but returned to end his international career at the 1952 Olympics.

Ron Pavitt, for many years utterly overshadowed by his Scottish
rival, pulled off a minor sensation in Helsinki by taking fifth position at 6 feet 4$\frac{3}{4}$ inches, the highest ever Olympic placing by an
English high jumper. Arthur Gold estimated Pavitt's jump was
worth a good 6 feet 7 inches but by the time the bar was raised to

6 feet 6 inches he was so tired that his spring and timing were impaired. Pavitt had previously made history in 1949 when, with his SEVENTEENTH jump of the competition, he became English record holder with 6 feet 6 inches. But not for long: Peter Wells, a fellow straddle exponent, leapt over 6 feet 6⅜ inches off grass a fortnight later. Wells decided to stay in New Zealand after competing at the 1950 Empire Games in Auckland and there he developed into a regular 6 feet 7 inches jumper, with a best of 6 feet 7½ inches —equalling Paterson's UK record—in 1954. He reached the Olympic finals of 1952 and 1956.

British high jumping in the last decade has been utterly dominated by two men . . . Crawford Fairbrother and Gordon Miller. It was Fairbrother, son of a Scottish international high jumper, who removed clubmate Paterson's name from the record list when he straddled 6 feet 8 inches, 6 feet 8⅜ inches and 6 feet 8¾ inches in quick succession in 1959. That middle performance was particularly memorable for although it was good only for third place in the USSR v. Britain match in Moscow behind Igor Kashkarov and Robert Shavlakadze it did equal the height achieved by the latter, who just a year on was to win the Olympic gold medal. Miller, who in 1959 (when 19) set an English record of 6 feet 7⅜ inches using a Western roll, reverted to the straddle for the 1960 season and conjured up visions of seven feet in the near future when he equalled the UK record of 6 feet 8¾ inches and reached the Olympic final. But although he has shown brilliant form on occasion—he cleared 6 feet 9½ inches and 6 feet 10 inches in May 1964—a long history of injuries and illness has thus far prevented his fulfilling his potential. Fairbrother, Britain's most 'capped' male international, jumped 6 feet 9½ inches in September 1964 and has cleared 6 feet 8 inches and upwards on 19 occasions. Perhaps his finest performance was in the 1962 Britain v. Poland match when, from a waterlogged take-off that reduced the opposition (both 6 feet 10 inches-plus performers) to 6 feet 2¾ inches and 6 feet 0¾ inch, he raised himself over 6 feet 7 inches.

Pole Vault

Pole vaulting for height, as distinct from distance, was pioneered in the mid-nineteenth century by members of the Ulverston (Lancashire) Cricket and Football Club. Pole vaulting then bore little resemblance to the event as we know it today. Utilising a heavy ash, cedar or hickory pole with three iron spikes in the base, the early vaulter would thrust the implement into the ground some three feet before the uprights, climb up it and endeavour to cross the bar in a sitting position. Montague Shearman described the technique of Tom Ray, a most distinguished exponent of the 'Lake District' school, in these terms: 'Grasping the pole about its middle, he takes his leap, and when the pole is perpendicular, poises it almost at a standstill, raises himself clear up it by sheer force of arm, and shoots himself over the bar.'

This style was indigenous to England. Elsewhere, climbing was forbidden, the rules decreeing that the athlete must not move his upper hand once he had left the ground. English vaulters came into line with the rest of the world shortly before the turn of the century, but not before monopolising the 'world record' for the best part of twenty-five years. The first men to vault 10 feet were J. Wheeler in 1866 and A. Lubbock in 1868, while the honour of being the first to master 11 feet went to Ulverston's Edwin Woodburn, who cleared 11 feet 1 inch in 1876. At this date the best by a 'conventional' vaulter was a mere 9 feet 9 inches by Peter Fraser (USA) in 1869.

The previously mentioned Tom Ray began his long period of supremacy in 1879 when, aged 17, he succeeded H. E. Kayll as record holder with 11 feet 2¾ inches. He remained firmly on top for almost a decade, his finest season being 1888 when he won the AAA title for the seventh time and raised the record for the ninth time to 11 feet 8½ inches. The non-English best then stood at 11 feet 5 inches by Hugh Baxter (USA), whom Ray had defeated for the 1887 American championship. Ray was eclipsed in 1889 by E. L. Stones, a fellow Ulverston member. Stones, too, enjoyed the rare distinction of winning an American title (1889) and twice set British figures: 11 feet 7 inches in June 1888 (Ray regained the record three months later) and 11 feet 8½ inches, equalling Ray's mark, the following season. The next record holder, last of the great pole-climbers before the style fell into disuse, was Richard Dickinson. The Windermere man, AAA champion five times in six years, jumped 11 feet 9 inches in 1891—four inches better than the highest conventional mark. Throughout all the eras of vaulting to follow . . . bamboo, steel, aluminium and the current fibre-glass . . . British pole vaulters were never again to attain real world class.

Dickinson's height remained unmolested as the British highwater mark for thirty-seven years, and for most of that time there was no one able to clear even 11 feet. So pathetic was the standard that at the 1903 AAA Championships one S. Morris was allowed to win unopposed with 8 feet 6 inches and even as late as 1921—by which time the world record was at 13 feet 5 inches—W. Wihuri was able to place higher than any other Briton at the Championships with a vault of 9 feet 0 inch. Two years later, not one home athlete bothered to challenge the famous French *high jumper* Pierre Lewden for the pole vault title, which was practically a permanent foreign possession anyway.

Dickinson's record finally fell by the wayside in 1928 when L. T. Bond vaulted 11 feet $10\frac{1}{4}$ inches. Although Bond never won an AAA title and was only fifth in the 1930 Empire Games he was far and away the best British vaulter in the early thirties in matters of heights cleared. In four further instalments he hoisted the record to 12 feet $7\frac{1}{2}$ inches in 1931, though competitively he was over-shadowed by Howard Ford, runner-up in the 1930 Empire Games.

The first international class vaulter produced in this country in the twentieth century was Richard Webster, son of F. A. M. Webster, the celebrated coach and writer. Actively encouraged by his father, young Webster began vaulting at the age of four (!), represented his county at 14 (his best then was 8 feet 10 inches) and won his international colours at 17. His progress was steady: 11 feet 3 inches in 1932, 11 feet 11 inches in 1933, 12 feet 3 inches in 1934, 12 feet $6\frac{1}{2}$ inches in 1935. He chose the Olympic year of 1936 to depose Bond as UK record holder, starting off with 12 feet 8 inches in July and ending, in Berlin the next month, with 13 feet $1\frac{1}{2}$ inches —a height that gained him a tie for sixth place with ten other athletes. He narrowly failed at 13 feet $7\frac{1}{2}$ inches, dislodging the bar with his fingers on the way down. It was a highly commendable performance in a field of thirty, and to this day no British vaulter has ever placed as high in Olympic competition. Webster, who was 6 feet 3 inches tall, never did surpass that but he cleared 13 feet 0 inch twice in 1937 and placed fourth in the 1938 Empire Games with 12 feet 9 inches. He resumed competition after the war and terminated his thirty-year vaulting career at the Wembley Olympics in 1948.

Another vaulter who at least scaled the foothills of world class was Geoff Elliott. He possessed all the qualities necessary to shine in this most technical of events: good speed (10.1 for 100 yards) and spring (6 feet 0 inch high jump), strength, acrobatic prowess and fine competitive ability. He made his international bow in 1950 and was an automatic choice for the next nine years. In 1952 Elliott accomplished the first of his seventeen British record performances by equalling the 1951 mark of 13 feet 6 inches by Scotland's Norman Gregor and two years later he achieved the eagerly awaited 14-footer. That 1954 season was a successful one for Elliott: he became Commonwealth champion at 14 feet 0 inch, tied for the bronze medal at the European Championships with a record 14 feet 1¼ inches, defeated former European champion and record holder Ragnar Lundberg (Sweden), and beat two formidable Russians in the London v. Moscow match. His self confidence was evident for at the European Championships he opened at an unprecedented 13 feet 1½ inches and cheekily declined to attempt 13 feet 9½ inches, opting instead for 14 feet 1¼ inches. He vaulted 14 feet 1¼ inches again on four occasions between 1957 and 1959 and retained his Commonwealth title in 1958.

Just how far behind world standards British vaulters had been dropping was emphasised in the 1963 Britain v. USA match. Trevor Burton was suitably inspired to set a national record of 14 feet 4 inches . . . but the competition was won by John Pennel with a world record 16 feet 10¼ inches! It was Burton who won the race to 15 feet, in July 1964, but Scotsman David Stevenson replied soon afterwards with 15 feet 1¾ inches. Stevenson improved to 15 feet 4 inches in 1966 but the record passed to Northern Ireland's Mike Bull who, while still 19, vaulted 15 feet 6 inches for the silver medal at the Commonwealth Games. Bull, whose competitive record is more impressive than the heights he has so far achieved, raised the UK record to 15 feet 9 inches in 1967 and cleared 16 feet 1¼ inches indoors in March 1968.

Long Jump

The winner of the English long jump title in 1869 was an Oxford undergraduate, Alick Tosswill, with what now seems the laughable distance of 19 feet 7 inches. That hardly merits recalling but the name of Tosswill does, for 'amidst intense applause (he) cleared the unusual distance of 21 feet 4 inches, in 1868 and the following year became the first amateur to better 22 feet. The trail towards 23 feet was blazed by Jenner Davies (significant surname), who leapt 22 feet 7 inches at the 1872 English Championships and 22 feet 10½ inches in 1874. The latter mark did not exist as a world's and British best for long, as in Dublin six weeks later the short and sturdy John Lane cut the sand at 23 feet 1½ inches to defeat Davies (22 feet 10 inches). This distance, although ratified as an Irish record, was never accepted as an official British record.

Meanwhile, in 1873 the English title had been carried off by Charles Lockton who at 16 became, and remains, the youngest athlete to win a national championship. He was indeed a precocious performer, clearing 22 feet 8½ inches the following year—which seems to have remained as his best mark.

The next important figures on the scene were two Irishmen and a Scot. Pat Davin, already featured in the high jump chapter, bettered his countryman Lane's world's best with 23 feet 2 inches— off grass and from behind a white line—in August 1883, a distance he duplicated the following month. Davin had, at the 1881 AAA meeting, won both high (6 feet 0½ inch) and long (22 feet 11 inches) jump titles and a similar feat was accomplished in 1883 when John Parsons, of Edinburgh University, recorded winning efforts of 6 feet 0¼ inch and 23 feet 0¼ inch. In the same competition, another of Parsons' jumps carried him clean beyond the pit. He rolled back into the sand but his heel marks were measured at 24 feet 4 inches from the board! The other Irish star of the period was John Purcell who, on August 26th 1886, twice matched the world figures of 23 feet 3 inches by the American, Malcolm Ford.

The pendulum swung back to England with the emergence of Charles Burgess Fry, one of the great all-rounders in sporting history. Quite apart from his casual flirtation with athletics he was an outstanding batsman for England from 1899 to 1912, played at full back in England's soccer team in 1901 and at three-quarter back for Blackheath and Barbarians. C. B. Fry was only 19 when he shook the athletics world in 1892 by adding two inches to Purcell's British record—reputedly taking off some nine inches behind the board! The following year, at the Oxford University sports on March 4th, 1893, he went one better by equalling the world record of 23 feet 6½ inches held by Charles Reber (USA). It was unfortunate for athletics that Fry did little more jumping, but before turning his attention to the other sports he did leap 23 feet 0½ inch in 1893. His other track and field accomplishments included running 100 yards in 'evens' and high jumping 5 feet 10 inches.

Even Fry's record proved ephemeral; after only eighteen months

Irish born J. J. Mooney jumped 23 feet 8 inches. Another Irishman, William Newburn, laid claim to the world's best before the turn of the century. He enjoyed a glorious spell in 1898, setting a record of 23 feet 9⅜ inches on June 18th, winning the AAA title by almost two feet with 23 feet 7 inches on July 2nd, and extending the record to 24 feet 0½ inch against Scotland in Dublin on July 16th. Two days later he was credited with 24 feet 6¾ inches but for one reason or another it never found its way into the record book; neither did his 24 feet 6 inches on August 1st. Newburn, 6 feet 3 inches tall and heavily built, was also Irish 100 yards champion from 1897 to 1899 . . . and reappeared in 1912 to win the Irish 56 pounds weight slinging title.

This century moved off to an auspicious start when Peter O'Connor not only smashed Newburn's figures but regained for Ireland the world's best which had in the meantime slipped back to the United States. The Wicklow born O'Connor, who used the 'sail' style of jumping, reached 24 feet 7¾ inches on August 29th 1900 one month after Alvin Kraenzlein (USA) had won the Olympic title with 23 feet 6⅞ inches. Inexplicably, O'Connor did not compete at the Paris Games, where he must have stood a great chance of victory. Pat Leahy, of high jumping fame, placed third with 22 feet 9½ inches. O'Connor had a remarkable season in 1901: four times he improved upon his own world record, eventually clearing the magnificent but frustrating distance of 24 feet 11¾ inches in Dublin on August 5th. The previous month he had topped the magical 25-foot mark by half an inch, but the runway was found to be downhill. O'Connor was a consistent competitor as well as prolific record breaker. He won the AAA long jump six times (and the high jump twice) and, at the age of 34, finished second with 23 feet 0½ inch to the 1904 Olympic champion, the USA's Myer Prinstein, in the Athens Games of 1906 after leading until the final round.

In a letter to Sir Sidney Abrahams, the 1913 AAA long jump champion and brother of the Olympic 100 metres champion, written in 1953 O'Connor reminisced over his career. 'I never had a trainer', he wrote. 'I was never massaged, nor I ever changed my ordinary food. I was always, and am still, a heavy pipe smoker. I had a natural gift of spring and I was very excitable and determined to beat opponents. I sprang always from my left foot and during my eight years in competition I sprained it on seven occasions and several times so badly that I could not compete for a considerable time. During my time and yours we had to jump off a hard board and at the landing pit side there was a channel about four inches wide and four or five inches deep, and if one's foot encroached too much over the board take off it meant to me generally a slight or badly hurt ankle. I was never certain of hitting the board accurately at full speed.' O'Connor remained a keen athletics enthusiast throughout his long life and attended every Olympic Games from 1924 to 1948: he was a long jump judge at the Los Angeles celebration.

Proof of the exceptional merit of O'Connor's 24 feet $11\frac{3}{4}$ inches is afforded by the fact that it survived as the world record until 1921, as the European record until 1928 and as a British best until as recently as 1960! The only athlete from the British Isles who seriously challenged this formidable target in the first half century of its existence was Tim Ahearne, from Tipperary. His big year was 1908. Having won the Irish title with 23 feet $1\frac{1}{2}$ inches he was expected to give a good account of himself at the London Olympics but was below form in placing eighth with 22 feet $0\frac{3}{4}$ inch. This disappointment was forgotten three days later as he triumphed in the triple jump with a world record effort of 48 feet $11\frac{1}{4}$ inches. Inspired by this success Ahearne jumped 24 feet 10 inches shortly after returning to Ireland. The following year he registered the breathtaking distance of 25 feet $3\frac{1}{2}$ inches in his home town of Athea but it was ruled out by the downhill runway.

The next breakthrough to relate was the demise, after no less than thirty years, of C. B. Fry's English record. The man responsible had as early as 1915 been described by F. A. M. Webster as 'phenomenal' after jumping 18 feet $1\frac{1}{2}$ inches at the age of 15 (a performance that today is considered unremarkable by a girl of that age!). In 1919, having witnessed his 21 feet 3 inches in the Cambridge Freshmen's sports, the same observer predicted with uncanny foresight that the young man in question—Harold Abrahams—was destined to jump 24 feet. Abrahams reached 22 feet 7 inches in 1920 but in that year's Olympics he recorded an abysmal 19 feet $10\frac{1}{4}$ inches. It was in 1923 that he began fulfilling his early promise. He broke Fry's record with 23 feet $7\frac{1}{4}$ inches in March, while in July's AAA Championships he had no fewer than three jumps of 23 feet $8\frac{3}{4}$ inches. The following June, one month before his Olympic 100 metres triumph, he landed at 24 feet $2\frac{1}{2}$ inches, a mark that was itself to stand for over thirty years as the English record. Hopes that Abrahams would go on to clear 25 feet were dashed when, while jumping in May 1925, he tore clean through the nerves and muscles behind his right knee. His leg was permanently damaged and his active career was over.

While the world record was rising steadily from 25 feet 5¾ inches in 1924 to 26 feet 8¼ inches in 1935, British standards were at best stagnant. About the only crumbs of comfort were offered by Ulsterman Edward Boyce, who jumped 24 feet 1½ inches in 1932 and 24 feet 2 inches (measured with a cloth tape) in 1934, and William Breach, who followed up his 23 feet 11¾ inches in 1937 with sixth place in the 1938 European Championships.

Not before time, Abrahams' English record was bettered in June 1954 when Ken Wilmshurst jumped 24 feet 3 inches, only because of a technicality (he was born in Calcutta) he was never officially credited with the record. Later in the season Wilmshurst won both the long jump (24 feet 8¾ inches) and triple jump (50 feet 1½ inches) at the Commonwealth Games but illness kept him out of the European Championships, the long jump at which was won at 24 feet 7¾ inches. Roy Cruttenden, a dependable performer for many years, struck his best form at the age of 31 in 1956 and achieved 24 feet 10¾ inches soon after the Melbourne Olympics in which he placed ninth. The honour of becoming the first Briton to reach 25 feet fell to John Howell, with 25 feet 0½ inch in 1960. Two years later Welshman Lynn Davies leapt 25 feet 4 inches for fourth place in the Commonwealth Games for the first of (to date) eight UK record instalments. Davies, who was born at Nantymoel, near Bridgend, on May 20th 1942, deserves a chapter to himself. Few British athletes can point to such a brilliant record of achievement . . . and his momentous career is not yet over. Here, in his own words— adapted from an interview I tape recorded at the end of 1966—is how Lynn Davies described his progress towards the Tokyo Olympics:

'For fun I entered the school sports in 1960 at the age of 18. My first ever long jump was along the side of a rugby field, from an old grass run-up and with hardly any sand in the pit. As I ran down I didn't know which leg I was going to take off on. I eventually took off on my left leg and I did 21 feet 2 inches. I think all my jumps that day were over 20 feet although I had never long jumped before in my life. After this success I felt I could get somewhere in athletics. I trained seriously for the first time prior to the 1962 season; I did no really specific training for 1961' [*in which year he jumped 23 feet 5¼ inches and finished last in his first international, Britain 'B' v. Switzerland, with 22 feet 0½ inch*].

'The 1962 Commonwealth Games were my first major Games and I went out to Australia really believing I could get a medal without really knowing what was involved. I was thrilled to bits with my series and when I got up to 25 feet 4 inches I thought I had reached the ultimate! Right up until the final round I was in third place and I could feel the bronze medal in my hand. When Mike Ahey (Ghana) did 26 feet 5 inches on his last jump, making me fourth, I could have cried; I've never felt so disappointed in all my life. I used the hang technique in Perth, by the way, and my run-up then was seventeen strides consisting of 114 feet. Now it's nineteen strides consisting of 133 feet 2 inches.

'I changed from the hang to the hitchkick after seeing Igor Ter-Ovanesyan (USSR) in action at the 1962 European Championships [*in which Davies placed eleventh with 24 feet 0½ inch*]. I've never been so impressed by anyone long jumping; I was inspired by him at Belgrade. I was standing right by the side of the pit when he did 26 feet 10½ inches and I suddenly saw what it was all about; he gave me a completely new insight into long jumping. In 1963 I was still experimenting with weight training and was still working on a 1½ hitchkick with the hang technique. It was a very bad year and it was only after Volgograd [*when Davies produced a season's best of 25 feet 0 inch and was only just beaten by Ter-Ovanesyan*] that I began to see what was involved in my preparation. The 2½ hitchkick technique I use now was working in the winter of 1963. I decided that if I was to improve significantly in Olympic year I would have to double my capacity for work. It was at this time that Ron Pickering, my coach, was most valuable to me in that he helped me to push up my sights in training.'

Davies opened the 1964 season in dazzling fashion by jumping 25 feet 6½ inches indoors. One month later, at the Whitsun British Games, he joined the ranks of the long jumping greats with a wind-assisted 26 feet 4¼ inches and legal 26 feet 3¼ inches—and also demonstrated his spectacularly improved sprinting powers by winning the 100 yards in 9.5. He finished no higher than sixth in the American Championships (25 feet 8¾ inches), won by the reigning Olympic champion Ralph Boston with 26 feet 7½ inches, but this taste of high pressure competition was valuable experience. Back

Lynn Davies in action at the Tokyo Olympics where he won the long
jump with 26 ft. $5\frac{3}{4}$ in.

Arthur Rowe, European and British Commonwealth shot-put
champion in 1962

in Britain he raised his Commonwealth record to 26 feet 4 inches and followed with unacceptable but none the less impressive marks of 26 feet 4½ inches (downhill) and 26 feet 5 inches (wind-assisted). Yet even this marvellous standard, which seemed all the more incredible in view of the generally low level prevalent in Britain, sufficed only to rank Davies fourth among Olympic contenders. Boston led the way with a world record 27 feet 4¼ inches, followed by Ter-Ovanesyan at 26 feet 10 inches and Gayle Hopkins (USA) at 26 feet 9¼ inches.

In his training diary Davies entered the figures 27 feet 4 inches on the page for October 18th 1964; it was a custom of his to set himself specific targets. But his challenge in Tokyo that day came perilously close to being ended in the qualifying round. Needing 24 feet 11¼ inches to reach the final, he opened with 24 feet 3 inches and followed with a foul. All depended on his last attempt . . . happily, he kicked his way out to 25 feet 6¼ inches.

Conditions for the final were deplorable: the runway was covered with puddles, the wind blew against the jumpers and the temperature was a chilly 13 degrees C. Not surprisingly the length of the jumps was affected and after four of the six rounds Boston led with 25 feet 10¼ inches from Ter-Ovanesyan (25 feet 7 inches) and Davies (25 feet 6¼ inches). Hopkins was out, having fouled three times. The bronze medal was as good as his but Davies sensed that a timely 26-footer could win the coveted gold medal. This was his opportunity: no one seriously expected him to beat Boston, who only the previous month had recorded the fantastic distance of 27 feet 10¼ inches, wind assisted or not, yet Davies knew he was being unsettled by the damp and dismal conditions to a lesser degree than his two more celebrated opponents.

Davies put his whole body and soul into the fifth jump and, generating a combination of speed, spring, strength and technique that would have spelt 27 feet in reasonable circumstances, he broke the sand at 26 feet 5¾ inches. Unbelievably, in spite of the adverse breeze, the state of the runway and the pressure of an Olympic final, he had managed to jump further than ever before while almost everyone else was falling a foot or more below their best! 'When I saw 8.07 metres go up', recalls Davies, 'I was at the same time tremendously delighted and numb: I couldn't take it all in. Boston reassured me that that jump would be the winner although he had one to go. In the back of my mind I had the feeling he could pull

M

something off and yet at the same time I had a sneaking suspicion that it wouldn't be beaten. The suspense was agony.' It was close, for Boston finished with 26 feet 4¼ inches and Ter-Ovanesyan with 26 feet 2½ inches.

Almost eighteen months elapsed before Wales' first Olympic champion resumed his progression. He admits he became somewhat blasé and lazy in his training in 1965, with the result that his best legitimate jump was only 25 feet 10¾ inches and he proved an easy victim for Boston and Ter-Ovanesyan. But the lure of the two major championships in 1966 was sufficient motivation for a return to his former dedication. The results were quickly apparent, for in February he jumped 26 feet 2 inches indoors and on a tour of South Africa in April he took advantage of the sunshine and high altitude to improve his national record to 26 feet 8¼ inches and 26 feet 10 inches. He was now the third longest jumper in history. Hopes of his joining Boston and Ter-Ovanesyan in the 27-foot 'club' in 1966 were not realised but it didn't matter for by winning both in Kingston (26 feet 2¾ inches) and Budapest (26 feet 2¼ inches on his very last jump) he became the first athlete to complete a hat-trick of gold medals: Olympic, Commonwealth and European.

Davies created a sensation while training in Mexico City for the 'Little Olympics' in October 1967 when he cleared 27 feet 7½ inches from take-off to landing (as measured by fellow Olympic champion Mary Rand)—two and a half inches beyond Boston's world record. In the actual competition, six days later, he registered his season's best of 26 feet 8 inches but fell 8¾ inches short of Ter-Ovanesyan.

Inevitably overshadowed by such a superlative contemporary have been two most capable performers in Fred Alsop and John Morbey. Alsop, primarily a triple jumper, reached the Olympic final in 1960 and recorded 25 feet 4¾ inches in 1964. Morbey, who interrupted Davies' reign as UK record holder for eight months with his 25 feet 4½ inches in August 1963, made the Tokyo Olympic final and—representing Bermuda, where he now lives—registered a personal best of 25 feet 10¾ inches in taking second place behind Davies at the 1966 Commonwealth Games.

Triple Jump

The early history of the triple jump is difficult to unravel owing to the parallel existence of two methods. One was the 'hop, step and jump' technique (the event's original name) which is the style used to the present day; the other, practised mainly by the Irish who were the early masters of this speciality, can best be described as the 'hop, hop and jump'. The second treatment usually yielded superior distances, and so performances recorded by this method should be treated with reserve when comparing them to 'conventional' marks.

The Irish trail blazers were Dan Shanahan and John Purcell. Shanahan covered 47 feet 7 inches the orthodox way in 1886 and reached 50 feet 0½ inch by the other method in 1888, winning by only three inches from P. D. Looney. Purcell, a great long jumper, accomplished what may now be termed a 'legal' 48 feet 3 inches in 1887 (remarkably, no Englishman did better until 1950) and an 'illegal' 49 feet 7 inches the same year. Shanahan's 50 feet 0½ inch stood as the best on record until Matthew Roseingrave landed at 50 feet 1 inch in 1895 and John Breshnihan at 50 feet 4 inches in 1906, although Tom Kiely (see the sub-section on hammer throwing!) attained 50 feet 9 inches from a downhill runway in 1892.

On the hop, step and jump plane, the towering figures were the Ahearne brothers from Limerick. The crowning achievement of Tim, the elder, was winning the 1908 Olympic title (representing Great Britain and Ireland) at the White City with a world record of 48 feet 11¼ inches—a mark that was to stand as the ultimate by a British athlete for nearly half a century. This prodigious performance by the 5 feet 7 inches, 126-pound Irishman followed three days after his disappointing showing in the long jump. Tim Ahearne, who thus became the first of Britain's three Olympic field event champions (Mary Rand and Lynn Davies, fifty-six years later, are the others), was 22 at the time. He displayed remarkable coolness in overtaking Canada's Garfield MacDonald (48 feet 5¼ inches) with his very last jump. He went on to win the AAA long jump the following year, shortly before emigrating to the USA, but was denied the opportunity of a British title in his best event for the simple reason that the triple jump was not introduced into the AAA programme until 1914. As late as 1925 one distinguished commentator described the triple jump as 'rather an anomalous and inconsequent event' and added: 'It is difficult to see why this "music hall" event is maintained.' This lingering opposition, or apathy at best, was reflected by the dismal performances achieved by even the best of the home-grown specialists until the last decade or so.

But back to the Ahearne brothers. Dan Ahearn (he dropped the

final letter on emigrating to the USA in 1909), two years younger
and considerably bigger at 5 feet 10 inches and 160 pounds, did
not emulate Tim's Olympic success but in many other respects was
the greater athlete of the two. Strictly speaking, Dan has no rightful
place in this book for his career was confined to the United States,
but as one of Ireland's most distinguished sporting sons he warrants
a paragraph to himself. Between 1910 and 1918 he won the American triple jump title eight times, he relieved his brother of the world
record in 1910 with 49 feet $7\frac{1}{4}$ inches and made even more indelible
history by improving to 50 feet 11 inches the following season, a
mark that withstood all challenges for thirteen years. His best using
the other—two hops and jump—method was 51 feet 7 inches in
1910. It is not being unreasonable to suppose that Dan would have
won an Olympic title in 1912 (won at 48 feet 5 inches) and/or 1916
but he was denied the chance: in 1912 he was not yet eligible to
represent the USA (and there was no independent Irish team) and,
of course, the world had other things on its mind four years later.
He did qualify for the 1920 team but, at 32, he was past his prime
and had to struggle for sixth place with 46 feet $2\frac{1}{4}$ inches.

Returning to the mainstream of British triple jumping one finds,
as in so many of the field events, a vacuum following the departure
of the great Irish pioneers. Not until 1923 did an Englishman exceed
even 46 feet, when J. Odde leapt 46 feet $4\frac{1}{2}$ inches in the AAA
Championships. The English record was improved to 46 feet 9
inches in 1926 by Jack Higginson, the most distinctive feature of
this being that his son was to equal it in 1937 and advance to 47
feet 4 inches the next season. In the meantime, Ulster's Edward
Boyce crashed the 47 and 48 feet barriers simultaneously with his
48 feet $5\frac{1}{2}$ inches in 1934.

The advent of Ken Wilmshurst brought new hope to this sadly
neglected event. A good sprinter, hurdler and high jumper and a
first-rate long jumper, Wilmshurst monopolised it for several seasons
in the fifties and established himself as the first British triple jumper
of international stature since Tim Ahearne. He made a remarkable
international debut against France in 1953 . . . by improving 20
inches on his previous best to win with 48 feet $9\frac{1}{4}$ inches. The following Whitsun he set a UK record of 50 feet $1\frac{1}{2}$ inches, a distance he
duplicated when winning the Commonwealth title in Vancouver. He
also won the long jump with a lifetime best of 24 feet $8\frac{3}{4}$ inches.
That 50 feet $1\frac{1}{2}$ inches effort would have gained second place in the

European Championships later in the month but Wilmshurst was an absentee due to an attack of mumps. He progressed to 50 feet 8 inches in 1955 and 51 feet 2¼ inches in 1956 and was close to his national record at the Melbourne Olympics with 50 feet 11¾ inches in ninth place.

Somewhat reminiscent of Wilmshurst six years earlier, Fred Alsop burst into prominence overnight at the 1959 Essex Championships: he jumped nearly two and a half feet further than ever before in reaching 49 feet 0¼ inch which, in view of Wilmshurst's Indian birthplace, was officially an English record. Alsop never looked back and has remained a sheet anchor of the British team ever since. He broke the UK record with 51 feet 4¼ inches in the qualifying round of the 1960 Olympics and jumped 50 feet 9¾ inches for twelfth place in the final. He also reached the long jump final, the only competitor to achieve that double distinction. Time and again Alsop surpassed himself in the most important contests. Typically it was on such heady occasions as the 1962 Commonwealth Games and 1964 Olympics that he pulled out all the stops and unleashed new national records. In Perth he finished third with 52 feet 7 inches and in Tokyo he placed fourth with his opening jump of 54 feet 0 inch, a distance which held second position for two rounds and third for four rounds. It was easily the closest approach to an Olympic medal in this event since Ahearne 56 years earlier and, by any standards, was a magnificent achievement. The UK record remains at 54 feet 0 inch but in 1965 Alsop stretched out to the extraordinary measurement of 54 feet 7½ inches with the following wind only just above the permissible limit at 2.47 metres per second. Family bereavement and injuries held him back in 1966 though, characteristically, he came up with a season's best of 52 feet 4½ inches at the Commonwealth Games for another bronze medal. He easily retained his domestic supremacy in 1967 with 52 feet 8 inches and continued to be a thorn in the flesh of many of the world's leading exponents.

The only other Briton to have exceeded 52 feet is Mike Ralph (52 feet 4¾ inches in 1964) but one who might have surpassed even Alsop's considerable accomplishments had he continued in the event—he gave it up because of the high risk of injury—is Lynn Davies. He attained 50 feet 7½ inches in 1962 at a time when his fastest 100 yards was 9.9 and his best long jump was 24 feet 9 inches. . . .

11

THE THROWS AND DECATHLON

Shot

THE history of championship shot-putting in England moved off to a somewhat embarrassing start when, at the 1866 Amateur Athletic Club meeting, it was discovered that the weight of the shot used was 18 pounds 10 ounces instead of the regulation 16 pounds! It was not until 1871 that 40 feet was beaten by an amateur, although four years earlier a professional, Donald Dinnie, had recorded 45 feet 7 inches. The 6 feet 6 inches tall E. J. Bor achieved 42 feet 5 inches at the 1872 English Championships, and that marked the end of British record breaking until 1884 when Ireland's J. Maxwell put exactly one foot further. The following season another Irishman, James O'Brien, carried the record out to 44 feet 10½ inches.

The first of Britain's two shot-putting *colossi* was Dennis Horgan, from County Cork. He won his first AAA title with 42 feet 9 inches in 1893 . . . and signed off nineteen years later, aged 43, with 44 feet 10 inches for his thirteenth English championship. His total, a record in itself, might have been greater still but for temporarily losing his amateur status in 1901–2. This boisterous, fun loving Irishman assumed the mantle of British record holder in 1894 (45 feet 3 inches) and world record holder in 1897 (48 feet 0½ inch). His best was 48 feet 10 inches in September 1904, three inches past the world record distance set by Ralph Rose (USA) in winning the Olympic title that year. Not only Horgan's athletic career, but his very life, nearly came to an end in 1907. Horgan, a New York policeman, had his skull broken by a shovel while he was trying to stop a brawl. The doctors did not hold out much hope of recovery, yet such was his resilience that the very next year—at the age of 39—he gained the silver medal for Great Britain and Ireland (at 44 feet 8¼ inches) behind Rose at the Olympics. This was, curiously, his Olympic debut. Horgan, whose weight rose from 165 pounds in 1893 to 238 pounds in 1908 for a height of 5 feet 10 inches, died in 1922. His records outlived him: his 48 feet 10 inches survived as the UK record until 1949 and no man has yet beaten his string of 13 AAA titles in one event. While on the subject of great Irish shot-putters, mention must be made of Pat McDonald, from County Clare, who—in USA colours—won the 1912 Olympic gold medal with 50 feet 4 inches.

Besides Horgan, Britain possessed two other shot-putters of an internationally respectable standard prior to the Great War. Tom Kirkwood, of Scotland, reached 45 feet 8½ inches in 1906 and lost to Horgan by only 7¼ inches at the 1908 AAA; while John Barrett, of the Royal Irish Constabulary, the fifth placer at the 1908 Olympics, hit 45 feet 2 inches in 1910 and was AAA champion as late as 1923. A word about the event's rules. Until 1908, the shot was put from a 7-foot square; superseded in that year by a circle of 7-feet diameter. The shot (or weight) itself is a ball made of any metal not softer than brass and weighing 16 pounds. The shot must not be thrown; it is put from the shoulder with one hand only.

The English record languished at an abysmal level for decades. Dr. Reginald Salisbury Woods, a 51 second quarter miler before 1914, set new figures of 44 feet 11 inches in winning the 1926 AAA title and, aged 35, improved to 45 feet 1½ inches the following year. Robert 'Bonzo' Howland pushed the record out to 46 feet 0 inch in 1929 and 48 feet 9 inches in 1935 but his main claim to fame was finishing second to foreign opposition in the AAA Championships on no fewer than eight occasions. He was even second in both the 1930 and 1934 Empire Games. Howland remained active for many years and was Cambridgeshire champion in 1950, when he was 45.

The first Briton to reach 50 feet was John Savidge, a 6 feet 7 inches tall Marine who, under the guidance of Geoff Dyson, had progressed at a startling rate. He was discovered by the Chief National Coach in June 1949, his best mark then being a paltry 43 feet 10 inches. In fact, Savidge believed the javelin to be his strongest event but Dyson got him to direct all his energy towards the shot. The benefits of skilled coaching and the introduction of weight training became apparent in November 1949 when he achieved 51 feet 4½ inches, an improvement of 7½ feet in less than six months! Savidge ruled the British shot-putting scene for many seasons and steadily worked the British record up to a highly

respectable 55 feet 2¾ inches which he registered on the same day—
May 8th 1954—that Parry O'Brien (USA) became the first man
over 60 feet. Savidge's all-time best was in fact 56 feet 8½ inches
but that was made in a demonstration in March 1953. He encountered mixed fortunes as a major championship competitor.
His 51 feet 5 inches qualifying put at the 1950 European Championships would have sufficed for the silver medal but, in the actual
final, he came only seventh with 48 feet 2½ inches. He fared much
better at the 1952 Olympics (sixth with 53 feet 1½ inches) and 1954
Commonwealth Games (winner with 55 feet 0¼ inch) but again
disappointed in the European Championships with only 52 feet
10 inches for fifth place.

Savidge made his final international appearance in 1957, finishing
second against France. The winner, at 54 feet 8¾ inches, was 20-
year-old Arthur Rowe, who a few days earlier had added an inch
to Barclay Palmer's 1956 British record of 55 feet 6 inches. Palmer,
6 feet 6 inches tall, never went on to fulfil his considerable promise
—and that left Rowe and Mike Lindsay, a Glasgow-born student at
Oklahoma University, to battle some 5,000 miles apart for the distinction of becoming the first British 60-footer.

Rowe, like Savidge, benefited enormously from the attentions of
Geoff Dyson. The first time he ever handled a shot was while waiting to bat in a cricket match; with his pads on he managed to heave
the junior (12 pounds) implement about 43 feet. It was hardly an
epoch-making effort by an 18-year-old but on the other hand it
wasn't bad for someone with no idea of technique. He was taken
in hand and won the Yorkshire junior title in 1955. Soon afterwards
he met Dyson, who told Rowe after seeing him reach 41 feet with
the 16-pounder at the end of their first session together: 'You can
be Europe's first 60-foot shot-putter'. Rowe worked hard and progress came swiftly: 51 feet 7 inches in 1956, 55 feet 7 inches in 1957.
By 1958 the 6 feet 1¾ inches, 220 pounds blacksmith was ready to
take on the world. He won the Commonwealth (57 feet 8 inches)
and European (58 feet 4 inches) titles, raised his UK record in seven
instalments to 58 feet 11¼ inches and reached 59 feet 8 inches in an
exhibition. Only four men stood ahead of him on that year's world
list.

Silvano Meconi of Italy beat Rowe to Europe's first 60-footer
but three months later, in August 1959, the Yorkshireman seized
the European record with exactly 61 feet. Again he occupied fifth

place in the world rankings. The 20-year-old Lindsay, meanwhile, had been making up ground; during the season he advanced from 53 feet $2\frac{1}{2}$ inches to 58 feet $2\frac{1}{4}$ inches and such was the rate of his progress in the USA that for a while it seemed possible he would reach 60 feet before Rowe.

Judging by a mighty exhibition toss of 64 feet 6 inches in June 1960 and a new UK record of 62 feet 1 inch just before the Olympics, Rowe seemed assured of fourth place at the very worst, behind the American trio, but the Rome Games proved to be as monumental a flop for Rowe as they were for Pirie and all too many others in the British team. There was nothing wrong with his 62 feet $11\frac{1}{2}$ inches training put the day after arriving in the Italian capital but during the succeeding days he was weakened, he claims, by a combination of tummy troubles and lack of appetite brought on by the considerable heat and humidity. Ten pounds lighter than when he arrived, Rowe was indeed a pathetic sight in the qualifying competition. All that was needed to make the final was 54 feet $11\frac{1}{2}$ inches but the best he could muster was 54 feet $8\frac{3}{4}$ inches. Lindsay, however, rose splendidly to the occasion to finish fifth in the final with 58 feet $4\frac{3}{4}$ inches, as did Martyn Lucking with eighth place at 57 feet $2\frac{1}{4}$ inches. The title was won by world record holder Bill Nieder with 64 feet $6\frac{3}{4}$ inches, fourth place going at 58 feet $8\frac{3}{4}$ inches.

So dejected was Rowe that he considered retiring there and then but on reflection he decided to continue, determined to establish himself as the world's number one. Soon after returning from Rome he attained 64 feet 11 inches in training and, on a bitterly cold and windy October day in East Berlin, amid pouring rain, he lengthened the European record to 62 feet $8\frac{1}{2}$ inches. He carried all before him in 1961; undefeated all season he improved to 63 feet $9\frac{1}{4}$ inches and 64 feet 2 inches. Just one man threw further that year, Dallas Long (USA) with 64 feet $7\frac{3}{4}$ inches; and only one other had ever bettered Rowe's 64 feet 2 inches . . . Nieder at 65 feet 10 inches. Rowe was now truly among the greats and, especially after a 66 feet $1\frac{1}{2}$ inches training put, there was a distinct possibility of his becoming world record holder in 1962 as well as the near-certainty of his retaining both Commonwealth and European titles. Unhappily, none of these prizes came his way for in July 1962 he signed professional rugby forms. It was a decision he was to regret, for his new career lasted only a few weeks. He knew he had not reached his limit with the shot put but, frustrated, had to stand aside as Hungary's Vilmos Varju took away his European title with 62 feet 4¾ inches and Martyn Lucking his Commonwealth championship with 59 feet 4 inches. Rowe's own official best for the season was 63 feet 11¼ inches, while as a professional he recorded 64 feet 0 inch.

Lucking (61 feet 1¼ inches), ranked ninth in the world in 1962, and Lindsay (60 feet 8½ inches in 1963) became the second and third Britons to surpass 60 feet but neither man ever made a habit of it and Rowe's successor is still awaited. Alan Carter, who hit 61 feet 0 inch indoors in 1965 at the age of 20, showed tremendous promise but has yet to reproduce that form. Indeed, British shot-putting in 1966 and 1967 reached its lowest ebb for many years with Lucking's 57 feet 2¾ inches the best during those two seasons. The world record, in the meantime, had shot out to 71 feet 5½ inches!

Discus

The history of British discus throwing, judged by international standards, has been one of almost unrelieved gloom. It got off to a bad start for although the event formed part of the inaugural modern Olympic Games in 1896 the AAA, in its wisdom, waited until 1914 before introducing the discus into its championship programme. In that year the world record of 158 feet 4½ inches stood to the credit of Finland's Olympic champion Armas Taipale; the UK best was exactly thirty feet less and was held by the poet and novelist Walter Henderson, who was really better as a high jumper. That yawning gap was never to close to any appreciable extent.

Even the Irish were unable to dash to the rescue in this instance. True, the first of the all-time greats in discus throwing—Martin Sheridan, the 1904 and 1908 Olympic champion—was born in County Mayo but he became a naturalised American citizen in 1897 and played no part in British athletics. Even so, it was an Irishman who dominated the event in the British Isles between the wars: Paddy Bermingham of Dublin. He won the AAA title five times between 1924 and 1934, finished tenth of thirty-one competitors in the 1924 Olympics (representing Ireland) and posted a worthy personal best of 151 feet 6½ inches in 1927—less than seven feet away from Taipale's still surviving world record. Bermingham, however, cannot be considered as a holder of the UK record since his career followed the signing on December 6th 1921 of the treaty that created the Irish Free State.

One had to wait until 1930 for the first throw over 130 feet by a British subject, that much belated distinction falling to Kenneth Pridie with 131 feet 3 inches. The world record by then was up to 167 feet 5¼ inches. Pridie advanced to 135 feet 6¼ inches in 1931, and three years later Douglas Bell threw precisely 140 feet before improving to 142 feet 10½ inches in 1936. Bell, who had been a high jumper and low hurdler of some note at Cambridge, finished second in the 1934 Empire Games but never won an AAA title. In fact no British discus thrower succeeded at his own national championship from the time that G. T. Mitchell won in 1923 with a ludicrous 110 feet 3 inches until Mark Pharaoh's victory in 1952! Bell died of wounds in Normandy in 1944.

A Glasgow policeman, David Young, added over ten feet to Bell's record in 1938 with 153 feet 8 inches and followed up with a silver medal in the Empire Games. Ten years later came England's first 150-footer, to the very inch . . . Jack Brewer. He was 33 at the time, yet ten years later he produced his lifetime best of 151 feet 6 inches and he is still throwing close to 140 feet. An even later developer has been Polish-born Konstanty Maksimczyk, a naturalised Briton, who threw 160 feet 8 inches in 1966 at the age of 52!

Young's national mark, which at the time of its establishment was twenty feet short of the world record, lasted until shot-put expert John Savidge registered 154 feet 6½ inches in 1950—thirty-two feet below the contemporary world figures. Three years afterwards, Mark Pharaoh became the first to exceed 160 feet and in July 1956 reached 174 feet 0 inch. He created a minor sensation at the Melbourne Olympics by placing fourth immediately behind the three American representatives. He threw 172 feet 3½ inches in the first round for third place, fell back to fourth after three rounds despite improving to 174 feet 9 inches, produced a splendid UK record of 178 feet 0½ inch in the fifth round to regain third—only for Des Koch to snatch back the bronze medal with a final toss of 178 feet 5½ inches. Pharaoh's last effort went 174 feet 5 inches. Pharaoh's achievement, easily the finest in British discus history, can best be appreciated when one considers that (a) he beat the next best European by over six feet; (b) he improved upon his previous best by over four feet while everyone else, except for winner Al Oerter, was several feet below; (c) of the thirteen finalists, ten had pre-Olympic marks superior to Pharaoh's. Gerry Carr, tenth with 166 feet 5 inches, also excelled himself.

Pharaoh never bettered 170 feet again and Carr reigned supreme for a few years. He took possession of the UK record with 178 feet 11 inches in 1958 and, by now a student in California, boosted it to 181 feet 2½ inches in April 1960—in which month he was credited with a training throw of 193 feet. Just eleven days after his latest record Carr was dethroned by another American-based student, Scotsman Mike Lindsay. The latter, who had won the 1957 AAA title as an 18-year-old and who had set a world's junior best of 193 feet 5 inches with the 1.5 kilogramme platter that same season, finally realised some of his immense potential with a throw of 181 feet 6 inches, though even this was far short of the 195 feet efforts he had produced in training the year before. Lindsay might have carried the record beyond 190 feet but, instead, he concentrated on the shot, in which event he placed a notable fifth at the Rome Olympics.

Carr regained the record in 1964, with a best throw of 185 feet 0 inch, but as he did not return to Britain to try for selection Britain's only representative in Tokyo was Roy Hollingsworth, from Trinidad. This former 49.8 400 metres performer, with a best mark of 186 feet 0½ inch in 1963 (this is the official UK record although Hollingsworth spent only a few years in Britain and has since returned home), did creditably to place tenth in the Olympic final with 176 feet 8½ inches. Carr, who had become a permanent American resident, threw 187 feet 0 inch in 1965, but this mark has not been accepted as a national record. Bill Tancred (182 feet 10 inches) and Arthur McKenzie (181 feet 1 inch), both in 1966, are the only others to have surpassed Pharaoh's 1956 mark.

Hammer

The hammer event as it is known today—a metal ball and chain thrown from a circle 7 feet in diameter, the thrower making three or four turns in the circle prior to releasing the implement—is a far cry from that of the pioneering days. Only the weight of the hammer (16 pounds) has remained unaltered throughout the event's evolution. When included in the first Oxford University sports of 1860 the hammer handle was wooden and an unlimited forward run was permitted, the throw being measured from the front foot at time of delivery. Six years later a scratch line was brought into operation. This 'freestyle' method lingered on at English universities until 1881 but elsewhere in England, from 1875 to 1886, the hammer (complete with 3 feet 6 inches long wooden handle) was thrown from a circle of 7 feet diameter. In 1887 the circle was enlarged to 9 feet and in 1896 the AAA permitted a metal handle to be used if desired. It was not until 1908 that the present rules came into force in Britain, although the Americans had operated them since 1887. Among later refinements a rule decreeing that the throw must land within a 90-degree sector came into being after the First World War (the current rule provides for a 60-degree sector), and the stipulation that the competitor must leave the circle after delivery from the rear half was activated in 1927.

It seems hardly necessary by now to point out that it was the Irish who controlled the event during the formative years. The first thrower of distinction from the Emerald Isle was the 6 feet 4 inches, 234 pounds Dr William Barry, from Cork. He won five AAA titles between 1885 and 1895 (plus three in the shot) and set record figures of 129 feet $3\frac{1}{4}$ inches in 1888. From the more advantageous 9 feet circle he attained 137 feet 9 inches in 1895. The other outstanding competitor during Barry's heyday was the 6 feet 0 inch, 233 pounds James Mitchel, from Co. Tipperary, who took the AAA title each year from 1886 to 1888. Mitchel emigrated to the USA in the latter year and went on to enjoy a very successful career there: American hammer champion no fewer than eight years running (1889–1896) and again in 1903. Mitchel raised the world record in several instalments from 1886, culminating with 145 feet $0\frac{3}{4}$ inch in 1892. At the age of 39 he placed fifth and last at the 1904 Olympics (for the USA) but gained a bronze medal in the 35 pounds weight throw.

Next in the glorious line of 'Irish Whales' were Tom Kiely, of Co. Tipperary, and John Flanagan, of Co. Limerick. Kiely, who had in 1892 'hop, hop and jumped' 50 feet 9 inches from a downhill runway and was a 23 feet 2 inches long jumper, won five AAA titles in the period 1897–1902 and in 1899 carved his niche in hammer throwing history by becoming the first man in the world to reach 160 feet—162 feet 0 inch in fact. The record lasted a mere six weeks as the dispossessed Flanagan quickly rose to this challenge to his established supremacy. Kiely did not compete in the hammer at the St Louis Olympics of 1904 but he did win a gold medal in the 'all round' event, as related in the decathlon subsection of this chapter.

Kiely may perhaps be considered lucky to win an Olympic gold medal in such an esoteric event but Flanagan certainly proved himself a true world's champion. Three times he was crowned Olympic hammer king—a feat that remained unparalleled until Al Oerter clinched his third consecutive discus title in Tokyo. Flanagan was 27 when he triumphed for the first time at the Paris Games of 1900. The hammer (from a 9 feet circle) attracted only three entrants, all from the USA (to which Flanagan had emigrated in 1896), and Flanagan's winning throw was 163 feet 2 inches. Four years later he threw 168 feet 1 inch for his second gold medal. His final success in London in 1908 was easily the greatest for he overtook team-mate Matt McGrath, the man who was to succeed him as Olympic champion and world record holder, with a final round toss of 170 feet 4¼ inches. Flanagan was truly a giant of his age, for over a period of fourteen years from 1895 to 1909 he lengthened the world record by nearly 40 feet! He was the first man over 150 feet (in 1897), 170 feet (1901) and 180 feet (1909) and his final figures of 184 feet 4 inches would have won the Olympic title in 1948. Like so many of his Irish colleagues, Flanagan was most agile for his size and was credited with a 22 feet 0 inch long jump and 46 feet 1 inch triple jump. He returned to his homeland in 1911 and died there in 1938.

Several other brilliant Irish-born exponents of the event followed Flanagan. There was Matt McGrath, from Co. Tipperary, setter of world records of 173 feet 7 inches in 1907 and 187 feet 4 inches in 1911 and winner of the 1912 Olympic title for the USA by the colossal margin of twenty feet. He finished second in the 1924 Olympics, his fourth Games, at the age of 46! There was Con Walsh, from Co. Cork, who despite a reluctance to train was a bronze medallist for Canada at the 1908 Olympics and threw 177 feet 6½ inches in 1911. There was Pat Ryan, from Co. Limerick, whose world record of 189 feet 6½ inches in 1913 withstood all assaults for twenty-four years and who retained the Olympic title for the USA in 1920. There was Dr Pat O'Callaghan, from Co. Cork: Olympic champion—wearing the green of Ireland—in 1928 and 1932 and world record breaker (at 195 feet 4¾ inches) in 1937. And there was Bertie Healion, of Dublin, who reportedly threw 202 feet 1 inch in an exhibition as a professional in New York in 1950.

From these dizzy heights we must descend to the more mundane level of English and Scottish throwing history. Indeed so poor was the standard at the turn of the century that it was only by a vote of 19–16 that a proposal for the event to be dropped from the AAA Championships was defeated. The first figure of any international significance was an Ayrshire farmer, Tom Nicolson. He was AAA champion six times between 1903 and 1912, finished fourth in the 1908 Olympics only 16¼ inches behind bronze medallist Walsh, and was sixth in the 1920 Games. Among his finest performances was defeating Ryan by 161 feet 6 inches to 149 feet 2 inches in the 1913 match between Ireland and Scotland—the year of Ryan's great world record. Nicolson continued as one of Britain's foremost throwers until he was 50, and his personal best of 166 feet 9½ inches in 1908 stood as a Scottish native record until 1947.

Nicolson's mark lasted as a UK best (not counting the Irish who settled in North America) until Malcolm Nokes broke new ground with throws of 172 feet 0¼ inch and 173 feet 1 inch in 1923. The latter performance, in turn, defied every other British thrower for twenty-four years. Nokes, who began throwing in 1920 (finishing last in the AAA with 101 feet 0 inches), was definitely in world class. He performed with distinction at the 1924 Olympics to take the bronze award with 160 feet 4 inches behind the American stars Fred Tootell (174 feet 10 inches) and McGrath (166 feet 9½ inches). In fact he came tantalisingly close to winning, for one of his four foul throws landed at around 180 feet. He defeated O'Callaghan by over eleven feet in the 1927 Triangular International and was champion at both the 1930 and 1934 Empire Games. Nokes, who won the Military Cross in the 1914–18 War, was a decent runner too and at one time held the official English native discus record of 126 feet 1 inch. He later became a prominent figure in coaching circles.

Before passing on to the mid-1940s, for after Nokes there were no British throwers of class until then, mention should be made of the remarkable A. E. Flaxman. In spite of a physical stature (5 feet 9 inches, 150 pounds) that seemed incompatible with the demands of the event Flaxman bettered 150 feet using four turns. In his book *Athletics of Today* (1929) F. A. M. Webster wrote: 'Given the weight of Flanagan, Nicolson or McGrath, there is little doubt that he would have beaten 200 feet for, as it was, he threw more than a foot in distance for every pound of his own light weight.' The artistically inclined Flaxman, a fine all-round athlete who won the AAA pole vault in 1909, fell during the first Somme offensive in July 1916.

While Nokes's English record lingered on until 1951 two burly Scots helped bring British hammer throwing back to international standard. Duncan Clark, who had placed third in the 1939 AAA, ranked ninth in the world in 1945 with his 170 feet 11 inches, and in the following year's European Championships he excelled in taking the bronze medal (168 feet 4½ inches), one place ahead of the Olympic champion and world record holder apparent, Hungary's Imre Nemeth. Clark brought off another splendid competitive *coup* in 1947 when he defeated European champion Bo Ericson on the Swede's home ground with a UK record of 178 feet 8 inches. After winning the 1950 Empire title in Auckland Clark settled in New Zealand and it was there, in March 1950, that he set his lifetime best of 183 feet 9½ inches. He continued in competition for many years and at the age of 48 he threw 160 feet 3½ inches for third place in the 1964 New Zealand Championships. The other Scottish star was Ewan Douglas. Highlights of his career were a victory over Karl Storch and Karl Wolf (second and sixth in the previous year's Olympics) in 1953 and a UK record of 192 feet 6 inches in 1955.

Back among the Sassenachs meanwhile, Peter Allday (then weighing a mere 158 pounds) broke the long standing English record with 172 feet 11 inches and 173 feet 3½ inches in 1951; Don Anthony led the way past 180 feet in 1955; and a rather bulkier Allday surpassed Douglas's figures with 195 feet 7 inches in 1956, shortly before placing ninth in the Olympics with 190 feet 3½ inches. The following season Mike Ellis, undoubtedly the greatest hammer talent yet produced in England, zoomed not only to the forefront in domestic competition but established himself as one of the world's outstanding performers.

Ellis had the perfect physique for the event (he stood 6 feet 3¾ inches and weighed 210 pounds while only 18) and in Dennis Cullum he was fortunate in possessing as coach one of the world's foremost authorities on the complex business of twirling a 16-pound ball and chain to the best advantage. Ellis came to the event as a 16-year-old schoolboy in November 1952. Cullum recalls: 'He was keen and worked hard but was rather tall and "gangly" and a bit unco-ordinated, and like so many top class athletes-to-be he did not at once show promise.' Carefully nursed through a programme of *(right)* What the well dressed woman athlete was wearing in 1924: the great pioneer sprinter, hurdler and jumper Mary Lines

(below left) Anne Smith *en route* to her world record shattering 4 min. 37 sec. mile in 1967

(below right) Ann Packer at the start of the Britain v. Poland 400 metres in 1964; later that year she scored a sensational win in the Olympic 800 metres

The first British woman ever to win an Olympic gold medal: Mary Rand. She leapt 22 ft. 2¼ in., a world record, in the long jump at Tokyo in 1964

graduated hammer weights (12 pounds, 14 pounds, 15 pounds, 16 pounds), the object being to maintain speed and distance at each stage, Ellis made his début in senior competition in August 1954, aged 17, and threw 158 feet 6 inches for eleventh place in the season's rankings. He progressed only slightly to 163 feet 10 inches the following year but in 1956 he leapt forward to 187 feet 11 inches.

As both Allday and Anthony had exceeded 190 feet during the Olympic season the race for the first British 200-footer was on in earnest, and it was 20-year-old Ellis who gained the distinction in 1957. It came about at the Britain v. USSR match in London in August and the throw measured no less than 205 feet 9 inches. This superb effort fell nearly seven feet short of the winning throw by former world record holder Mikhail Krivonosov but it was good enough to rank Ellis thirteenth on the world's all-time list and prompted his great Soviet rival to predict that Ellis was capable of reaching 73 metres (239 feet 6 inches). The world record at that date was 224 feet $10\frac{1}{2}$ inches by the American, Harold Connolly! The previous month Ellis had, in fact, defeated Connolly in one of three clashes with the Olympic champion. Once Ellis had broken through the 200-feet barrier he rarely fell below it and in September 1957 he strengthened his position among the world's élite by recording 206 feet 3 inches and 210 feet $11\frac{1}{2}$ inches against Poland and 211 feet $9\frac{1}{2}$ inches against West Germany. With another three years in which to mature fully, Ellis looked an extremely bright Olympic prospect.

The 1958 season, however, proved something of an anti-climax. He exceeded 204 feet in only one meeting, the Commonwealth Games (he won with 206 feet $4\frac{1}{2}$ inches), and was a disappointing ninth in the European Championships (195 feet $10\frac{1}{2}$ inches), won by Poland's Tadeusz Rut—whom Ellis had easily beaten in Warsaw the previous year. He resumed his progress in 1959, throwing 213 feet 1 inch (the current UK record) for seventh spot on the world year list, but was destined for a bitter experience at the Rome Olympics. He started off magnificently with the fourth best throw in the qualifying round (at 207 feet $4\frac{1}{2}$ inches it was beyond Connolly's 1956 Olympic record) but in the final, after two fouls of about 207 feet, his only valid throw spun out of his hands after only two turns and carried to a mere 177 feet $10\frac{1}{2}$ inches. Thus he finished fifteenth and last whereas in his very best form he could have aspired to fourth place.

N

Although still very young and inexperienced by hammer-throwing standards Ellis retired at the end of the 1960 season, re-emerging in 1964 for just one competition in which he threw 192 feet 4½ inches—13 feet behind his successor as Britain's number one, Howard Payne. Born in South Africa and a representative of Rhodesia at the 1958 Commonwealth Games, Payne made his international début for Britain in 1960, won the Commonwealth title for England in 1962 and 1966, and has thrown over 200 feet in more than thirty competitions with a best of 208 feet 10 inches in 1962. Although the world record now stands at over 240 feet only one other Briton (Peter Seddon with a best of 202 feet 6 inches in 1967) has surpassed 200 feet.

Javelin

Of all the many and diverse events that go to make up the sport of athletics probably none has yielded so little success for Britain as javelin throwing. At least in the pole vault a Briton once tied for sixth in the Olympics, there was a discus thrower who finished fourth and a decathlete who placed ninth; in the javelin the highest position on record by a British thrower in Olympic competition is . . . fourteenth.

Although the Scandinavians revived this ancient skill in the 1890s, the British were very slow to follow suit. The event appeared in the AAA Championships for the first time in 1914 and it was not until 1923 that a home athlete even placed in the first three . . . and it so happened there was no foreign opposition that year. Jock Dalrymple was the winner with the princely distance of 148 feet 9½ inches, over twenty yards short of the world record. The 5 feet 5 inches tall Dalrymple, who had been invalided out of the Army as an 80 per cent disability, was the first Briton to surpass 170 and 180 feet, his best being 186 feet 5½ inches in 1924. Bill Land, the former high jump prodigy, breached 190 feet in 1935 (191 feet 7 inches) and the 200 feet landmark was reached by James McKillop with 202 feet 2½ inches in 1939.

Malcolm Dalrymple, Jock's son, made his modest mark on javelin history too. He threw 202 feet 8½ inches in 1944 in an exhibition with his father and set a UK record of 210 feet 9½ inches in 1948. He failed to qualify for the Olympic final at Wembley but the following year he did succeed in becoming the first Briton to win the javelin event in an international match. The occasion was the fixture against France and his winning throw was 182 feet 5½ inches. The Olympic season of 1952 was, relatively speaking, a vintage one for British spearmen. The youthful Mike Denley carried the UK best out to 216 feet 1 inch, a mark that lasted precisely one week until Ulsterman Dick Miller came up with 221 feet 11½ inches. Miller placed fourteenth of the twenty-seven competitors at the Helsinki Games with 209 feet 2 inches after throwing 213 feet 11 inches in the qualifying round. That was his international début but many years of fairly mediocre performances flitted by before Miller made a dramatic advance late in athletic life. He reached 238 feet 6 inches in 1961 and 243 feet 9 inches in 1963 (aged 34) but by then he had long since been replaced as the nation's top javelin thrower.

Clive Loveland was the first over 230 feet (231 feet 0 inch in 1956) and Peter Cullen, runner-up to Ken Wilmshurst in the 1956 inter-counties triple jump, won the 1957 AAA title with 236 feet 7 inches. Cullen was speedily dislodged as UK record holder by Colin Smith, who shot up from 212 feet 6 inches to 246 feet 7 inches during 1957. The big throw came in the West Germany v. Britain match in Hannover and it provided him with an unexpected victory over Heiner Will, then the tenth-ranking performer of all time at 263 feet 2 inches. Smith won the Commonwealth title next year with 233 feet 10½ inches and only narrowly failed to defend successfully in 1962 (he finished second 6½ inches behind with a personal best of 255 feet 8½ inches) but never competed in an Olympics and drew a blank in two European Championships. In 1967, by now a successful javelin coach in his own right, he returned to the international side.

Two seemingly exceptional young talents arose in the persons of left-hander John McSorley, Smith's successor as national record holder with 256 feet 1 inch and 260 feet 0 inch in 1962, and John Greasley, record equaller with 260 feet 0 inch in 1963. These distances stood on the fringe of world class (the world record then was 284 feet 7 inches) but persistent injuries prevented either of them from topping 240 feet in subsequent years. Number one in 1964 was John FitzSimons, whose best of 247 feet 10½ inches against Finland fell only 16 inches short of the distance recorded by Pauli Nevala, the Olympic winner three months later. FitzSimons improved to 253 feet 9 inches in 1965 but that year's most successful competitor was Dave Travis, only just 20, who summoned up a personal best of 250 feet 10 inches in winning against West Germany. FitzSimons was dominant in 1966, winning the Commonwealth title with a UK record of 261 feet 9 inches and ending the season with victories against strong opposition in Sweden (257 feet 3 inches), France (259 feet 11 inches) and Cuba (260 feet 1 inch). His was the most outstanding campaign of any British javelin thrower in history. He enrolled at the University of Southern California after the 1966 season but despite training throws of about 270 feet his best in competition in 1967 was 251 feet 10 inches. Travis, recovered from nagging injuries, threw a personal best of 252 feet 7 inches soon after returning from Tokyo, where he won the World Student Games title.

Decathlon

Rather surprisingly, in view of the traditional emphasis placed on all-round sporting ability at many schools, the decathlon has attracted scant interest in this country, although the situation is now improving. The decathlon consists of four track and six field events spread over two consecutive days: 100 metres, long jump, shot, high jump and 400 metres on the first; 110 metres hurdles, discus, pole vault, javelin and 1,500 metres on the second. Points are awarded for each individual performance and the winner of the competition is the athlete with the highest aggregate score.

Possibly the earliest all-round competition held in Britain was reported by *Bell's Life* in 1853. Two amateurs endured this arduous sequence of events: running a mile, walking a mile backwards, running a coach wheel a mile, leaping over fifty 3 feet 6 inches hurdles, stone picking and weight putting. Even that programme appears relatively straightforward (apart from the walking!) compared to the contents of the 'all-round' championship held after the 1904 Olympics in St. Louis: 100 yards, shot, high jump, 880 yards walk, hammer, pole vault, 120 yards hurdles, 56-pound weight, long jump and mile—and all on one day! The winner, representing Tipperary and Ireland, was hammer throwing and triple jumping expert Tom Kiely, who turned down an invitation to compete for Great Britain in this ordeal. This particular competition was labelled as the world's championship and not accorded official Olympic status but Kiely, who finished first in four of the events, was awarded a genuine Olympic gold medal for his herculean labours.

The next prominent all-rounder from the British Isles was another Irishman, Bob Tisdall. At the 1932 Olympics, a few days after his amazing 400 metres hurdles victory, he finished a worthy eighth in the decathlon with these performances: 11.3 100 metres, 21 feet 7¾ inches long jump, 41 feet 3¼ inches shot, 5 feet 5 inches high jump, 49.0 400 metres, 15.5 110 metres hurdles, 109 feet 3½ inches discus, 10 feet 6 inches pole vault, 148 feet 6 inches javelin and 4:34.0 1,500 metres. Scoring by the tables currently in use (they were introduced in 1962) Tisdall would have totalled 6,560 points, which no UK athlete bettered until 1960. In this survey, by the way, all scores have been converted to the present tables; otherwise comparison would be meaningless.

The first Englishman to win an AAA decathlon title was Tom Lockton, grandson of long jumping pioneer Charles Lockton. This success came in 1938, only the third occasion on which the championship was held, and his score converts to 5,524 points. Harry Whittle, the Olympic 400 metres hurdles and long jump finalist, scored 5,983 in 1949 and 6,040 in 1950. The latter year was notable also for the eleventh place in the European Championships of 19-year-old Geoff Elliott, later to develop into Britain's most eminent pole vaulter. Elliott's greatest decathlon achievement was placing ninth in the 1952 Olympics with 6,541 points, made up as follows: 11.4 100 metres, 21 feet 1½ inches long jump, 40 feet 8 inches shot, 5 feet 8⅞ inches high jump, 53.0 400 metres, 15.7 110 metres hurdles, 112 feet 3 inches discus, 13 feet 5½ inches pole vault, 162 feet 7 inches javelin and 5:03.6 1,500 metres.

Eight years elapsed before the next advance with Colin Andrews scoring 6,638, but in the last few years there has been an encouraging upsurge in interest and performances. The UK record has risen thus: 6,699 by Derek Clarke in 1964, 6,736 by Scotsman Norman Foster in June 1965, 6,791 by javelin expert Dave Travis and 6,840 by Foster in the AAA Championship in August 1965, 7,002 by Clarke in September 1965. Best of all has been Clive Longe, from Guyana. Representing Wales on a residential qualification, this powerfully built and dedicated all-rounder excelled at the 1966 Commonwealth Games by taking second place with 7,123 points, and again at the European Championships where he finished ninth with 7,160. Always at his best in major international competitions Longe continued to develop in 1967 and his latest UK record of 7,392 was accomplished at the USA v. British Commonwealth

match in Los Angeles. His performances: 11.1 100 metres, 22 feet
1½ inches long jump, 48 feet 4 inches shot, 5 feet 8⅞ inches high
jump, 49.9 400 metres, 15.3 110 metres hurdles, 143 feet 8 inches
discus, 13 feet 5½ inches pole vault, 195 feet 2 inches javelin and
4:49.4 1,500 metres.

12

THE WALKS

WALKING may be one of the most basic of human activities but *race* walking is almost a contradiction in terms. One's instinct when walking speed proves insufficient is to break into a run; but in competitive walking that urge must be controlled and correct walking form adhered to at all times. What has bedevilled the sport for so many years is the question of what constitutes fair walking. The officially accepted definition is clear enough in theory . . . 'walking is progression of steps so taken that unbroken contact with the ground is maintained, i.e. the advancing foot must make contact with the ground before the rear foot leaves the ground'. It is not so simple in practice, particularly in short track events when a walker can be travelling at nine miles per hour.

British walk judges are generally acknowledged to be the most scrupulous in the world but, alas, standards are not always so high in some other countries and the history of international walking is riddled with controversial judging decisions. It was because of these eternal disputes that track walking was banished from the Olympic programme in 1928, 1932, 1936 and ever since 1952. The two international championship distances on the road are now 20 kilometres (12 miles 753 yards) and 50 kilometres (31 miles 122 yards), while in Britain national titles are at stake each year in those two events plus 2 and 7 miles on the track and 10 and 20 miles on the road.

The sport of walking in its earlier days usually took the form of man against time and distance rather than man against man, and almost invariably a wager was at stake. As early as 1589 it is recorded that Sir Robert Carey walked from London to Berwick for a bet. The two most celebrated professional walkers were Foster Powell, from Yorkshire, and Captain Robert Barclay, a Scot. Powell, famous also as a long distance runner, achieved such exploits as walking 100 miles in 22 hours (1789) and the 402 miles from London to York and back in 5 days 13 hours 35 minutes in 1792 at the age of 56. Captain Barclay ruled from 1796, when at 17 he walked six miles in the hour, until 1808, when he successfully completed 1,000 miles in 1,000 consecutive hours—the stipulation being that he cover one mile in each hour, day and night. That effort, spread over a period of 42 days, netted him a purse of 1,000 guineas.

The inaugural English Championships in 1866 included a 7 miles walk, won by the Cambridge rowing 'Blue' John Chambers in a modest 59:32. Later champions were to cover the distance much faster but whether all of them were fair walkers is questionable. H. Webster, the 1877 winner in 53:59.6, was described by a contemporary as having 'trotted away' from his rivals; while the following year he and Harry Venn (champion in 52:25) 'both ran most of the way', according to the same observer. Venn's time, indeed, was later rejected as a record by the AAA. This practice seems to have persisted for some years and that astute commentator Montague Shearman wrote in his book, published 1886: 'Walking races are hardly so satisfactory now as ten years ago, for judges are lenient and walkers aspire to fast times, consequently most of the walking seen on the running-path is of shifty character and, if not absolutely a run, is more like a shuffle than a fair heel-and-toe walk.'

Dubious styles or not, 53 minutes for 7 miles was not officially bettered by an amateur until Harry Curtis won the 1890 AAA title by a clear two minutes in 52:28.4. The professional record, though, was lowered to 51:04 in 1883 by a former AAA champion, J. W. Raby. In 1894 Curtis won the first 4 miles championship, a distance that the AAA substituted for the traditional '7' until 1901. Curtis apart, the only man ever to win the '4' was Bill Sturgess, whose best time was 28:24.8 in 1897, compared to Raby's 'pro' record of 27:38 in 1883. Sturgess had, in 1895, set new 7 miles figures of 51:27 during a one hour record of 8 miles 274 yards.

The man who broke Sturgess's records, and practically every other performance in the books, was George Larner—the Alf Shrubb of walking. Born at Langley, Buckinghamshire, in 1875, Larner was 28 before he took up the sport but he soon made up for lost time. In 1904, only his second season, this Brighton policeman won both the AAA 2 miles (instituted in 1901) and 7 miles titles, and among his records were 6:26 for a mile (still the fastest by a Briton) and 13:11.4 for 2 miles (which lasted until 1960). Larner retired after an equally devastating 1905 season during which he covered 8 miles 438 yards in the hour and clocked 50:50.8 for 7 miles. Happily, he came back in 1908 to win the first two Olympic walks in history: he took the 3,500 metres (2 miles 306 yards) event in 14:55 (passing 2 miles in 13:43.4) and the 10 miles in 75:57.4. This latter was a world's amateur best but 72.4 seconds outside Raby's 25-year-old 'pro' record. Runner-up, if one may use the term in this context, in both races was compatriot Ernie Webb with times of 15:07.4 (13:53 at 2 miles) and 77:31. Webb was a particularly colourful figure. A Londoner by birth, he ran away to sea at the age of 12 and later served in the British cavalry in the retreat to Ladysmith during the Boer War. He became a walker in 1906 at the age of 34 and, after winning several AAA titles, climaxed his career with a third Olympic silver medal in the 1912 10,000 metres (46:50.4). He eventually settled in Canada.

In 1913, the year in which the International Amateur Athletic Federation issued its first list of world records, Larner was credited as holder of ten records from one to ten miles, plus the hour! Britain possessed other records too, including the 2 hours mark of 15 miles 128 yards by Harold Ross in 1911 and Tom Griffith's 20 miles time of 2:47:52 which had stood since 1870 and was destined to survive as a record until 1934! Not surprisingly, a mysterious 2 miles time of 12:53.2 by A. T. Yeomans in Swansea in 1906 did not appear on the list. Yeomans was AAA champion that year, but in 14:20.4.

Other notable performances were the ultra-long distance efforts recorded by Tommy Hammond. At the White City in 1908 he walked 131 miles 580 yards in 24 hours and the following year marched from London to Brighton (52 miles) in 8:08:18. Another prolific record breaker was Bobby Bridge, seven times an AAA champion, who covered 15 miles 701 yards in two hours in 1914. More Olympic medals came Britain's way after the war. C. E. J. Gunn, only third in 14:49 in the AAA 2 miles, gained the bronze in the 1920 10,000 metres and G. R. Goodwin took the silver four years later, though the winning times on both occasions were about a minute slower than Webb in 1912.

Following a number of incidents in 1924, walking was dropped altogether from the 1928 Olympic programme but, thanks largely to pressure by British officials, a 50 kilometres road event was introduced in 1932. Fittingly, the winner in Los Angeles was a

Briton: 39-year-old father of four, Tommy Green. Slowed by very hot weather, Green's time of 4:50:10 was nearly quarter of an hour slower than when he won the inaugural national championship in 1930, but what really mattered is that he finished seven minutes ahead of his nearest rival.

This newly established Olympic tradition was brilliantly upheld four years later in Berlin by Harold Whitlock. Only ninth after 20 kilometres he moved into third place by the halfway mark, second position at 30 kilometres and took the lead just before 35 kilometres. A severe case of sickness at 38 kilometres caused Whitlock's lead to shrink but he recovered well to finish almost 1½ minutes clear in 4:30:41.4. This magnificent and always fair competitor completed a rare double by winning the European title in 4:41:51 two years later. Whitlock's career was as long as it was distinguished. He first came into prominence in 1931 with second place in the national 50 kilometres and it was not until 1952 (aged 48) that he bowed out as an international, placing eleventh in the Olympics in 4:45:12.6. Between 1933 and 1939 he won the national '50' on six occasions with a fastest time of 4:30:38 in 1936. Other honours included a world 30 miles track record of 4:29:31.8 en route to 50 miles in 7:44:47.2 and the distinction of being the first to walk from London to Brighton in under eight hours.

Meanwhile, at the shorter distances the top men during the thirties were Alf Pope, Fred Redman and Bert Cooper. All three posted official world records: 35:47.2 for 5 miles, 44:42.4 for 10,000 metres, 50:28.8 for 7 miles and 8 miles 474 yards in the hour by Pope in 1932; 74:30.6 for 10 miles by Redman in 1934; 12:38.2 for 3,000 metres and 21:52.4 for 5,000 metres by Cooper in 1935. Cooper's other claim to fame was his sequence of seven victories in the AAA 2 miles with a best of 13:39.8 in 1933.

H. Forbes and C. Megnin filled second and third places in the 1946 European 50 kilometres but it was Harry Churcher who attracted the most attention in the early post-war days. He was tipped as a possible Olympic 10,000 metres winner in 1948 on the strength of his world 5 miles record of 35:43.4 but at Wembley he was subdued by a judge's warning and finished no higher than fifth in 46:28. One place ahead was team-mate C. J. Morris (46:04) who had clocked 45:10.4 in his heat—faster than the final winning time. A bronze medal was gained in the 50 kilometres through 48-year-old T. Lloyd Johnson (4:48:31) who conceded second place only in

the last two miles. Johnson's career as a leading walker stretched
back over quarter of a century. He had in 1923 finished third in
the national '20' and in 1926 had placed third in the AAA 2 miles
(14:43) at the meeting made memorable by the epic half-mile duel
between Otto Peltzer and Douglas Lowe. Even this belated Olympic
success did not mark the end of Johnson's active days: he won the
national title in 1949 and no less than ten years later he won a 50
kilometres race from Luton to London on a hot day in 5:11:15!

Harold Whitlock's younger brother, Rex, held second place at
35 kilometres in the Wembley race but was obliged to retire shortly
afterwards. He came back at Helsinki in 1952 with an excellent
fourth in 4:32:21, only 4¼ minutes behind the winner. Those Games,
however, spelt the end of Britain's medal-at-every-Olympics record
in walking. Roland Hardy, the 5 miles world record holder at 35:15
and author of other super-fast times like 2 miles in 13:27.8, 10,000
metres in 44:37.4 and 7 miles in 49:28.6, was the favourite of many
but—exactly as in the European Championships two years earlier—
he and second string Lol Allen suffered disqualification. What irri-
tated British supporters even more was the blatant 'lifting' by the
Swiss and Soviet athletes who finished second and third in the final
yet neither of them was pulled out. The furore provoked by these
controversial disqualifications led to the final removal of track
walking from the Olympic programme. As from 1956 the 20 kilometres road event replaced the 10,000 metres 'sprint'.

Although disillusioned by their summary treatment abroad,
Hardy and Allen returned to competition. Hardy won national
titles in 1956 at 10 miles in 74:31 (with a youngster name of Ken
Matthews twenty-third in 81:12) and 20 miles in the extremely fast
time of 2:38:27; while Allen was national 20 miles champion in
1958. Hardy (who was still active in 1967) finished eighth in the
1956 Olympic 20 kilometres in 1:34:40.4 but two of the men ahead
of him were team-mates. Stan Vickers, in his international debut,
placed fifth in 1:32:34.2, only 66.8 seconds behind the winner, while
39-year-old George Coleman (fifth in the 1952 10,000 metres) was
seventh in 1:34:01.8. In the 50 kilometres Britain's big hope was
Don Thompson who, during 1956, had won the national championship in a British best of 4:24:39 and walked from London to Brighton in 7:45:32, but he had the misfortune to succumb to the 90
degrees F. temperature in Melbourne and collapsed at 42 kilometres while in fifth place. Ironically, the Olympic title was won

by an Englishman, Norman Read . . . but in New Zealand's colours. This former English junior mile (1950) and 5 miles (1951) champion brought off a stunning upset by winning in 4:30:42.8.

The 20 kilometres event superseded the 10,000 metres at the 1958 European Championships and the first victor was none other than Vickers, who scored handsomely by nearly two minutes in 1:33:09. 'I decided', said Vickers, 'not to make the same mistake as in Melbourne when I cut out the early pace—to the advantage of my opponents. The last kilometre was agony because of tendon strain in my left foot. But moments like this make everything worthwhile'. The 50 kilometres was a very fast race and despite a time of 4:25:09 Thompson placed no higher than fifth. One position ahead, in 4:20:31.8, was Tom Misson whose other great achievement until then had come about the previous year when he won a 100 kilometres (62 miles) race in 9:40:03, nine minutes ahead of Thompson with Italy's Abdon Pamich—the most consistently great long distance walker of all time—fourth. Another exceptional 'marathon' effort in the autumn of 1957 was Thompson's London to Brighton record of 7:35:12 over a course measured at 53 miles 129 yards—an average of seven miles per hour.

Vickers may have proved himself Europe's top speed walker but his reputation held few terrors for Ken Matthews, a man who ever since defeating the Olympic trio of Vickers, Coleman and Hardy in a final pre-Melbourne tune-up race over 10 miles had enjoyed a reputation as a giant killer. Only a week or two after the European Championships he beat Vickers at 5 miles—35:36.6 to 35:42.4. In March 1959 Matthews won his first national title, covering 10 miles on the road in a phenomenal 71:00.4, two minutes ahead of Vickers. The European champion gained revenge in May by winning a 25 kilometres event in East Berlin in 1:55:59, nine places and over ten minutes ahead of Matthews, who was making his international debut. But from the Whitsun British Games onwards it was all Matthews. He triumphed in the inter-counties 2 miles (13:37.2) and 7 miles (49:47.4) championships, literally walked away with the AAA 2 miles in 13:19.4, placed second over 20 kilometres against the USSR in 1:26:05.2 (suggesting a short course) and set a world's best 5 miles time of 34:26.6. Vickers finished well behind in each of these races.

Matthews displayed even more formidable form in 1960. Performances of the calibre of 42:35.6 for 10,000 metres, 70:57 for 10 miles (road) and 1:28:15 for 20 kilometres (road) suggested a possible Olympic victory but in Rome he fell victim to a combination of the after effects of 'flu, his own ruthless pace and the searing heat. The result was that he collapsed and was taken to hospital. Vickers sportingly eased up to help Matthews but his colleague urged him on . . . 'You go on, my legs are turning to rubber'. Vickers went on to finish third in 1:34:56.4, less than a minute behind the winner. As for Matthews, he lost little time in re-establishing himself. Later in the month he set a UK hour record of 8 miles 1,018 yards (with record figures of 48:53 for 7 miles on the way) and in another race he reduced his 5 miles world best to 34:21.2, a minute ahead of Vickers and 1½ minutes in front of Australia's Olympic silver medallist Noel Freeman.

The great success of 1960 was, of course, Don Thompson. Remembering his ordeal in the sun at Melbourne and determined to be prepared for any climatic extremes, Thompson spent many hours sweating it out in a bathroom heated to a temperature of 100 degrees F. Known to Italian fans as il topolino ('the little mouse') ever since he won a 100 kilometres race there in 1955, Thompson proved a vastly popular winner of the 50 kilometres gold medal. He captured the hearts of everyone in the stadium as he wiggled around the final lap to snap the tape seventeen seconds ahead of Swedish veteran John Ljunggren in 4:25:30. The glorious tradition established by Tommy Green and Harold Whitlock (Thompson's own adviser) lived on. Modestly, Thompson described his performance as 'quite an ordinary one . . . which was, however, sufficient for the occasion'. Thompson wasted no time resting upon his laurels. Just ten days afterwards he won the London to Brighton race in 7:37:42, followed up with a UK 50 kilometres track record of 4:17:29.8 in October and finished no less than twenty-five minutes ahead of Pamich in November's Milan 100 kilometres classic.

Before leaving 1960, truly a memorable year for British walking, one must mention the remarkable AAA 2 miles duel between Vickers and Matthews. The start of a walking race at the White City always provokes amusement among the spectators but the guffaws very quickly gave way to applause and gasps of admiration as these two great athletes drew away from the field at dazzling speed. Vickers won in the extraordinary time of 13:02.4, with Matthews 7.2 seconds behind.

The major event of 1961 was the inauguration of an IAAF international walking competition for the Lugano Trophy. The final was between Britain, Sweden, Italy and Hungary, and Britain emerged as the narrow winners. On the individual plane Matthews took the 20 kilometres in 1:30:54 and Thompson finished second to Pamich in the 50 kilometres. Earlier in the season Matthews had reduced his UK 7 miles record to 48:24.0. Matthews carried all before him during the remainder of his momentous career and showed what a superlative 20 kilometres competitor he was by winning the 1962 European title in 1:35:54.8, the 1963 Lugano Trophy final in 1:30:10 (Britain retained the trophy) and, finally, the Olympic crown by over $1\frac{1}{2}$ minutes in 1:29:34. He scored numerous successes, too, from the stopwatch angle—notably 48:22.2 for 7 miles (1964) and 2:38:39 for 20 miles on the road (1962).

Thompson added another medal to his collection by placing third in the 1962 European 50 kilometres; but next to Matthews the most successful British walker of the mid-sixties has been Paul Nihill, who rose superbly to the occasion at the Tokyo Olympics by finishing second, a mere nineteen seconds down on Pamich, in the 50 kilometres with a time of 4:11:31.2. Born in Essex but of Irish descent, Nihill has also established himself as one of the world's finest short distance walkers and in 1965 he won national titles at 2 miles, 7 miles, 10 miles, 20 kilometres and 20 miles. Only defeat in the 50 kilometres (in which, suffering from a cold, he finished fifth) prevented an unprecedented clean sweep. Nihill retired temporarily in 1966 and the inaugural Commonwealth Games 20 miles event went to Ron Wallwork in 2:44:42.8. No medals were gained in the European Championships a few weeks later.

13

THE RELAYS

RELAY racing is one of the few components of the athletics programme not to have originated, or been initially revived, in the British Isles. The first relay race on record was a two miles event in California in 1883 but it was not until September 1895 that an inaugural 'flying squadron' race was organised at Stamford Bridge. The event was over two miles, the stages being 440 yards, $\frac{3}{4}$ mile and mile. The runners passed not a baton, but a flag, to each other and Finchley Harriers won in 8:57.4. This new fangled form of racing from America did not catch on to any notable extent and another sixteen years passed before the AAA assessed there was sufficient interest to warrant the institution of a mile medley (880, 220, 220, 440) championship.

The following year, 1912, British relay racing received a tremendous boost when medals were gained in both the Olympic relay events. In the 4 × 100 metres race Jacobs, Macintosh, d'Arcy and Applegarth took advantage of the Americans' absence from the final (they were disqualified in their heat) by winning in 42.4, only a tenth of a second away from Germany's world record; and in the 4 × 400 metres Nicol, Henley, Soutter and Seedhouse placed third behind the USA (3:16.6) and France (3:20.7) in 3:23.2. Unfortunately, Nicol was injured and handed over well down; otherwise the team, which had won its heat in 3:19.0, would probably have been second.

Another set of Olympic gold medals was obtained in 1920. On this occasion it was the 4 × 400 metres quartet who triumphed, with Griffiths, Lindsay, Ainsworth-Davis and Butler winning comfortably in 3:22.2 ahead of South Africa, anchored by the English-born 400 metres champion Rudd. This season was a most auspicious one, for at the famed Penn Relays in Philadelphia an Oxford and Cambridge team set world figures of 7:50.4 for the 4 × 880 yards. The runners were Tatham, Stallard (who transformed a twenty-yard deficit into a twenty-yard lead), Milligan and Rudd.

Although deprived of the services of Liddell, because of his refusal to run on a Sunday, both British relay teams finished among the medals at the 1924 Olympics. After setting a short-lived world record of 42.0 in the heats, Abrahams, Rangeley, Royle and Nichol clocked 41.2 for second place in the final behind the Americans. In the longer race Butler, on the anchor leg, made a brave attempt to make up several yards leeway on his American counterpart. He got to within a yard or so after 200 metres but the effort took its toll and Britain eventually finished third in 3:17.4.

At the next Games in 1928, Leigh-Wood, Craner, Rinkel and Lowe produced a 4 × 400 metres time of 3:16.4 but this sufficed only for fifth. It was a pity that Lord Burghley, the 400 metres hurdles champion, was not selected; his presence might have pushed Britain up to third. In the sprint relay Gill, Smouha, Rangeley and London finished third in 41.8.

The thirties will always be remembered as the era of outstanding British quarter-mile relay runners. Brown and Roberts, second and fourth in the 1936 Olympic 400 metres, were in the highest world class individually but men like Rampling and Lord Burghley surpassed themselves when grasping a baton. This inspiring period can be said to have begun in Cologne in 1931, when England (as Great Britain was styled prior to 1933) scored desperately exciting victories in both the 4 × 400 metres and the 1,600 metres medley in the match against Germany. The hero each time was Rampling. In the 4 × 400 metres, following good work by Brangwin, Lord Burghley and Hanlon, Rampling took over just ahead of Metzner and succeeded in winning by two yards in 3:15.0. His leg was timed at 47.0. Later in the afternoon Rampling received the baton for the final 400 metres stint of the medley relay a good half-dozen yards behind Metzner. It seemed an impossible task, but the 22-year-old Englishman timed his effort to perfection to win on the post, having taken just 46.6 for his stage. This was four-tenths faster than the official world record though of course he was helped by a flying start. Although Germany won the match by 7½ events to 4½, further glory came England's way when Harris, Hedges, Cornes and Thomas slashed 15.8 seconds from the Finnish-held world record in the 4 × 1,500 metres with a time of 15:55.6.

The 1932 Olympic squad of Stoneley (48.8), Hampson (47.6), Lord Burghley (46.7) and Rampling (48.1) was inside the previous world record with a magnificent 3:11.2 in Los Angeles but even it was no match for the United States team who set what was then considered the simply sensational time of 3:08.2. Rampling had a similar experience to Butler in 1924: he set off a dozen yards behind the 400 metres champion and world record holder Carr and gallantly cut the deficit by half before paying the penalty for his suicidal pace. Two years later Rampling anchored the English 4 × 440 yards team to victory in 3:16.8 at the Empire Games but as Britain were non-participants in the first European Championships later in 1934 Germany won the 4 × 400 metres unpressed in 3:14.1.

Never mind, the greatest glory of all awaited Rampling and Co. at the 1936 Olympics. For some strange reason best known to the selectors, the 400 metres gold and bronze medallists Williams and LuValle were omitted from the USA foursome; yet even so the best 400 metres times of the American team added up to 3:07.2 as against Britain's 3:09.6. Theoretically, then, the USA ought to have won by around twenty yards . . . but fortunately athletic results are not based upon mathematical calculations. Bearing in mind the quality and fighting spirit of the last three runners Britain could win providing the weak link in the chain, Wolff (best time of only 48.6), could stay within reasonable distance of 46.5 performer Cagle on the first leg. Rampling (personal best of 47.5), Roberts (46.8) and Brown (46.7) could be relied upon to do the rest.

Wolff, drawn in the sixth and outside lane, did his difficult job well. True, he took 49.2 for his leg and handed over a good ten yards behind Canada but what mattered was that he finished merely four yards down on his American rival. The situation was tailor-made for Rampling and, with a time of 46.7, he swept Britain into a three yard lead over the USA. There was no stopping them now: Roberts (46.4) added another two yards and Brown (46.7) drew right away to snap the tape fifteen yards clear in a superb 3:09.0, second fastest time on record.

One week afterwards, at the White City, Roberts, Rampling and Brown joined forces with Canadian Fritz (fifth in the Olympic final) under the banner of the British Empire to defeat an all-star American team of Williams, Fitch, Hardin and LuValle by inches in 3:10.6. It was a world record for 4 × 440 yards but unacceptable as the team was a composite one. The race was a thriller all the way and decided only in the last few strides when Brown, who had taken over some yards behind LuValle, came through with one final irresistible burst. His time . . . 45.9! Brown, whose sister Audrey won a silver medal in the 4 × 100 metres relay in Berlin and whose brother Ralph was 440 yards hurdles bronze medallist at the 1934 Empire Games, contributed another heroic performance in the Britain v. Germany match at the White City in 1937. As the final event, the mile medley, came under starter's orders the scores were level at 66 points each. Roberts (440), Sweeney (220) and Pennington (220) laid the foundations for ultimate success and Brown completed the job by totally outpacing Harbig (destined shortly to become one of the all-time greats of athletics) over the last 880 yards stage.

After all this heady stuff the 1938 season proved a let-down. Barnes, Baldwin, Pennington and Brown clocked only 3:14.9 for second place at the European Championships, well beaten by the Harbig-anchored German team. A relatively better performance was the close third in 41.2 by the 4 × 100 metres squad of Scarr, Brown (again!), Sweeney and Page. Roberts, who had missed these championships, collected a European silver medal of his own in 1946 when he ran a storming anchor to finish only inches behind the victorious French team. The time for the team of Ede, Pugh, Elliott and Roberts was 3:14.5. Anchored again by Roberts, now 36, Britain improved to 3:14.2 at the Wembley Olympics but this was not quite fast enough to qualify for the final—though three of the teams that did get through in the other heats clocked 3:17 or slower. Second place in the final went to France . . . in 3:14.8! The 1948 Games, however, were by no means a write-off for thanks to some slick baton passing McCorquodale, Gregory, Ken Jones and Archer collected the silver medals seven yards behind the Americans in 41.3. Indeed, Britain were at first proclaimed winners of the 4 × 100 metres in view of an alleged takeover infringement by the Americans but study by the Olympic Jury of film of the pass in question proved everything was legal and the USA were named champions.

Britain's flagging 4 × 400 metres tradition was revived in 1950 when Pike (49.2), Lewis (47.2), Scott (47.6) and Pugh (46.2) carried off the European title in 3:10.2 but floundered again at the 1952 Olympics when a time of 3:10.0 was found to be good enough only for fifth place over 50 yards behind the great Jamaican and American teams. In the shorter event Britain placed a sound fourth in 40.6.

A feature of the floodlit international meetings which did so much to popularise athletics during the fifties was the world relay record attempts. Two major successes came about in 1951 and 1953.

Firstly, a 4×880 yards team of Nankeville (1:53.4), Webster (1:52.8), Evans (1:53.6) and Parlett (1:50.8) took nearly four seconds off the University of California's ten-year-old record with 7:30.6; secondly, Ralph Dunkley (3:53.4), Law (3:50.0), Pirie (3:50.2) and Nankeville (3:53.6) set 4×1,500 metres figures of 15:27.2. Another world record was achieved in the 4×1 mile event in 1953 by Chataway (4:11.8), Nankeville (4:06.6), Seaman (4:15.0) and Bannister (4:07.6). Their time of 16:41.0 existed until 1958 when Blagrove (4:05.4), Clark (4:06.6), Ibbotson (4:08.6) and Hewson (4:10.0) collaborated to produce 16:30.6.

Meanwhile, at the 1954 European Championships Britain, as represented by Peter Higgins (47.7), Dick (47.3), Fryer (47.0) and Johnson (46.2), had suffered the mortifying experience of finishing first (in a brilliant 3:08.2) only to be disqualified because of a collision between Fryer and a Hungarian runner. Many thought it an unjust decision against the team which, as England, had won the Commonwealth 4×440 yards title in 3:11.2 a few weeks earlier. In the 4×100 metres Box, Ellis, Ken Jones and Shenton placed second in 40.8. Two years later, at the Melbourne Olympics, there was a special satisfaction attached to Britain's third place in the 1,600 metres: the first European team to finish. Salisbury (47.6), Wheeler (46.8), Higgins (46.3) and Johnson (46.5) totalled 3:07.2 for a British record.

Both relay teams excelled themselves at the 1958 European Championships. Sampson (47.5), MacIsaac (47.9), Wrighton (46.2) and Salisbury (46.3) recorded a winning 3:07.9 while Radford, Sandstrom, Segal and Breacker were only just caught by Germany in the 4×100 metres and finished second in the same time (a UK record) of 40.2. Earlier, at the Commonwealth Games, the same sprint relay quartet had won in England's colours in 40.7 (4×110 yards) and Sampson (48.2), Johnson (47.5), Wrighton (47.5) and Salisbury (46.4) were second to South Africa in 3:09.6.

Radford, Dave Jones, Segal and Whitehead were, frankly, doubly lucky to receive bronze medals in the 1960 Olympic 4×100 metres. They actually finished fourth in 40.2 but were elevated to third after the USA had been disqualified; however, film indicates that the first changeover between Radford and Jones was made outside the permitted zone and thus Britain, too, ought to have been ruled out. The UK record of 40.1 was equalled in a heat. Another national record—3:07.0 for 4×400 metres—was set by

Yardley, Jackson, Wrighton and Brightwell at a minor meeting but in Rome, following a 3:07.5 heat, they could produce only 3:08.3 in fifth place.

The 1961 season, though, saw a talented collection of youthful quarter milers, all aged between 19 and 22, place Britain top of the world in the relay department. They kicked off with a 4 × 440 yards victory against the USA, no less, in the European record time of 3:07.0 . . . Futter 48.2, Jackson 47.3, Brightwell 46.2 and, in the best Rampling-Brown tradition, Metcalfe 45.3. Against Hungary there was a British 1,600 metres record of 3:05.8—Jackson 47.2, Yardley 46.8, Brightwell 46.0, Metcalfe 45.8. The next victims were West Germany and the UK 4 × 400 metres record tumbled to 3:04.9, with Jackson showing 46.2, Yardley 47.0, Brightwell 45.8 and Metcalfe 45.9. The season concluded with further metric victories against Poland (with Wilcock substituting for Yardley) in 3:09.3, the Russian Federal Republic in 3:06.4 and France in 3:06.8. A secondary highlight of the season was the European 4 × 1 mile record of 16:24.8 by a Northern Counties team of Taylor (4:10.0), Anderson (4:05.0), Simpson (4:05.0) and Hall (4:04.8).

Highest honours in 1962 and 1963 fell to the sprint formation. At the European Championships Jones (Dave), Jones (Ron), Jones (Berwyn) and Meakin twice clocked national record figures of 39.8 and placed third in the final, while later in 1962 England (Radford, Carter, Meakin, Dave Jones) retained the Commonwealth 440 yards title in 40.6. The metric record was trimmed to 39.7 in 1963 by Radford, Meakin, Dave Jones and Berwyn Jones but the highspot— and probably Britain's greatest sprint relay exploit since the 1912 Olympic victory—was the unforeseen win by Radford and the three Joneses (running second, third and fourth in the order Ron, Dave and Berwyn) against the USA national team anchored by none other than the world's fastest human, Hayes. As if that were not enough, the time of 40.0 equalled the world record for 4 × 110 yards around two turns!

Returning to the one-lap specialists, Jackson (47.5), Wilcock (47.0), Metcalfe (46.6) and Brightwell (44.8!) were very narrowly beaten by Germany in the European Championships (3:05.8 to 3:05.9) after an unfunny comedy of errors but in 1963 the best time slumped to 3:06.6. By 1964, though, a glorious new 4 × 400 metres team had taken shape. The line-up of Graham, Cooper, Metcalfe and Brightwell made a promising debut in beating Finland by eighty yards in 3:08.6 and eleven days later 'brought the house down' at the White City by narrowly defeating a starry USA/Jamaica team in a UK record-tying 3:04.9. Graham handed over just ahead of Hardin (son of the great hurdler) in 47.0; Metcalfe (47.3), struggling to regain form, was passed by Kerr but fought back to finish only a short way behind; Cooper, a hurdler whose best official 440 yards time is 47.9, clung like a leech to Larrabee, the Olympic champion-to-be, and was timed in an absolutely staggering 45.9; and Brightwell judged his effort beautifully to shoot past Cassell a dozen yards from the tape. His stage: 44.7.

And so to Tokyo for the Olympics. Three-quarters of the team had shown great form in the individual events: Brightwell had equalled the UK record of 45.7 in the 400 metres, Graham had exceeded everyone's wildest hopes in finishing sixth in 46.0 and Cooper had taken the 400 metres hurdles silver medal in national record time. The big question mark hovered over Metcalfe, who had not even reached the semi-finals of the 400 metres. The team's best individual times added up to 3:04.9 but the calibre of the opposition can be judged by the fact that the USA foursome's best times totalled an amazing 3:00.9, Trinidad's 3:03.7, Germany's 3:05.4 and Jamaica's 3:05.6.

The USA won the first heat in 3:05.3, Trinidad the second in 3:05.0 and Britain the third in a UK record of 3:04.7, followed by Germany (3:04.9) and Jamaica (3:05.3). The 'splits' were Graham 46.7, Metcalfe 46.5, Cooper 45.8 and Brightwell 45.7. Clearly an epic final was in prospect, and so it proved. Graham, in the outside lane, again surpassed himself by running the opening leg in 45.9, a yard ahead of the USA (Cassell) and Trinidad (Skinner). Metcalfe, showing a timely return to form, went hell for leather and built up a lead of five yards over Larrabee. The newly crowned Olympic champion surged past at the beginning of the finishing straight but Metcalfe, operating at 45.5 pace, handed over in third place five yards behind the USA but only two behind Trinidad and one ahead of Jamaica. On the third stage Cooper ran himself out with a magnificent 45.4, yet such was the strident tempo of the race that he actually conceded a place to Jamaica. Here is how I described that fantastic last lap for *Athletics Weekly*. . . .

'At the final changeover the position was USA first by about five yards, from Trinidad and Jamaica, with Britain fourth just behind. As Britain was drawn on the outside, some ground was lost to begin with, and Robbie Brightwell set out two or three yards behind the West Indians, Wendell Mottley (Trinidad) and George Kerr (Jamaica), and some seven yards in arrears of Henry Carr. Excitement ran high as Mottley, covering the opening furlong at a furious pace, drew up to Carr's shoulder by the halfway mark. At that point, the 200 metres champion decided that like Garbo he wanted to be alone and proceeded to draw cleanly away. Entering the final straight, Carr was out of any possible danger and looking good, but Mottley and Kerr were beginning to buckle. Now was Brightwell's chance . . . and he took it. Striding out to text-book perfection— chest held high, knees well up, arms working powerfully—Robbie edged up on his two adversaries. He caught Kerr sixty yards from the tape, the exhausted Jamaican leaning out towards Robbie as he went by, and took Mottley just five yards from the line in as stirring a finish as one can remember. The crowd rose to Robbie in admiration for one of the guttiest performances of the Games. From fourth to second in fifty yards—the British fighting spirit, so much in evidence in Tokyo, had won through again. How Robbie and his men deserved their silver medals . . . they had run 3:01.6 (45.4 average) for them! The times for that final, pulsating leg: Carr 44.7, Brightwell 44.8, Mottley 45.1.'

The final result was: 1, USA 3:00.7 (world record); 2, Britain 3:01.6 (European record); 3, Trinidad 3:01.7; 4, Jamaica 3:02.3; 5, Germany 3:04.3; 6, Poland 3:05.3. The first three teams in this never to be forgotten race broke the previous world record. On a much more modest level a truly British 4 × 100 metres team excelled too, with Radford (English), Ron Jones (Welsh), Campbell (Scottish) and Davies (Welsh) setting a UK record of 39.6 for eighth and last place in the final.

The only medals gained in 1966 were Commonwealth bronze awards by a reconstructed English 4 × 440 yards team of Winbolt Lewis (47.6), Adey (46.3), Warden (47.1) and Graham (45.5) who clocked a European record of 3:06.5. But at the European Championships, despite another fine anchor by Graham (45.4), only fifth place was obtained. On the sprint front, Wales finished a highly creditable fourth in Kingston in 40.2, three places ahead of England; and the British team were fifth in Budapest in 40.1. The year was notable, though, for a superb 4 × 880 yards race at the Crystal Palace, won in the world record shattering time of 7:14.6 by a British team of Grant (1:49.5), Varah (1:48.9), Carter (1:48.0) and

Boulter (1:48.2). Unfortunately the runners did not receive official credit for their grand work as the record was disallowed on the grounds that Boulter received assistance, an infringement of IAAF Rule 142, Paragraph 11. What happened was that National Coach John Le Masurier called out Boulter's first lap time as 52 seconds although in fact it was an almost suicidal 49.8. Consequently, the world record plaques went instead to the defeated Soviet Union team (7:16.0), an extraordinary state of affairs.

Solid if unspectacular performances were registered by both relay teams in 1967. The sprinters clocked 39.8 for 4 × 100 metres and defeated Hungary, Poland and West Germany; the quarter-milers recorded 3:06.2 for 4 × 400 metres and provided glimpses of another vintage team in the offing.

14

A CENTURY OF LANDMARKS

In this chapter are listed year by year since 1866, the most significant happenings in British men's athletics history, including details of all the world records or best performances at standard events; Olympic, European and Commonwealth Games gold medals achieved by athletes from the United Kingdom; and results of all full international matches.

1866: The Amateur Athletic Club was formed, and on March 23rd at the grounds of Beaufort House, London, promoted the first 'English Championships' which were, however, restricted to 'gentlemen amateurs' drawn from the Services and professional classes. The winners were—100 yards: T. M. Colmore 10.5; 440 yards: J. H. Ridley 55.0; 880 yards: P. M. Thornton 2:05.0; Mile: C. B. Lawes 4:39.0; 4 miles: R. C. Garnett 21:41.0; 120 yards hurdles: T. Milvain 17.8; high jump: T. G. Little and J. H. T. Roupell 5 feet 9 inches; pole vault: J. Wheeler 10 feet 0 inch; long jump: R. Fitzherbert 19 feet 8 inches; shot (18 pounds 10 ounces by error): C. Fraser 34 feet 6 inches; hammer: W. J. James 78 feet 5 inches; 7 miles walk: J. G. Chambers 59:32.0. During the year world records were set by W. Collett (23.0 220 yards turn) and in the high jump as above.

1867: The first cross-country race, other than at public schools, was organised by the Thames Rowing Club over a 2¼ mile course at Wimbledon Common. World records set by E. J. Colbeck (22.8 220 yards turn), F. Pelham (2:02.5 880 yards), W. K. Gair (2:01.0 880 yards), R. L. N. Michell (9:59.0 2 miles), J. Morgan (15:38.0 3 miles), T. G. Little (5 feet 9 inches high jump, equals record) and J. Stone (37 feet 7 inches shot).

1868: World records set by C. A. Absalom (10.0 100 yards), W. M. Tennent (10.0 100 yards, equals record), E. J. Colbeck (50.4 440 yards), W. M. Chinnery (4:29.6 mile), W. Gibbs (4:28.8 mile), J. Morgan (15:20.3 3 miles), A. C. Tosswill (21 feet 4 inches long jump) and J. Stone (37 feet 11 inches shot).

1869: World records set by A. C. Tosswill (22 feet 2 inches long jump), R. Waltham (38 feet 0 inch shot) and W. Trehair (38 feet 6 inches shot).

1870: World records set by J. G. Wilson (10.0 100 yards, equals record), W. Bullock (38 feet 9 inches shot) and T. Griffiths (2:47:52 20 miles walk).

1871: World records set by J. Scott (9:54.0 2 miles and 15:08.6 3 miles), R. J. C. Mitchell (5 feet 9½ inches high jump) and D. Lundie (41 feet 0 inch shot).

1872: World records set by W. A. Dawson (10.0 100 yards, equals record), G. A. Templer and T. Christie (2:01.0 880 yards, equals record), E. J. Davies (22 feet 7 inches long jump) and E. J. Bor (42 feet 5 inches shot).

1873: World records set by G. H. Urmson (10.0 100 yards, equals record), J. H. A. Reay (22.8 220 yards turn, equals record), A. Pelham (1:59.8 880 yards), W. E. Fuller (34:42.0 6 miles and 58:58.4 10 miles) and T. Davin of Ireland (5 feet 10¼ inches high jump).

1874: World records set by E. J. Davies (10.0 100 yards, equals record, and 22 feet 10½ inches long jump), W. Slade (4:26.0 mile), J. Warburton (9:51.0 2 miles), M. J. Brooks (5 feet 11 inches high jump) and J. G. Lane of Ireland (23 feet 1½ inches long jump).

1875: World records set by W. Slade (4:24.5 mile and 9:50.0 2 miles), J. Warburton (9:51.0 2 miles), T. Duckett (9:46.5 2 miles), W. E. Fuller (33:58.0 6 miles and 56:07.0 10 miles) and M. G. Glazebrook (5 feet 11 inches high jump, equals record).

1876: The first English cross-country championship was held in Epping Forest but all thirty-two runners went off course and the race was declared void. A team from London Athletic Club won a match in Ireland (billed as England v. Ireland), the first recorded instance of international match. World records set by B. R. Martin of Ireland (10.0 100 yards, equals record), F. T. Elborough (22.6 220 yards turn and 1:57.5 880 yards), W. Slade (1:58.2 880 yards and 9:42.0 2 miles) and M. J. Brooks (6 feet 2½ inches high jump).

1877: P. H. Stenning became the inaugural English cross-country champion over an 11¾ miles course at Roehampton; there were thirty-three starters. World records set by J. Shearman (50.4 440 yards, equals record), J. Gibb (14:46.0 3 miles, 32:07.0 6 miles and 54:49.0 10 miles) and G. H. Hales (110 feet 0 inch hammer).

1878: World records set by W. P. Phillips (10.0 100 yards, equals record, and 22.0. 220 yards straight) and S. Palmer (16.0 120 yards hurdles, equals record).

1879: Growing dissatisfaction with the AAC culminated in members of the powerful London Athletic Club boycotting the AAC Championships and holding their own so-called national championships later in the season. World records set by J. Warburton (31:12.5 6 miles and 54:06.5 10 miles).

1880: The AAC died when a meeting was held at Oxford on April 24th to discuss the future of the English Championships. The outcome was the Amateur Athletic Association, an amateur definition ('Any person who has never competed for money with or against a professional for any prize, and who has never taught, pursued, or assisted in the practice of athletic exercises as a means of obtaining a livelihood'), and an agreement that the English Championships (to be known as the AAA Championships) be thrown open to all amateurs and be held in the summer instead of spring as previously. The inaugural AAA Championships attracted eighty entries and were held at the Lillie Bridge Grounds in London on July 3rd. The meeting cost £91 16s. 2d. to stage and made a loss of £31 2s. 2d. The winners were—100 yards: W. P. Phillips 10.2; 440 yards: M. Shearman 52.2; 880 yards: S. K. Holman 2:00.4; mile and 4 miles: W. G. George 4:28.6 and 20:45.8; 10 miles: C. H. Mason 56:07.0; steeplechase: J. Concannon; 120 yards hurdles: G. P. C. Lawrence 16.4; high jump: J. W. Parsons 5 feet 9¾ inches; pole vault: E. A. Strachan 10 feet 4 inches; long jump: C. L. Lockton 22 feet 2 inches; shot: W. Y. Winthrop 37 feet 3 inches; hammer: W. Lawrence 96 feet 0 inch; 7 miles walk: G. P. Beckley 56:40. World records set by W. G. George (4:23.2 mile) and P. Davin of Ireland (6 feet 2¾ inches high jump).

1881: The second AAA Championships made a profit of £325, the event attracting over 10,000 spectators to Birmingham's Aston Lower Grounds. World records set by W. Snook (9:33.4 2 miles), W. G. George (14:42.8 3 miles) and G. A. Dunning (1:24:24 15 miles).

1882: World records set by W. G. George (4:19.4 mile, 9:25.6 2 miles, 30:49.0 6 miles and 52:56.5 10 miles).

1883: The English Cross-Country Union was founded. World records set by W. G. George (52:53.0 10 miles) and P. Davin (23 feet 2 inches long jump).

1884: World records set by J. M. Cowie (10.0 100 yards, equals record), W. G. George (4:18.4 mile, 9:17.4 2 miles, 14:39.0 3 miles, 30:21.5 6 miles, 51:20 10 miles and 11 miles 932 yards in one hour), J. Maxwell of Ireland (43 feet 5 inches shot) and O. Harte of Ireland (114 feet 2 inches hammer).

1885: World records set by J. M. Cowie (22.2 220 yards turn), J. O'Brien of Ireland (44 feet 10½ inches shot) and W. J. M. Barry of Ireland (116 feet 10 inches hammer).

1886: World records set by A. Wharton of Jamaica (10.0 100 yards, equals record), C. G. Wood (22.2 220 yards turn, equals record), C. F. Daft (16.0 120 yards hurdles, equals record), S. Morris (59.0 440 yards hurdles), J. Purcell of Ireland (23 feet 3 inches long jump), D. Shanahan of Ireland (47 feet 7 inches triple jump) and W. J. M. Barry (119 feet 0 inch hammer).

1887: World records set by C. G. Wood (21.6 220 yards straight) and J. Purcell (48 feet 3 inches triple jump).

1888: World records set by F. J. K. Cross (1:54.4 880 yards), J. J. Mooney of Ireland (25.0 220 yards hurdles) and W. J. M. Barry (129 feet 3¼ inches hammer).

1889: World records set by H. C. L. Tindall (48.5 440 yards) and J. Kibblewhite (14:29.6 3 miles).

1890: World records set by W. H. Morton (1:23:49.6 15 miles and 1:47:01.2 30,000 metres).

1891: World record set by G. B. Shaw (57.2 440 yards hurdles).

1892: World records set by S. Thomas (30:17.8 6 miles and 1:22:15.4 15 miles) and D. D. Bulger of Ireland (15.8 120 yards hurdles, equals record).

1893: World records set by S. Thomas (14:24.0 3 miles) and C. B. Fry (23 feet 6½ inches long jump, equals record).

1894: The first international team match in England was held between Oxford and Yale Universities. World records set by G. Crossland (1:46:00 30,000 metres) and J. J. Mooney (23 feet 8 inches long jump).

1895: The first relay race was staged in Britain. World records set by C. A. Bradley and A. Downer (9.8 100 yards, equals record), E. C. Bredin (48.5 440 yards, equals record), F. E. Bacon (4:17.0 mile), J. M. Ryan of Ireland (6 feet 4½ inches high jump) and J. J. Flanagan of Ireland (145 feet 10½ inches).

1896: After an interval of fifteen centuries the Olympic Games were revived in Athens. A few British athletes competed at their own expense but so poorly publicised were the Games that C. B.

Fry, who had equalled the world long jump record at Oxford three years earlier, was not even aware of their existence.

1897: World record set by D. Horgan of Ireland (48 feet 2 inches shot).

1898: The first international cross-country race, between France and England at Ville d'Avray, resulted in a clean sweep by England: all eight members of the team finishing before the first Frenchman. World record set by W. J. M. Newburn of Ireland (24 feet 0½ inch long jump).

1899: World record set by T. F. Kiely of Ireland (162 feet 0 inch hammer).

1900: Olympic winners in Paris: A. E. Tysoe (2:01.2 800 metres and 5,000 metres team race), C. Bennett (4:06.2 1,500 metres and 5,000 metres team race), J. T. Rimmer (12:58.4 4,000 metres steeplechase and 5,000 metres team race), S. J. Robinson (5,000 metres team race) and S. Rowley of Australia (5,000 metres team race). World records set by Bennett (4:06.2 1,500 metres and 15:20.0 5,000 metres) and P. J. O'Connor of Ireland (24 feet 7¾ inches long jump).

1901: World record set by P. J. O'Connor (24 feet 11¾ inches long jump).

1902: World records set by F. Appleby (1:06:42.2 20,000 metres and 1:20:04.4 15 miles).

1903: The inaugural International Cross-Country Championship was held on Hamilton Park Racecourse in Scotland; England, Scotland, Wales and Ireland were represented and A. Shrubb led England to victory. World records set by Shrubb (9:11.0 2 miles and 14:17.6 3 miles).

1904: No official British representation at St Louis Olympics but T. F. Kiely of Ireland won a gold medal in the 'all-round' event. World records set by A. Shrubb (9:09.6 2 miles, 14:17.2 3 miles, 29:59.4 6 miles, 31:02.4 10,000 metres, 50:40.6 10 miles and 11 miles 1,137 yards in one hour), D. Horgan (48 feet 10 inches shot) and G. E. Larner (13:11.4 2 miles walk). England retained International Cross-Country Championship.

1905: World records set by G. E. Larner (50:50.8 7 miles walk and 8 miles 438 yards in one hour). England retained International Cross-Country Championship.

1906: Winners at the unofficial Olympics in Athens: H. Hawtrey (26:26.2 5 miles) and C. Leahy of Ireland (5 feet 9 inches high jump). England retained International Cross-Country Championship.

1907: The AAA Championships were held away from London for the last time. The Road Walking Association (later the Race Walking Association) was founded. England retained International Cross-Country Championship.

1908: The Olympics were held at the White City Stadium, London, and for the first time constituted a truly international sports festival. A crowd estimated at 70,000 packed the stadium to watch the finish of the marathon. Winners: W. Halswelle (50.0 400 metres), J. E. Deakin, A. J. Robertson and W. Coales (3 miles team race), E. R. Voigt (25:11.2 5 miles), A. Russell (10:47.8 3,200 metres steeplechase), T. J. Ahearne of Ireland (48 feet 11¼ inches triple jump) and G. E. Larner (14:55.0 3,500 metres walk and 1:15:57.4 10 miles walk). World records set by H. A. Wilson (3:59.8 1,500 metres), Robertson (15:01.2 5,000 metres), Ahearne (as above) and Larner (10 miles walk as above). England retained International Cross-Country Championship.

1909: England retained International Cross-Country Championship.

1910: World record set by G. R. L. Anderson (56.8 440 yards hurdles). England retained International Cross-Country Championship.

1911: World record set by H. V. L. Ross (15 miles 128 yards two hours walk). England retained International Cross-country Championship.

1912: Olympic winners in Stockholm: A. N. Strode-Jackson (3:56.8 1,500 metres) and D. Jacobs, H. M. Macintosh, V. H. A. d'Arcy and W. R. Applegarth (42.4 4 × 100 metres). World record set by Applegarth (21.8 220 yards turn, equals record). England retained International Cross-Country Championship.

1913: World record set by W. R. Applegarth (21.6 220 yards turn). England retained International Cross-Country Championship.

1914: World record set by W. R. Applegarth (21.2 220 yards turn). England retained International Cross-Country Championship.

1920: Olympic winners in Antwerp: A. G. Hill (1:53.4 800 metres and 4:01.8 1,500 metres), P. Hodge (10:00.4 3,000 metres steeplechase) and C. R. Griffiths, R. A. Lindsay, J. C. Ainsworth-Davis and G. M. Butler (3:22.2 4 × 400 metres). World record set by Oxford and Cambridge team of W. G. Tatham, H. B. Stallard, W.

Milligan and B. G. D'U. Rudd (7:50.4 4 × 880 yards). England retained International Cross-Country Championship.

1921: The first international match between England (prior to 1933 all British teams were styled as 'England') and France was staged in Paris; Britain won 123–118. Following the signing on December 6th of the treaty that set up the Irish Free State, southern Irishmen became ineligible for British teams and records. England retained International Cross-Country Championship.

1922: The first full international match at home was held at Stamford Bridge, London; Britain beat France 57–42. England lost International Cross-Country Championship after nineteen years to France.

1923: English Championships, open only to athletes of English birth or parentage, were held at Northampton but the AAA discontinued them after 1925. Britain beat France 69–42. The number of starters in the English Cross-Country Championship exceeded 300 for the first time.

1924: Olympic winners in Paris: H. M. Abrahams (10.6 100 metres), E. H. Liddell (47.6 400 metres) and D. G. A. Lowe (1:52.4 800 metres). World record set by Abrahams, W. Rangeley, L. C. Royle and W. P. Nichol (42.0 4 × 100 metres). England regained International Cross-Country Championship.

1925: The Schools Athletic Association was founded. Britain lost to France 53–58. England retained International Cross-Country Championship.

1926: Britain beat France 63–48.

1927: World record set by Lord Burghley (54.2 440 yards hurdles). Britain beat France 66–45. Over 400 starters in English Cross-Country Championship for the first time.

1928: Olympic winners in Amsterdam: D. G. A. Lowe (1:51.8 800 metres) and Lord Burghley (53.4 400 metres hurdles).

1929: World record set by E. Harper (1:23:45.8 25,000 metres). Britain lost to France 58–62 and Germany 4–8 (events).

1930: Winners at the first British Empire Games in Hamilton: S. E. Englehart (21.8 220 yards), T. Hampson (1:52.4 880 yards), R. H. Thomas (4:14.0 mile), S. A. Tomlin (14:27.4 3 miles), D. McL. Wright (2:43:43 marathon), G. W. Bailey (9:52.0 steeplechase), Lord Burghley (14.6 120 yards and 54.4 440 yards hurdles), M. C. Nokes (154 feet 7½ inches hammer), and English team of Lord Burghley, K. C. Brangwin, R. Leigh-Wood and H. S. Townend

(3:19.4 4 × 440 yards). Britain lost to France 55–65. England regained International Cross-Country Championship.

1931: The inaugural AAA Junior Championships were held. World record set by English team of A. A. Harris, H. W. Hedges, J. F. Cornes and R. H. Thomas (15:55.6 4 × 1,500 metres). Britain beat France 67–53 and Italy 83½–62½, lost to Germany 4½–7½. England retained International Cross-Country Championship.

1932: The British Amateur Athletic Board was formed and replaced the AAA as Britain's representative on the International Amateur Athletic Federation. The AAA Championships were held at the White City for the first time. Olympic winners in Los Angeles: T. Hampson (1:49.7 800 metres) and T. W. Green (4:50:10 50 kilometres walk). World records set by Hampson (as above), A. H. G. Pope (44:42.4 10,000 metres walk, 50:28.8 7 miles and 8 miles 474 yards in one hour), and A. E. Plumb (2:43:38 20 miles walk). England retained International Cross-Country Championship.

1933: Britain beat France 65¼–54¾, lost to Germany 59–75 and Italy 62–85. England retained International Cross-Country Championship.

1934: Winners at the Empire Games in London: A. W. Sweeney (10.0 100 yards and 21.9 220 yards), G. L. Rampling (48.0 440 yards), W. J. Beavers (14:32.6 3 miles), A. W. Penny (31:00.6 6 miles), S. C. Scarsbrook (10:23.4 steeplechase), D. O. Finlay (15.2 120 yards hurdles), F. A. R. Hunter (55.2 440 yards hurdles), M. C. Nokes (158 feet 3½ inches hammer), and English teams of E. I. Davis, W. Rangeley, G. T. Saunders and Sweeney (42.2 4 × 110 yards) and D. L. Rathbone, C. H. Stoneley, G. N. Blake and Rampling (3:16.8 4 × 440 yards). World record set by F. J. Redman (1:14:30.6 10 miles walk). Britain beat France 66½–53½. England retained International Cross-Country Championship.

1935: AAA inaugurated indoor championships at Wembley. World records set by A. A. Cooper (12:38.2 3,000 metres walk and 21:52.4 5,000 metres), and H. H. Whitlock (4:29:31.8 30 miles walk). Britain beat France 64–56, lost to Finland 70–78 and Germany 61–75. England retained International Cross-Country Championship.

1936: Olympic winners in Berlin: H. H. Whitlock (4:30:41.4 50 kilometres walk) and F. F. Wolff, G. L. Rampling, W. Roberts and A. G. K. Brown (3:09.0 4 × 400 metres). England retained International Cross-Country Championship.

1937: World record set by S. C. Wooderson (4:06.4 mile). Britain beat France 66–54 and Germany 69–67, lost to Finland 67–82 and Norway 65–74. England retained International Cross-Country Championship.

1938: Empire Games winners in Sydney: C. B. Holmes (9.7 100 yards and 21.2 220 yards), W. Roberts (47.9 440 yards) and J. W. Ll. Alford (4:11.6 mile). European Championship winners in Paris: A. G. K. Brown (47.4 400 metres), S. C. Wooderson (3:53.6 1,500 metres), D. O. Finlay (14.3 110 metres hurdles) and H. H. Whitlock (4:41:51 50 kilometres walk). World records set by Wooderson (1:48.4 800 metres and 1:49.2 880 yards). Britain beat Norway 72–67 and France 70–50. England retained International Cross-Country Championship.

1939: Britain lost to Germany $42\frac{1}{2}$–$93\frac{1}{2}$.

1945: Britain lost to France 29–73.

1946: European champions in Oslo: J. Archer (10.6 100 metres) and S. C. Wooderson (14:08.6 5,000 metres). The AAA Coaching Scheme came into existence. Britain beat France 72–57.

1947: G. H. G. Dyson appointed by AAA as England's first national coach. Britain lost to France 56–73.

1948: No British winners at Olympic Games held at Wembley, where crowds of up to 85,000 watched the athletics events. World record set by H. G. Churcher (35:43.4 5 miles walk).

1949: World record set by H. G. Churcher (35:33.0 5 miles walk). Britain beat France 82–65.

1950: Empire champions in Auckland: H. J. Parlett (1:53.1 880 yards), L. Eyre (14:23.6 3 miles), J. T. Holden (2:32:57 marathon), T. D. Anderson (13 feet 0 inch pole vault) and D. McD. M. Clark (163 feet $10\frac{1}{4}$ inches hammer). European champions in Brussels: B. Shenton (21.5 200 metres), D. C. Pugh (47.3 400 metres), H. J. Parlett (1:50.5 800 metres), J. T. Holden (2:32:13.2 marathon), A. S. Paterson (6 feet $5\frac{1}{8}$ inches high jump) and M. W. Pike, L. C. Lewis, A. W. Scott and Pugh (3:10.2 4 × 400 metres). Britain beat France 106–99.

1951: World records set by E. McD. Bailey (10.2 100 metres, equals record), R. G. Hardy (35:24.0 5 miles walk) and G. W. Nankeville, A. Webster, F. Evans and H. J. Parlett (7:30.6 4 × 880 yards). Britain beat France 115–89, Yugoslavia $102\frac{1}{2}$–$89\frac{1}{2}$, Greece 96–84 and Turkey 103–75. England regained International Cross-Country Championship.

1952: World records set by J. H. Peters (2:20:42.2 marathon) and R. G. Hardy (35:15.0 5 miles walk). Britain beat France 120–85.

1953: World records set by D. A. G. Pirie (28:19.4 6 miles), J. H. Peters (2:18:34.8 marathon), R. H. Dunkley, D. C. Law, Pirie and G. W. Nankeville (15:27.2 4 × 1,500 metres) and C. J. Chataway, Nankeville, D. C. Seaman and R. G. Bannister (16:41.0 4 × 1 mile). Britain beat France 127–79, lost to West Germany 94–112 and Sweden 103–109. England regained International Cross-Country Championship.

1954: Commonwealth champions in Vancouver: D. J. N. Johnson (1:50.7 880 yards), R. G. Bannister (3:58.8 mile), C. J. Chataway (13:35.2 3 miles), P. B. Driver (28:09.4 6 miles), J. McGhee (2:39:36 marathon), G. M. Elliott (14 feet 0 inch pole vault), K. S. D. Wilmshurst (24 feet 8¾ inches long jump and 50 feet 1½ inches triple jump), J. A. Savidge (55 feet 0¼ inch shot) and English team of F. P. Higgins, A. Dick, P. G. Fryer and Johnson (3:11.2 4 × 440 yards). European champion in Berne: Bannister (3:43.8 1,500 metres). World records set by Bannister (3:59.4 mile), F. Green and Chataway (13:32.2 3 miles), Chataway (13:51.6 5,000 metres) and J. H. Peters (2:17:39.4 marathon). England retained International Cross-Country Championship.

1955: World record set by C. J. Chataway (13:23.2 3 miles). Britain beat West Germany 111–95, France 128–85 and Czechoslovakia 117–95, lost to Hungary 93½–116½ and USSR 93–137. Over 500 starters in English Cross-Country Championship for the first time. England retained International Cross-Country Championship.

1956: Olympic winner in Melbourne: C. W. Brasher (8:41.2 3,000 metres steeplechase). World records set by D. A. G. Pirie (7:52.8 3,000 metres and 13:36.8 5,000 metres). Britain beat Czechoslovakia 119–93, lost to Hungary 104–108.

1957: World record set by G. D. Ibbotson (3:57.2 mile). Britain beat France 118–94, lost to USSR 93–119, Poland 101–111 and West Germany 92½–119½. Over 700 starters in English Cross-Country Championship for the first time.

1958: Commonwealth champions in Cardiff: G. M. Elliott (13 feet 8 inches pole vault), A. Rowe (57 feet 8 inches shot), M. J. Ellis (206 feet 4½ inches hammer), C. G. Smith (233 feet 10½ inches javelin) and English team of P. F. Radford, D. H. Segal, E. R. Sandstrom and A. Breacker (40.7 4 × 110 yards). European champions in Stockholm: J. D. Wrighton (46.3 400 metres), M. A. Rawson (1:47.8 800 metres), B. S. Hewson (3:41.9 1,500 metres), A. Rowe (58 feet 4 inches shot), S. F. Vickers (1:33:09 20 kilometres walk) and E. J. Sampson, J. MacIsaac, Wrighton and J. E. Salisbury (3:07.9 4 × 400 metres). World record by English team of M. T. Blagrove, P. R. Clark, G. D. Ibbotson and Hewson (16:30.6 4 × 1 mile). Britain beat France 124–88, lost to Commonwealth 162–199. England regained International Cross-Country Championship.

1959: Britain beat Finland 126–104, lost to West Germany 95–117, Poland 99–106 and USSR 95–129. England retained International Cross-Country Championship.

1960: Olympic winner in Rome: D. J. Thompson (4:25:30 50 kilometres walk). World record by P. F. Radford (20.5 220 yards turn). Britain beat France 116½–95½. England retained International Cross-Country Championship.

1961: World record by B. B. Heatley (47:47.0 10 miles). Britain beat Hungary 110–102, lost to USA 88–122, West Germany 98–113, Poland 105–106 and France 99–113. Britain won inaugural Lugano Trophy walking competition.

1962: European champions in Belgrade: R. I. Brightwell (45.9 400 metres), M. B. S. Tulloh (14:00.6 5,000 metres), B. Kilby (2:23:18.8 marathon) and K. J. Matthews (1:35:54.8 20 kilometres walk). Commonwealth champions in Perth: Kilby (2:21:17 marathon), M. T. Lucking (59 feet 4 inches shot), A. H. Payne (202 feet 3 inches hammer) and English team of P. F. Radford, L. W. Carter, A. Meakin and D. H. Jones (40.6 4 × 110 yards). AAA Indoor Championships were revived at Wembley after 23 years. Britain beat West Germany 69–56½ (indoors), lost to Poland 104–108. England regained International Cross-Country Championship.

1963: World record set by P. F. Radford, R. Jones, D. H. Jones and T. B. Jones (40.0 4 × 110 yards, two turns). Britain beat Sweden 126–86, Russian Federal Republic 112–99 and Hungary 106½–105½, lost to West Germany 58–92 (indoors), USA 91–120 and West Germany (101–109). Britain retained Lugano Trophy. Over 800 starters in English Cross-Country Championship for first time.

1964: Olympic winners in Tokyo: L. Davies (26 feet 5¾ inches long jump) and K. J. Matthews (1:29:34 20 kilometres walk). World records set by M. R. Batty (47:26.8 10 miles), J. N. C. Alder (1:34:01.8 30,000 metres) and B. B. Heatley (2:13:55 marathon). Britain beat Finland 59–47 (indoors), Finland 129–83 and France

110–102, drew with Poland 106–106. England regained International Cross-Country Championship.

1965: World records set by R. Hill (1:12:48.2 15 miles and 1:15:22.6 25,000 metres) and T. F. K. Johnston (1:32:34.6 30,000 metres). Britain finished sixth in inaugural European Cup competition. Britain beat Finland 64–42 (indoors) and Hungary 114–96, lost to USA 47–70 (indoors), Poland 93–118 and West Germany 91–121. Over 900 starters in English Cross-Country Championship for first time. England retained International Cross-Country Championship.

1966: Commonwealth champions in Kingston: J. N. C. Alder (2:22:07.8 marathon), D. P. Hemery (14.1 120 yards hurdles), L. Davies (26 feet 2¾ inches long jump), A. H. Payne (203 feet 4 inches hammer), J. H. P. FitzSimons (261 feet 9 inches javelin) and R. Wallwork (2:44:42.8 20 miles walk). European champions in Budapest: J. J. Hogan (2:20:04.6 marathon) and L. Davies (26 feet 2¼ inches long jump). World records set by Hogan (1:32:25.4 30,000 metres) and—unofficially—G. D. Grant, G. P. M. Varah, C. S. Carter and J. P. Boulter (7:14.6 4 × 880 yards). Britain beat Finland 122–90, lost to USSR 87–134, Sweden 100–112 and France 98–113. England retained International Cross-Country Championship.

1967: Britain eliminated in semi-finals of European Cup. Britain beat Hungary 113–99 and France (2nd, 3rd and 4th strings) 210–198, lost to France 57–71 (indoors), Poland 99–113, USA 84–139 and West Germany 90–121. Full-scale junior matches inaugurated; Britain beat France 200½–187½ and Sweden 225–163. England retained International Cross-Country Championship.

1968: Britain lost to West Germany 67–78 (indoors). England retained International Cross-Country Championship. J. Whetton won the 1,500 metres at the European Indoor Games for the third consecutive year.

15

WOMEN'S ATHLETICS

ATHLETICS for women dates back to the days of Ancient
Greece, for although prohibited on pain of death from even watching the Olympic Games women held their own four-yearly Heraea
Games, named after Hera, wife of Zeus. The events included foot
races of about 165 yards. Women participated in the sports meetings held at English fairs and wakes in the eighteenth and early
nineteenth centuries but it was not until after the First World War
that women's athletics began to be organised on a national basis.
One of the first recorded performances is a 58.8 4 × 110 yards relay
time by the Women's Royal Air Force at Stamford Bridge on
September 9th 1918; while in 1919 Elaine Burton (later an M.P.
and now Baroness Burton of Coventry) won what was styled the
Northern Counties 100 yards championship in exactly 13 seconds.

March 10th 1921 was a historic date, for the first women's international meeting was held then at Monte Carlo. Five countries were
represented and the team of seven British athletes accounted for
six of the ten events. Team captain Mary Lines, aged 27 and in her
first year of competition, dominated the proceedings as she won the
60 metres in 8.2, the 250 metres in 36.6 and the long jump with
15 feet 5 inches, and assisted in two relay victories. The other
British success was provided by Hilda Hatt (17), who high jumped
4 feet 7 inches. Later in the year an unofficial match was staged
between France and Britain in Paris, with the visitors winning
53–40. Again Mary Lines was the star, winning the 100 yards in
11.6 and 300 metres in 43.8—both world bests. Next day the
Fédération Sportive Féminine Internationale was formed to govern
this quickly developing side of the sport. Co-founders with Britain
and France were Czechoslovakia, Italy, Spain and the United
States.

With women's athletics now established internationally it was
time for Britain to put her own affairs in order. The Amateur
Athletic Association's General Committee decided in 1922 that it

would be advisable for women's athletics to be governed by a separate body. In other words, it wanted no part of an activity that many members deemed unfeminine. Consequently the Women's AAA was founded and at about the same time the first exclusively women's club in Britain, London Olympiades, came into existence.

The highlight of the 1922 season was the 'Women's Olympic Games', later known as the first World Games following objections by the International Olympic Committee and the International Amateur Athletic Federation to the use of the word Olympic. The meeting, held in Paris, was organised as a gesture of defiance after the FSFI's demand for women's events to be added to the 1924 Olympic programme was rejected by the IOC. Five nations participated and British victories were gained by Nora Callebout (12.0 100 yards), Mary Lines (44.8 300 metres and 16 feet 7 inches long jump), Hilda Hatt (4 feet 9$\frac{1}{8}$ inches high jump) and the 440 yards relay team of Miss Lines, Miss Callebout, Daisy Leach and Muriel Porter, whose time of 51.8 equalled the world's best.

Another year of great significance in the evolution of women's athletics was 1923. The WAAA staged its first full-scale championships at Bromley; the winners were Mary Lines (12.0 100 yards, a world record 62.4 440 yards, 18.8 120 yards hurdles and 16 feet 3$\frac{1}{2}$ inches long jump), Eileen Edwards (27.0 220 yards), Edith Trickey (2:40.2 880 yards and 4:35.0 880 yards walk), Hilda Hatt (4 feet 9 inches high jump), Florence Birchenough (53 feet 0$\frac{1}{2}$ inch shot, two handed aggregate, and 78 feet 10 inches discus) and Sophia Elliott-Lynn (later Lady Heath) of Ireland (117 feet 4 inches javelin, two handed aggregate). The following month, in Paris, Britain defeated France 60–37 in the first official international match, the highlight of which was the world record equalling 11.4 100 yards by Rose Thompson, whom Mary Lines had beaten in the championships. Another British winner was Vera Palmer (later Mrs Searle, to this day a prominent official), who set a world 440 yards record of 60.8 during the season.

One of the standouts of 1924 was Eileen Edwards, who recorded new global figures of 11.3 for 100 yards and 26.2 for 220 yards and equalled Vera Palmer's 440 yards mark, but she met defeat at the hands of Rose Thompson in the 100 yards at an international meeting the novelty of which drew 25,000 spectators to Stamford Bridge. Yet there was still much male opposition to overcome. One famous athlete of the day was representative of a large and influential body of opinion when he wrote: 'I do not consider that women are built for really violent exercise of the kind that is the essence of competition. One has only to see them practising to realise how awkward they are on the running track.' Nevertheless, women's athletics had come to stay and now, some forty years later, it is accepted by all as a perfectly natural and appropriate sport for females. The jibes and ridicule suffered by the pioneers in their knee length 'shorts' and flapping shirts, were not in vain. What follows is a *resumé*, year by year, of the outstanding athletes and their achievements.

1925: The WAAA Championships were notable for world records by Edith Trickey, whose 2:26.6 880 yards equalled versatile Mary Lines' 1922 figures, and schoolgirl Phyllis Green (5 feet 0 inch high jump). Miss Trickey later clocked 2:24.0 in a meeting with Canada and Czechoslovakia at Stamford Bridge, and other world marks set during the season were 26.0 for 220 yards by Eileen Edwards and 33.8 for 250 metres by Vera Palmer.

1926: British winners at the second World Games in Gothenburg, supported by eight nations, were Eileen Edwards (250 metres in world record 33.4), Edith Trickey (1,000 metres in 3:08.8), Daisy Crossley (1,000 metres walk in world record 5:10.0) and the 4 × 110 yards relay team (world record 49.8) of Doris Scouler, Florence Haynes, Miss Edwards, and Rose Thompson. Other world records were posted by Miss Edwards (25.8 220 yards) and Phyllis Green (5 feet 1⅛ inches high jump).

1927: Eileen Edwards scored a brilliant world record sprint double in Berlin, covering 100 metres in 12.4 (equalling the record) and 200 metres in 25.6 following a 25.3 heat. Other records during the year were a 25.8 220 yards (equal) by Miss Edwards and an 18 feet 4½ inches long jump by Phyllis Green, who also raised her British high jump record to 5 feet 2¼ inches but lost the world mark. The first national cross-country championship was staged.

1928: Women's athletics made its bow at the Amsterdam Olympics but Britain was conspicuous by her absence as the WAAA disapproved of the IAAF's grudging offer of only five events—the 100 metres, 800 metres, 4 × 100 metres, high jump and discus. During the season Edna Potter added her name to those who had run 220 yards in 25.8 and Florence Haynes became the third 60.8 quarter-miler. Other highlights included a 12.2 100 metres (equal to the Amsterdam winning time) by Daisy Ridgley and an 18 feet

7¾ inches long jump victory by Muriel Gunn, the pioneer hitch-kicker, over world record holder Kinue Hitomi of Japan in the WAAA Championships.

1929: Britain lost to Germany 53½–45½ in Dusseldorf, her first match defeat and the last until 1952. Marian King became the first quarter-miler to break the minute with 59.2. The 80 metres hurdles became a standardised event, replacing the numerous other distances previously contested.

1930: Seventeen nations took part in the third World Games in Prague and Britain's only winner was Gladys 'Sally' Lunn, who took the 800 metres in 2:21.9. Three weeks earlier she had set a world 880 yards record of 2:18.2. Other records were achieved by Nellie Halstead (25.2 220 yards) and Muriel Gunn, who in addition to equalling the world 80 metres hurdles mark of 12.2 improved her UK long jump figures to 19 feet 2½ inches—which stood until 1952. Britain beat Germany 51–47.

1931: England beat France and Belgium, with Gladys Lunn the individual winner, in the first international cross-country race, held at Douai. A British team of four captured seven of the twelve events at 'The Olympiad of Grace' in Florence, which was supported by eleven countries. Nellie Halstead won the 60 metres in 8.0 and the 200 metres in 25.8, Muriel Gunn the 80 metres hurdles in 13.0 and long jump with 17 feet 11 inches, and three victories were gained in the relays. Miss Halstead won the 100, 220 and 440 yards (in a world record 58.8) at the WAAA Championships, while Constance Mason in clocking 7:45.6 became the first woman to walk a mile inside eight minutes. Britain beat Germany 53–48.

1932: A British women's team participated in the Olympic Games for the first time and the relay squad of Eileen Hiscock, Gwendoline Porter, Violet Webb (mother of Janet Simpson, one of today's top sprinters) and Nellie Halstead won the bronze medals in 47.6. The highest individual placing was fifth by Miss Hiscock in the 100 metres and 17-year-old Miss Webb in the hurdles. Ethel Johnson, who had the misfortune to injure herself at the Los Angeles Olympics, beat the British 100 yards record by three-tenths with 11.0 at the WAAA Championships but even this was overshadowed by Miss Halstead's 56.8 quarter-mile . . . a mark that remained unbeaten throughout the world until 1954!

1933: The WAAA Championships went metric, a progressive move that existed until 1951. This was the first year during which no world records were set by British girls—a sign of the high standards.

1934: The Empire Games included women's events for the first time; English victories were provided by Eileen Hiscock (11.3 100 yards and a world record 25.0 220 yards), Gladys Lunn (2:19.4 880 yards and 105 feet 7¼ inches javelin!), Phyllis Bartholomew (17 feet 11¼ inches long jump) and the 440 yards medley relay team of Nellie Halstead, Miss Hiscock and Elsie Maguire. A more significant international tournament was held also at the White City the following week: the fourth and final World Games. Nineteen nations sent teams and, for the first time, there were no British successes. Best placed was Mary Milne, runner-up in the high jump at 5 feet 0 inch, but intrinsically the finest performance was the 2:14.2 800 metres in third place by Miss Lunn, which stood as a British record for 20 years.

1935: The amazingly versatile Nellie Halstead, an 11.4 100 yards performer and world record holder at 440 yards, won the first of two national cross-country titles! World records were set in the 4 × 110 yards (49.1) by Ethel Johnson, Elsie Maguire, Lilian Chalmers and Eileen Hiscock and in the 220 yards (24.8) by British-born South African-resident Barbara Burke. Miss Hiscock set a national 100 metres mark of 11.9 and Miss Burke equalled the 100 yards figures of 11.0. A 15-year-old schoolgirl by the name of Dorothy Odam high jumped 5 feet 0 inch for second place in the WAAA Championships.

1936: Dorothy Odam established herself as Britain's most successful athlete. In June she set a national record of 5 feet 5 inches, a mere quarter-inch below the world record, and won at an international meeting in Blackpool with 5 feet 4 inches, while at the Berlin Olympics in August she jumped 5 feet 3 inches—the same height as the winner—for second place. Under the present rules for deciding ties Dorothy would have won. Silver medals were gained also by the 4 × 100 metres team of Eileen Hiscock, Violet Olney, Audrey Brown (Godfrey Brown's sister) and Barbara Burke with a time of 47.6. Elsewhere, Olive Hall posted a world 880 yards record of 2:17.4 (which did not gain official recognition by the IAAF until 1951!). The mile became a championship event, with Gladys Lunn winning the inaugural title in 5:23.0.

1937: Barbara Burke tied the hurdles world record of 11.6 and Gladys Lunn broke new ground in the mile with 5:17.0.

1938: Dorothy Odam won the Empire title in Sydney with a jump of 5 feet 3 inches but did not compete at the first European Championships in Vienna. The best placed British competitors there were Dorothy Saunders (12.3 100 metres), Dorothy Cosnett (5 feet 2¼ inches high jump) and Ethel Raby (17 feet 10 inches long jump)—all fourth.

1939: Dorothy Odam was in splendid form all season and her reward was a world record of 5 feet 5⅜ inches. Evelyne Forster ran the mile in 5:15.3, a time which stood until 1952, and Bevis Reid improved her British shot-put record by over two feet with 40 feet 6 inches.

1946: Winifred Jordan, the 1937 WAAA 100 metres champion, placed second in both sprints (12.1 and 25.6) at the European Championships in Oslo, with Maureen Gardner (17) fifth in the 100 metres in 12.2.

1947: In her first season at the event and coached by future husband Geoff Dyson, Maureen Gardner accomplished the British 80 metres hurdles record time of 11.5 on four occasions. Britain beat France 26–24 in the first official international match since 1931.

1948: The Dutch housewife, Fanny Blankers-Koen, dominated the Wembley Olympics but, in her slipstream, silver medals went to Dorothy Manley (12.2 100 metres), Audrey Williamson (25.1 200 metres) and Maureen Gardner (11.2 hurdles). Neither of the two British sprinters had ever competed internationally before (and Miss Williamson never did again). Miss Gardner, beaten merely by inches, sliced three-tenths off her British record. Yet another silver medal came Britain's way in the high jump where Dorothy Tyler (*née* Odam) displayed the greatest form of her career in clearing a national record 5 feet 6⅛ inches and losing only on the fewer failures rule.

1949: Barbara Burke's 14-year-old British 220 yards record was broken at last by Sylvia Cheeseman with 24.5. Anchored by Valerie Ball, a Southern Counties team set an inaugural world record of 7:07.8 for the 3 × 880 yards relay.

1950: Dorothy Tyler retained the Empire title she had held since 1938 with a jump of 5 feet 3 inches and at the European Championships cleared 5 feet 4⅛ inches for the silver medal behind team-mate Sheila Alexander (same height). The latter, the first woman to use a straddle, had earlier raised the UK record to 5 feet 6⅝ inches. Maureen Dyson again finished second to Mrs Blankers-Koen in the hurdles (11.6) and Bertha Crowther placed second in the pentathlon (200 metres, hurdles, shot, long jump and high jump). June Foulds, aged 16, and Dorothy Hall (*née Manley*) gained a bronze medal apiece in the sprints (12.4 and 25.0 respectively) and together with Elspeth Hay and Jean Desforges triumphed in the relay in 47.4. Britain beat France 58–45.

1951: Sheila Lerwill (*née* Alexander) established a world high jump record of 5 feet 7⅝ inches at the WAAA Championships. Mrs Tyler, meanwhile, changed her style after twenty years of jumping —forsaking the scissors for the Western roll. During the season she set a British pentathlon record of 3,953 points. A WAAA team comprising Sylvia Cheeseman, Barbara Foster, Margaret Brian and Dorothy Hall set a 4 × 220 yards world record of 1:41.4. Britain beat France 61–43.

1952: Sheila Lerwill jumped 5 feet 5 inches for second place at the Helsinki Olympics with 16-year-old Thelma Hopkins fourth and Dorothy Tyler seventh, both at 5 feet 2¼ inches. Shirley Cawley removed a twenty-two-year-old British record in long jumping 19 feet 5 inches for third place, and bronze medals were gained also in the relay (46.2) by Sylvia Cheeseman, June Foulds, Jean Desforges (who had clocked a wind-assisted 10.9 in her hurdles semifinal) and Heather Armitage. A paradoxical situation arose during the season in the half-mile. Valerie Ball was credited with a world record of 2:14.5, yet Enid Harding became British record holder only with her 2:14.4 of 18 days earlier—the reason being that Harding's time was made off scratch in a handicap race. Other world records fell in the 4 × 200 metres (1:39.7) to a Southern Counties foursome of Ann Johnson, Miss Foulds, Shirley Hampton and Miss Cheeseman, in the 3 × 880 yards (7:00.6) to an Ilford AC team anchored by Phyllis Green and, unofficially, in the mile (5:11.0) to Anne Oliver. Britain beat France 60–43 but lost to Italy 46–47.

1953: Two more world relay records: Anne Pashley (currently a well known opera singer), Jean Newboult, Shirley Hampton and Ann Johnson clocked 1:39.9 for 4 × 220 yards; while Norah Smalley, Chris Slemon and Diane Leather returned 6:49.0 for 3 × 880 yards. Miss Leather also ran the fastest mile on record (5:02.6). Jean Desforges became the first Briton to long jump over twenty feet (she had a quarter-inch to spare) and also amassed a British pentathlon record score of 3,997. Beryl Randle walked a mile faster (7:44.0) than anyone else. Britain beat France 69–33 and West Germany 49–47.

1954: The only domestic success at the Commonwealth Games came in the high jump, won by Yorkshire-born Thelma Hopkins (representing Northern Ireland) with 5 feet 6 inches. As at the 1938 and 1950 Games, Dorothy Tyler cleared 5 feet 3 inches, this time placing second. Miss Hopkins completed a fine double by taking the European title at 5 feet 5¾ inches and Jean Desforges (who later married Ron Pickering, who was to become Lynn Davies' coach) won the long jump with 19 feet 9¾ inches. Diane Leather was second in the 800 metres (2:09.8) and bronze medals went to Anne Pashley (11.9 100 metres), Shirley Hampton (24.4 200 metres) and Pam Seaborne (11.3 hurdles). This was also a bumper season for records. World marks were set by Miss Leather (2:09.0 880 yards, 4:59.6 mile and a record equalling 56.6 440 yards) and a 3 × 880 yards trio of Miss Leather, Anne Oliver and Norah Smalley with 6:46.0. Beryl Randle improved her mile walk time to 7:38.4 and other national standards included 10.9 for 100 yards by Heather Armitage and Miss Pashley and 11.0 for the hurdles by Miss Seaborne (who later married pole vault champion Geoff Elliott). Britain beat Hungary 59–54 and Czechoslovakia 58–48.

1955: The 5 feet 10¼ inches tall Diane Leather improved her mile time to 4:50.8 and 4:45.0 and also set British 400 and 800 metres figures of 56.3 and 2:06.9 respectively. Other national records included 10.8 for 100 yards by Margaret Francis, 24.3 for 220 yards by Jean Scrivens and a 4,289 pentathlon score by Thelma Hopkins. Britain beat West Germany 53–50, Hungary 60–53, France 60–46 and Czechoslovakia 58–48 but lost to the USSR 48–83.

1956: Thelma Hopkins, who had set a world record of 5 feet 8½ inches earlier in the year, maintained Britain's 20-year sequence of silver medals in the Olympic high jump with a clearance of 5 feet 5¾ inches while Dorothy Tyler, in her farewell international appearance, placed twelfth with 5 feet 3 inches. The relay quartette of Anne Pashley, Jean Scrivens, June Paul (*née* Foulds) and Heather Armitage distinguished itself by finishing second in 44.7, which was inside the previous world record. Unfortunately the 400 metres was not on the Olympic schedule, for Janet Ruff—destined to become one of England's greatest hockey players—broke the world 440 yards record with 56.5. British records included 10.8 for 100 yards

(equal) by Miss Pashley and Mrs Paul, 11.6 for 100 metres by Mrs
Paul, Miss Pashley and Miss Armitage, 23.8 for 200 metres by
Mrs Paul, 20 feet 2 inches long jump by Sheila Hoskin and 45 feet
11¼ inches shot and 154 feet 3 inches discus by Suzanne Allday
(wife of hammer thrower Peter Allday). Britain beat Czechoslovakia 58–46 and Hungary 70–43.

1957: British records fell to Heather Young (*née* Armitage) with
24.2 for 220 yards (she also tied the 100 yards mark of 10.8), Janet
Ruff with 56.4 for 440 yards and Diane Leather with 2:06.8 for
800 metres. The latter scored a rare WAAA championship double
when she took the 880 yards (2:09.4) and mile (4:55.3) titles on the
same afternoon. The ever astonishing Dorothy Tyler, now 37, came
within an eighth of an inch of her best with 5 feet 6 inches. At the
other end of the age scale Mary Bignal, aged 17, set an English
pentathlon record of 4,046 points and made her international debut
as a high jumper, placing fourth and last (at 5 feet 3 inches) against
the USSR. Another to make her international bow during the season was 16-year-old Dorothy Hyman, who finished third in the 100
yards (11.9) against France. Fourth in the English Schools intermediate 150 yards championship in 18.0 was a 15-year-old by the
name of Ann Packer. Britain beat France 68–38 and Poland 57–49,
lost to the USSR 40–73 and West Germany 48½–58½.

1958: Pride of place at the Commonwealth Games went to the
English sprinters, Heather Young, June Paul, Dorothy Hyman and
Madeleine Weston, who joined forces to win the 4 × 110 yards relay
in a world record 45.3. On the individual plane, Mrs Young was
second in the 100 yards (10.6) and third in the 220 yards (23.9),
both British records. Other outstanding results were realised by
Sheila Hoskin (19 feet 9 inches) and Mary Bignal (19 feet 7 inches),
first and second in the long jump; Suzanne Allday (150 feet
7½ inches), the discus winner; and Carole Quinton, runner-up in
the hurdles with a wind assisted 10.7. The following month Mrs
Young became the first British woman to win an individual track
title at the European Championships by taking the 100 metres in
11.7. Torn ligaments in her foot forced her to withdraw from the
200 metres and relay and it was equally unfortunate that Mrs Paul,
who had shown great form in clocking 24.0 in her semi-final, broke
down in the 200 metres final with an Achilles tendon injury. This
prevented her, too, from running in the relay and in the circumstances it was a worthy effort by the team of Miss Weston, Miss

Hyman, Marianne Dew and Miss Quinton to finish second in 46.0. Other European medallists were Diane Leather (second in 800 metres in UK record of 2:06.6), Molly Hiscox (third in 400 metres in 55.7) and Dorothy Shirley (third in high jump at 5 feet 5¾ inches). Mrs Allday gave a boost to the traditionally weak 'heavy events' by placing fifth in the shot with a British record of 48 feet 1¼ inches and Miss Bignal set a national pentathlon record of 4,466 points in filling seventh position. Miss Hiscox, a prominent sprinter, had earlier created a sensation by breaking the world 440 yards record with 55.6 on a rainsoaked White City track. It was her first race at the distance and she admitted she had no idea of how to run it properly! Other British records included 55.5 for 400 metres by Gordon Pirie's wife Shirley (*née* Hampton), 10.9 for the hurdles by Miss Quinton, 156 feet 6 inches discus by Mrs Allday and 158 feet 1½ inches javelin by Averil Williams. Britain beat France 68–38 and lost to the Commonwealth 84–91.

1959: Mary Bignal established herself as one of the world's foremost long jumpers with a British record of 20 feet 4 inches against West Germany and 20 feet 2¼ inches against the USSR. In the latter match she also won the hurdles in 11.0, inches ahead of Irina Press—the future Olympic champion and world record holder. Other British records included 54.0 for 400 metres by Molly Hiscox, 2:08.1 for 880 yards by Joy Jordan, 49 feet 1 inch shot by Suzanne Allday, 162 feet 10½ inches javelin by Susan Platt and a 4,679 pentathlon by Miss Bignal. Dorothy Hyman continued to progress steadily: she won both WAAA sprint titles and registered times of 10.8 for 100 yards and 24.1 for 220 yards. Ann Packer won the English Schools 100 yards and clocked sprint times of 11.0 and 25.7; she was also fifth in the Southern long jump championship with 17 feet 10¾ inches—a competition won by Miss Bignal with a gale-assisted 20 feet 8¼ inches. Britain beat West Germany 64–51, lost to Poland 50–54 and the USSR 41–76.

1960: Olympic gold continued to elude Britain's women athletes but brilliant second place performances were achieved by Dorothy Hyman (wind-assisted 11.3 100 metres), Carole Quinton (UK record equalling 10.9 hurdles) and Dorothy Shirley (5 feet 7¼ inches high jump). Miss Hyman was also third in the 200 metres (24.7 against the wind). Mary Bignal placed fourth in the hurdles in 11.1, which compensated a little for her disappointment in the long jump where she led the qualifiers with a British record of 20 feet 9¼ inches but encountered run-up difficulties in the final and ended up only ninth with 19 feet 8½ inches. Equally heart-rending was the experience of Susan Platt in the javelin final. She threw over 177 feet, which would have earned the silver medal, but in the excitement of the occasion she unwittingly walked over the scratch line and thus annulled the great throw. Joy Jordan, who placed sixth in the 800 metres (2:07.8), later set a world 880 yards record of 2:06.1. Other British records included 11.5 for 100 metres and 23.7 for 200 metres by Miss Hyman and 169 feet 3½ inches javelin by Miss Platt. As for Ann Packer, she won her first WAAA title . . . as a long jumper. In the absence of Miss Bignal she leapt 18 feet 7½ inches for victory but, hindered by an ankle injury, cleared only 17 feet 3¾ inches for third place in her international debut against Italy. Britain beat Italy 58–45 and France 71–35.

1961: The only British record breakers were Jenny Smart (23.6 200 metres and a record-tying 11.5 100 metres) and Susan Platt, whose 178 feet 7½ inches javelin throw and several fine international performances confirmed her standing as Britain's greatest ever throwing event exponent. It was a poor year, though, for three of the brightest names in British athletics history: Dorothy Hyman was out injured; Mary Rand (*née* Bignal), who had earlier announced her retirement, did not compete as seriously as previously and had to be content with 20 feet 0½ inch for the long jump; and Ann Packer had a quiet season, her best mark being 11.1 for 100 yards. The eternal Dorothy Tyler, aged 41, ranked fifth among the high jumpers with 5 feet 4¼ inches! Britain beat the USA 56–50, Hungary 61–45 and France 73–33, and lost to West Germany 45–61 and Poland 46–60.

1962: Dorothy Hyman came back better than ever and at the European Championships won the 100 metres in a wind-aided 11.3, finished second in the 200 metres (23.7) and completed her set of medals by combining with Ann Packer, Daphne Arden and Mary Rand to clock 44.9 for third place in the relay. Other medallists were Joy Grieveson (second in the 400 metres in a UK record 53.9), 16-year-old Linda Knowles (third in the high jump with 5 feet 8⅛ inches) and Mrs Rand (third in the long jump with 20 feet 4¾ inches—only a few months after the birth of her daughter). Miss Arden finished fourth in both sprints (11.5 and 24.2), with Miss Packer creating a pleasant surprise by taking sixth in the 200 metres with 24.4 for many thought she was lucky to gain selection in the first place. Joy Jordan set a UK 800 metres record of 2:05.0 in fourth position, the consistent Dorothy Shirley high jumped 5 feet 5½ inches for fourth, and Mary Peters finished fifth in the pentathlon with 4,586. Miss Hyman was even more successful at the Commonwealth Games, winning the 100 yards against a strong wind in 11.2 and the 220 yards in 23.8. She, together with Miss Packer (who was sixth in the hurdles!), Miss Arden and Australian-born Betty Moore, made up the English team that came second in the relay in 46.6. Susan Platt won the javelin (164 feet 10½ inches) ahead of Rosemary Morgan (162 feet 9½ inches), Mrs Jordan set another UK record as she finished third in the 880 yards in 2:05.9, and Miss Knowles jumped 5 feet 8 inches for fourth. Other UK records set during the year included 10.6 for 100 yards and 11.5 for 100 metres (equalling the existing figures), 23.4 for 200 metres and 23.8 for 220 yards by Miss Hyman, and 54.4 for 440 yards by Miss Grieveson; while indoors an outstanding performance was the 5 feet 9 inches high jump by Frances Slaap. Mrs Moore, who represented Britain several times, equalled the world 80 metres hurdles record of 10.5—which still stands as the official UK record although she returned to Australia for good. Britain beat Poland 54–52, lost to West Germany indoors 43–52.

1963: A world record of 45.2 for the 4×110 yards relay by Madeleine Cobb (*née* Weston), Mary Rand, Daphne Arden and Dorothy Hyman in the match against the USA was the highlight of another eventful season. Miss Hyman, with UK records of 11.3 for 100 metres, 23.2 for 200 metres and 23.7 for 220 yards, proved herself the world's number one sprinter. Other national record setters included Joy Grieveson (53.2 400 metres), Pat Nutting (10.8 hurdles if one disregards Betty Moore) and Mrs Rand (10.8 hurdles, 21 feet 1¾ inches long jump and 4,726 pentathlon). Ann Packer made her bow as a quarter-miler and, astonishingly, recorded three 400 metres times in the 53.3–53.4 range—compared to the European record of 53.2 shared by Miss Grieveson and Maria Itkina (USSR). Britain beat the USA 65½–51½, West Germany 75½–63½ and the Netherlands 74–43, lost to West Germany indoors 42–64, the Russian Federal Republic 56–62 and Hungary 48–55.

1964: This was undoubtedly the greatest year in British women's athletics history. After thirty-two years of endeavour an Olympic gold medal finally came Britain's way; no not one, but two! Mary Rand utterly dominated the long jump and won with a world record

leap of 22 feet 2¼ inches; six days later Ann Packer, who had made
her two-lap debut only five months earlier, ran a flawless race to
win the 800 metres in the official world record time of 2:01.1. In
addition, Mrs Rand took second place in the pentathlon with 5,035
points (a performance bettered by only one other athlete in history)
and gained a third medal—bronze—in the relay, in which she
teamed up with Janet Simpson, Daphne Arden and Dorothy Hyman
to return the brilliant time of 44.0; while Miss Packer smashed the
European record in clocking 52.2 for second place in the 400
metres. Another splendid Olympic achievement was Mary Peters'
fourth in the pentathlon with 4,797 points. Miss Hyman, unfortunately, was not at her best following an untimely injury and in
the circumstances did well even to reach the 100 metres final. Other
British records during the year: the 10.6 100 yards mark was tied
by Miss Hyman, Mrs Rand and Miss Arden; Miss Arden ran 220
yards in 23.6; Miss Packer clocked 54.3 for 440 yards; prior to the
Olympics Anne Smith had set 800 metres figures of 2:04.8; Pat
Pryce (*née* Nutting) ran 10.7 for the hurdles; Frances Slaap high
jumped 5 feet 9¼ inches; Suzanne Allday put the shot 49 feet
9¾ inches; Rosemary Payne threw the discus 158 feet 3½ inches;
Susan Platt threw the javelin 179 feet 10 inches; Miss Peters fleet-
ingly held the pentathlon record at 4,801; and Judy Farr walked
1½ miles in 12:06.8. Britain beat the Netherlands 70–47, lost to
Poland 57–60.

1965: The retirement of Dorothy Hyman and Ann Packer
seriously depleted the British team's strength and in fact the season
proved a severe anti-climax. Only two national records were set:
Rosemary Payne's 166 feet 3 inches discus throw and Judy Farr's
7:36.2 mile walk. The outstanding competitor of the year was Anne
Smith, who went unbeaten over two laps and clocked times of
2:05.3 for 800 metres and 4:46.3 for the mile. In the inaugural
European Cup tournament Britain suffered the humiliation of
failing even to qualify for the final. Britain beat Hungary 63–52,
lost to the USA indoors 33½–38½, Poland 58–59 and West Germany
57–67.

1966: Only one victory at the Commonwealth Games (Mary Rand
with 20 feet 10½ inches long jump) and none at the European
Championships. Other medallists in Kingston were Jill Hall (third
in 100 yards in 10.8), Deirdre Watkinson (second in 440 yards in
UK record 54.1), Anne Smith (third in 880 yards in 2:05.0), Dorothy

Shirley (second in high jump at 5 feet 7 inches), Sheila Parkin (second in long jump with 20 feet 8 inches), Mary Peters (second in shot with 53 feet 5½ inches) and the English relay team (45.6) of Maureen Tranter, Janet Simpson, Daphne Slater (*née* Arden) and Miss Hall. The highest placed competitors in Budapest were Pam Piercy (2:04.1 800 metres) and Mrs Rand (4,711 pentathlon)—both fourth. In addition to Miss Watkinson, other British record breakers included Miss Smith (2:04.2 880 yards and 4:44.2 mile), Miss Peters (53 feet 6¼ inches shot, plus an unacceptable 56 feet 1½ inches) and Rosemary Payne—wife of the Commonwealth hammer champion—with 167 feet 1 inch in the discus. Britain beat France 59–57, lost to the USSR 53–71.

1967: Top honours were shared by Anne Smith and Lillian Board. Miss Smith, suspended from international competition for the year following her walk-out from the European Championships, twice broke the world mile record with 4:39.2 (laps of 70.0, 70.4, 70.0 and 68.8) and 4:37.0 (68.0, 69.8, 70.2 and 69.0). On the latter occasion she also beat all previous figures for 1,500 metres with 4:17.3. Miss Board, aged 18 and in only her second season of quarter-miling, recorded 52.8 for 400 metres in Los Angeles to defeat an immensely strong field and was Britain's only winner in the European Cup Final in which the team finished fifth. Rosemary Stirling, Pat Lowe and Pam Piercy set a 3 × 880 yards world record of 6:25.2 and also bettered the listed time for 3 × 800 metres with 6:20.0, while other best-on-record times were credited to Christine Perera (13.7 for the newly introduced 100 metres hurdles over 2 feet 9 inches barriers) and Pat Jones (27.3 for 200 metres hurdles). Miss Jones was also timed at 10.6 for 80 metres hurdles, fastest ever by a UK athlete. Britain beat Hungary 73–51 and West Germany 66–65, lost to Poland 55–62. Mary Rand won the 80 metres hurdles from Miss Jones (both 10.8) at the 'Little Olympics' in Mexico City.

1968: Pam Davies won the English cross-country title for the fourth successive year.

APPENDIX

TOP TEN BRITISH PERFORMERS
OF ALL TIME
(as at end of 1967 season)

100 YARDS

9.4 Peter Radford 1959
9.5 David Segal 1960
9.5 Alfred Meakin 1961
9.5 David Jones 1962
9.5 Ronald Jones 1963
9.5 Lynn Davies 1964
9.5 Menzies Campbell 1967
9.6 Ten men

100 METRES

10.2 Menzies Campbell 1967
10.3 Roy Sandstrom 1956
10.3 Peter Radford 1958
10.3 David Jones 1961
10.3 Berwyn Jones 1963
10.4 Arthur Sweeney 1937
10.4 Alistair McCorquodale 1948
10.4 Ronald Jones 1959
10.4 Alfred Meakin 1963
10.4 Barrie Kelly 1967
10.4 Lynn Davies 1967

220 YARDS

20.5 Peter Radford 1960
20.8 Menzies Campbell 1967
21.0* David Jones 1961
21.0* Robbie Brightwell 1962
21.0* Richard Steane 1967
21.1* David Segal 1958
21.2 William Applegarth 1914
21.2 Arthur Sweeney 1935
21.2 Cyril Holmes 1938
21.2* Michael Hildrey 1961
21.2* Brian Smouha 1961
21.2* Patrick Morrison 1965
21.2 Lynn Davies 1966
* 200 metres time plus 0.1

440 YARDS

45.9 Robbie Brightwell 1962
46.0* Adrian Metcalfe 1961
46.3* Timothy Graham 1964
46.6* John Wrighton 1958
46.8 Edward Sampson 1958
46.8* John Salisbury 1958
46.8* Barry Jackson 1962
46.9* Malcolm Yardley 1960
46.9* Colin Campbell 1967
47.0* Godfrey Brown 1936
* 400 metres time plus 0.3

880 YARDS

1:47.0* Christopher Carter 1966
1:47.2* John Boulter 1966
1:47.3* Derek Johnson 1957
1:47.7* Brian Hewson 1958
1:47.7* Michael Rawson 1958
1:48.1 William Cornell 1963
1:48.1 Robbie Brightwell 1964
1:48.2* James Paterson 1957
1:48.2 Michael Varah 1967
1:48.5 Anthony Harris 1964
* 800 metres time plus 0.7

1,500 METRES

3:39.1 Alan Simpson 1964
3:39.9 John Whetton 1964
3:40.4 John Boulter 1964
3:40.7 Michael Wiggs 1964
3:41.1 Brian Hewson 1958
3:41.6 Neill Duggan 1966
3:41.9 Derek Ibbotson 1957
3:41.9 Stanley Taylor 1962
3:42.2 Roger Bannister 1954
3:42.2 Michael Blagrove 1958
3:42.2 Andrew Green 1965

MILE

3:55.7	Alan Simpson	1965
3:56.1	Neill Duggan	1966
3:57.2	Derek Ibbotson	1957
3:57.5	Michael Wiggs	1965
3:57.7	John Whetton	1965
3:57.7	Andrew Green	1965
3:58.0	Stanley Taylor	1962
3:58.7	Allan Rushmer	1967
3:58.8	Roger Bannister	1954
3:58.9	Brian Hewson	1958

3 MILES

13:06.4	Ian McCafferty	1967
13:08.6	Michael Wiggs	1965
13:08.6	Allan Rushmer	1966
13:11.4	Richard Taylor	1967
13:12.0	Bruce Tulloh	1961
13:13.2e	Gordon Pirie	1956
13:13.8e	Bill Wilkinson	1966
13:15.6	Derek Graham	1965
13:17.6	John Hillen	1967
13:18.8	Geoffrey North	1966

e estimated time during 5000
metres race

5000 METRES

13:33.0	Michael Wiggs	1965
13:36.8	Gordon Pirie	1956
13:37.2	Allan Rushmer	1967
13:39.6	Bill Wilkinson	1966
13:42.6	Richard Taylor	1967
13:45.8	Ian McCafferty	1967
13:47.6	Derek Graham	1966
13:47.8	Stanley Eldon	1959
13:49.0	Fergus Murray	1964
13:49.4	Bruce Tulloh	1964
13:49.4	Dominic Keily	1965
13:49.4	Geoffrey North	1966

6 MILES

27:23.8	Bruce Tulloh	1966
27:24.8	Roy Fowler	1966
27:26.0	Ronald Hill	1966
27:26.0*	Michael Freary	1966
27:26.4	Michael Bullivant	1964
27:30.6	James Alder	1966
27:32.2	Allan Rushmer	1966
27:33.2	Michael Turner	1966
27:33.8	John Farrington	1966
27:35.0	James Hogan	1964

* 10,000 metres time less 60.0

MARATHON

2:13:45	Alastair Wood	1966
2:13:55	Basil Heatley	1964
2:14:12	Ronald Hill	1964
2:14:43	Brian Kilby	1963
2:14:44	James Alder	1967
2:15:37	Juan Taylor	1964
2:16:50	William Adcocks	1965
2:17:19	Donald Macgregor	1967
2:17:39	James Peters	1954
2:18:15	Denis O'Gorman	1960

3,000 METRES STEEPLECHASE

8:32.4	Maurice Herriott	1964
8:36.4	John Jackson	1967
8:37.0	Ernest Pomfret	1967
8:40.2	Gerald Stevens	1967
8:41.2	Christopher Brasher	1956
8:41.4	Anthony Ashton	1967
8:41.6	John Linaker	1966
8:43.8	Paul Lightfoot	1967
8:44.2	John Disley	1955
8:44.8	Laughlin Stewart	1966

120 YARDS HURDLES

13.9	Michael Parker	1963
13.9	David Hemery	1966
13.9	Alan Pascoe	1967
14.0	Robert Birrell	1961
14.1	Lawrence Taitt	1963
14.1	Michael Hogan	1963
14.1	Stuart Storey	1967
14.2	Rodney Morrod	1964
14.2	Andrew Todd	1967
14.3	Donald Finlay	1938
14.3	John Parker	1955
14.3	Peter Hildreth	1957

440 YARDS HURDLES

50.4*	John Cooper	1964
50.5*	John Sherwood	1967
51.0*	Peter Warden	1966
51.3*	Thomas Farrell	1960
51.3*	Christopher Surety	1961
51.4*	Andrew Todd	1967
51.6	Christopher Goudge	1958
51.6*	Michael Hogan	1964
51.6*	Robin Woodland	1966
51.8	Harry Kane	1954
51.8	David Hemery	1966

* 400 metres time plus 0.3

HIGH JUMP

6'	10"	Gordon Miller 1964
6'	9½"	Crawford Fairbrother 1964
6'	7½"	Alan Paterson 1947
6'	7½"	Peter Wells 1954
6'	7"	Richard Morris 1962
6'	7"	Michael Campbell 1967
6'	6¼"	David Wilson 1959
6'	6¼"	Lloyd Foster 1967
6'	6"	Six men

POLE VAULT

15'	9"	Michael Bull 1967
15'	4"	David Stevenson 1966
15'	0"	Trevor Burton 1964
14'	8"	Martin Higdon 1967
14'	7"	Gordon Rule 1967
14'	6"	Norman Foster 1967
14'	5"	Rex Porter 1963
14'	3"	Neal Willson 1966
14'	1¼"	Geoffrey Elliott 1954
14'	1¼"	Jeffrey Fenge 1967
14'	0"	Michael Bryant 1967
14'	0"	Stewart Seale 1967

LONG JUMP

26'	10"	Lynn Davies 1966
25'	10¾"	John Morbey 1966
25'	4¾"	Frederick Alsop 1964
25'	0½"	John Howell 1960
24'	10¾"	Roy Cruttenden 1956
24'	8¾"	Kenneth Wilmshurst 1954
24'	8½"	Alan Lerwill 1967
24'	8"	John Whall 1960
24'	7¾"	Peter Reed 1965
24'	7½"	Peter Templeton 1966

TRIPLE JUMP

54'	0"	Frederick Alsop 1964
52'	4¾"	Michael Ralph 1964
51'	11"	Derek Boosey 1964
51'	7¼"	John Vernon 1966
51'	2¼"	Kenneth Wilmshurst 1956
50'	9"	David Macbeth 1967
50'	7½"	Lynn Davies 1962
50'	3¾"	Anthony Wadhams 1966
50'	0½"	John Whall 1959
49'	11¾"	Peter Drew 1967

SHOT

64'	2"	Arthur Rowe 1961
61'	1¼"	Martyn Lucking 1962
60'	8½"	Michael Lindsay 1963
59'	11"	Alan Carter 1965
56'	4"	Jeffrey Teale 1967
56'	3¼"	Barry King 1965
55'	8¼"	William Tancred 1967
55'	7¼"	Nicholas Morgan 1961
55'	7"	Anthony Elvin 1966
55'	6"	Barclay Palmer 1956

DISCUS

187'	0"	Gerald Carr 1965
186'	0"	Roy Hollingsworth 1963
182'	10"	William Tancred 1966
181'	6"	Michael Lindsay 1960
181'	1"	Arthur McKenzie 1966
178'	0"	Mark Pharaoh 1956
177'	2"	Eric Cleaver 1962
176'	0"	Barry King 1966
174'	6"	John Hillier 1967
173'	7"	Michael Cushion 1967

HAMMER

213'	1"	Michael Ellis 1959
208'	10"	Howard Payne 1962
202'	6"	Peter Seddon 1967
198'	7"	Lawrence Bryce 1967
195'	7"	Peter Allday 1956
194'	3"	Bruce Fraser 1967
192'	6"	Ewan Douglas 1955
192'	1"	Lawrence Hall 1962
190'	9"	Donald Anthony 1956
189'	8"	Warwick Dixon 1961

JAVELIN

261'	9"	John FitzSimons 1966
260'	0"	John McSorley 1962
260'	0"	John Greasley 1963
255'	8"	Colin Smith 1962
252'	7"	David Travis 1967
245'	3"	Richard Perkins 1967
244'	7"	John Kitching 1960
244'	6"	Barry Sanderson 1966
243'	10"	Roger Lane 1960
243'	9"	Richard Miller 1963

DECATHLON

7392	Clive Longe 1967
7002	Derek Clarke 1965
6866	David Gaskin 1966
6840	Norman Foster 1965
6791	David Travis 1965
6662	Michael Bull 1966
6638	Colin Andrews 1960
6578	George McLachlan 1962
6575	Antony Tymms 1964
6572	Peter Gabbett 1967

20 KILOMETRES WALK

1:28:15	Kenneth Matthews 1960
1:31:13	Peter Fullager 1967
1:31:39	Paul Nihill 1964
1:31:43	Stanley Vickers 1960
1:32:30	Robert Clark 1961
1:32:41	Ronald Wallwork 1965
1:32:46	John Edgington 1964
1:33:28	John Paddick 1964
1:33:37	Eric Hall 1959
1:33:43	Roy Hart 1964

50 KILOMETRES WALK

4:11:31	Paul Nihill 1964	4:22:45	Charles Fogg 1965
4:12:19	Donald Thompson 1959	4:23:46	Ronald Wallwork 1963
		4:25:50	John Paddick 1965
4:14:03	Thomas Misson 1959	4:26:40	Albert Johnson 1958
4:16:43	Raymond Middleton 1963	4:26:56	Shaun Lightman 1967
		4:28:44	Kenneth Mason 1963

WOMEN'S EVENTS

100 YARDS

10.6	Heather Young 1958
10.6	Dorothy Hyman 1962
10.6	Mary Rand 1964
10.6	Daphne Arden 1964
10.7	June Paul 1958
10.7	Madeleine Weston 1958
10.7	Jennifer Smart 1960
10.7	Jill Hall 1965
10.7	Elizabeth Gill 1965
10.7	Elizabeth Parsons 1966
10.7	Maureen Tranter 1966
10.7	Wendy Kavanagh 1967
10.7	Anita Neil 1967
10.7	Denise Ramsden 1967

100 METRES

11.3	Dorothy Hyman 1963
11.4	Della James 1967
11.5	Jennifer Smart 1961
11.5	Daphne Arden 1964
11.6	June Paul 1956
11.6	Anne Pashley 1956
11.6	Heather Young 1956
11.6	Janet Simpson 1965
11.6	Elizabeth Gill 1965
11.6	Jill Hall 1965
11.6	Maureen Tranter 1966
11.6	Anita Neil 1967

220 YARDS

23.3*	Dorothy Hyman 1963
23.6	Daphne Arden 1964
23.7*	Jennifer Smart 1961
23.7	Janet Simpson 1964
23.8*	Ann Packer 1964
23.9*	June Paul 1956
23.9	Heather Young 1958
23.9*	Maureen Tranter 1965
23.9	Della James 1967
24.0*	Mary Rand 1967

* 200 metres time plus 0.1

440 YARDS

52.5*	Ann Packer 1964
53.1*	Lillian Board 1967
53.5*	Joy Grieveson 1963
54.1	Deirdre Watkinson 1966
54.3*	Moyra (Molly) Hiscox 1959
54.4	Rosemary Stirling 1966
54.7*	Patricia Kippax 1964
54.8*	Mary Green 1967
54.9*	Jean Dunbar 1961
55.3	Pamela Piercy 1962

* 400 metres time plus 0.3

880 YARDS

2:01.9* Ann Packer 1964
2:04.2   Anne Smith 1966
2:04.9* Pamela Piercy 1966
2:05.4   Rosemary Stirling 1966
2:05.8* Joy Jordan 1962
2:05.8   Patricia Lowe 1966
2:06.1* Mary Hodson 1964
2:07.1* Iris Lincoln 1967
2:07.4* Diane Leather 1958
2:07.7   Sheila Taylor 1967
    * 800 metres time plus 0.8

80 METRES HURDLES

10.6 Patricia Jones 1967
10.7 Patricia Pryce 1964
10.8 Mary Rand 1963
10.8 Ann Wilson 1967
10.9 Carole Quinton 1958
10.9 Ann Charlesworth 1961
11.0 Pamela Seaborne 1954
11.0 Maxine Botley 1964
11.0 Mary Peters 1964
11.1 Three girls

HIGH JUMP

5' 9¼" Frances Slaap 1964
5' 8½" Thelma Hopkins 1956
5' 8"   Linda Knowles 1962
5' 8"   Dorothy Shirley 1967
5' 7¾" Gwenda Matthews 1964
5' 7¾" Mary Rand 1964
5' 7½" Sheila Lerwill 1951
5' 7"   Rosemary Curtis 1964
5' 6¾" Iris Pegley 1960
5' 6½" Barbara Inkpen 1967

LONG JUMP

22' 2¼"   Mary Rand 1964
21' 0¾"   Sheila Parkin 1967
20' 6½"   Ann Wilson 1967
20' 2"   Sheila Hoskin 1956
20' 1"   Anita Neil 1967
20' 0¾"   Alix Jamieson 1964
20' 0½"   Thelma Hopkins 1956
20' 0¼"   Jean Desforges 1953
19' 10¾" Maureen Barton 1966
19' 10"   Susan Scott 1967

SHOT

53' 6¼" Mary Peters 1966
51' 1½" Brenda Bedford 1967
49' 9¾" Suzanne Allday 1964
45' 9½" Josephine Cook 1958
45' 9"   Jennifer Bloss 1967
45' 8"   Kathryn Duckett 1966
45' 1¼" Brenda Gill 1964
44' 9¼" Moira Kerr 1966
43' 3¼" Josephine Frampton 1967
43' 0"   Valerie Woods 1962

DISCUS

167' 1"   Rosemary Payne 1966
157' 6"   Hilda Atkins 1966
156' 6"   Suzanne Allday 1958
156' 4"   Brenda Bedford 1967
150' 3"   Maya Giri 1958
149' 3"   Josephine Frampton 1967
147' 8"   Maureen Arnold 1966
146' 10" Wendy Thomas 1964
144' 11" Maureen Burtenshaw 1958
143' 1"   Barbara Everitt 1964

JAVELIN

179' 10" Susan Platt 1964
177' 9"   Rosemary Morgan 1964
162' 5"   Averil Williams 1960
159' 3"   Anne Farquhar 1967
156' 2"   Barbara Nicholls 1963
152' 8"   Janet Baker 1966
150' 0"   Mary Tadd 1959
149' 6"   Monica Podmore 1960
148' 7"   Diane Coates 1952
148' 2"   Margaret Callender 1959

PENTATHLON

5035 Mary Rand 1964
4823 Mary Peters 1964
4676 Ann Wilson 1966
4441 Patricia Jones 1967
4419 Susan Scott 1967
4379 Thelma Hopkins 1961
4367 Susan Mills 1965
4302 Patricia Pryce 1964
4297 Brenda Gill 1963
4294 Ann Packer 1963

INDEX